# BETRAYAL TRAUMA

# BETRAYAL TRAUMA

The Logic of Forgetting Childhood Abuse

## JENNIFER J. FREYD

Harvard University Press

Cambridge, Massachusetts

London, England   1996

Designed by Marianne Perlak

*Library of Congress Cataloging-in-Publication Data*

Freyd, Jennifer J.
  Betrayal trauma : the logic of forgetting childhood abuse /
Jennifer J. Freyd.
      p.   cm.
  Includes bibliographical references and index.
  ISBN 0-674-06805-X (cloth : alk. paper)
  1. Child sexual abuse.  2. Betrayal—Psychological aspects.
3. Psychic trauma.  I. Title.
RJ506.C48F74   1996
616.85'82239—dc20      96-9059

*2-26-97*

*For JQ Johnson*
*and our children,*
*Theodore, Philip, and Alexandra*

# CONTENTS

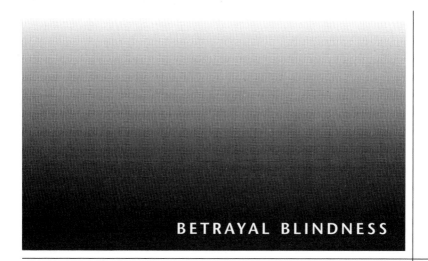

Our jet from St. Louis was landing at the Denver airport, heading west. The morning was sparkling clear. The air, dead still.

I sat in a window seat on the right side, near the front of the plane. With my forehead pressed against the cool plastic window, I admired the snowcapped Rockies glistening ahead and contemplated the houses and buildings down below, growing ever larger as we made our descent. I half-listened to the flight attendant on the intercom announcing connecting gate information.

The houses below me looked fresh and appealing in the November sunlight, still small enough to appear like toys, yet large enough to look worth exploring, a bright playroom of dollhouses. And then, fascinated, I found myself looking down on another jet.

That plane was a bit lower than ours, and I gazed upon its fat back for a moment or two before being hit with a horrifying jolt of awareness: There was not room for two planes! We were both headed for the same spot in midair! Yet the attendant was still on the intercom, talking on about connecting flights. I wondered, Should I scream? Does the pilot realize this? What do I *do?* Don't they realize the danger we are in?

I've wondered since then: For how long were these panicked questions bouncing about my mind? I doubt it was more than a fraction of a second, because suddenly our plane made an abrupt change in direction. Instead of continuing down, we headed up. And the flight attendant stopped talking.

As I looked out the window the houses and the other jet shrank as we made our escape. I looked around at the other passengers, wondering, Was anyone afraid? Were they relieved to be spared a midair collision? Had they even noticed our missed approach? I couldn't tell. At least the flight attendant must have noticed, I thought, for she *did* stop talking.

After perhaps a minute we leveled off. I watched eagerly as we circled the Denver airport and began our descent once again, this time heading due south, landing on a runway that I had been on many times—but only for takeoffs. I looked around for other planes but could find none. No planes were in the air near the airport. Nor were planes on the runways. Where, I wondered, had they gone?

To my amazement, the flight attendant resumed her announcement of connecting gates. She simply picked up where she had left off, as if nothing had happened.

Wait a minute! I silently protested. Haven't we just barely missed a midair or runway collision? Won't they say something about what just happened? Explain? Reassure us?

The plane parked at the gate. The attendant stopped talking. As I gathered my coat and carry-on bag, the man sitting in the seat two rows ahead of me caught my eye. We had been at the same conference in St. Louis and we recognized each other. He looked concerned and confused. He hesitated a bit before blurting out to me, "Did you notice anything strange? Weren't we heading down, about to land, when suddenly we went back up for awhile?"

"Yes," I agreed. "That did happen!" I looked around to see if others would chime in, but no one seemed to be paying us any attention. As I exited the plane a few moments later, I passed the flight attendant, who was standing in front of the cockpit, chanting, "Good-bye! good-bye!" in the standard cheery way. But instead of the door being open, as is usual after landing, this time the door was closed.

And that was that. Thanks to the crew's silence, most passengers on that flight disembarked blissfully blind to both the betrayal of safety and the betrayal of truth they had just suffered.

Today I wonder: What if my acquaintance had not asked if I noticed something strange? Would I now believe that I had seen us get so close to another plane? I might well say to myself, "Surely a near collision on a clear day, at a big American airport, seems a bit far-fetched. If it had really happened they would have explained it, acknowledge it at least, right? Maybe this was all a fantasy of mine—a false memory."

These doubts are tempting. The old Denver airport is no longer, but I have no choice: I must continue to use that airline and the new Denver airport—unless I give up flying to conferences or vacations, which would mean giving up large portions of my professional and family life. If the near disaster were simply a false memory, then I would not have to believe that I had been put into that kind of danger by people, technology, and a system that I *need to trust.*

It is not difficult to imagine what lay behind the pilot and crew's decision to remain silent about the event. By not acknowledging the missed approach perhaps the passengers would remain unaware, or at least unsure, of the danger that had been present. And if the event were not acknowledged, if no one made a "big deal" about it, maybe those passengers who did notice it would forget.

That missed approach into the Denver airport hardly ranks as a trauma next to other horrifying events: war, disasters, violence. Although I need to trust airlines and airports, the trust required of me is limited in time and scope and does not begin to compare with the trust that a young child needs to have for his or her caregivers. Nonetheless the same rule applies: See no betrayal. Hear no betrayal. Speak no betrayal.

## The Core Betrayal Trauma: Childhood Sexual Abuse

Consider the pressure on a child who is sexually abused by a parent or other adult who has power and authority over that child. The child *needs* to trust his or her parents and caregivers. Childhood sexual abuse, whether molestation or even penetration, usually leaves no lasting physical evidence. It is neither explained nor understandable to the child. It is often not even acknowledged by the perpetrator, except to say it didn't happen or wasn't what it seemed to be.

Sexual abuse perpetrated on a child by a trusted caregiver is a perfect opportunity for the victim to create information blockage. To know is to put oneself in danger. Not to know is to align oneself with the caregiver and ensure survival.

This book is about information blockage as a natural and inevitable reaction to childhood sexual abuse. It is about the logic of amnesia for abuse. Memory repression will be shown to arise not because it reduces suffering, but because not knowing about abuse by a caregiver is often necessary for survival.

This book is also about the ubiquity of the human response of not knowing, of not remembering, betrayals. Everyday betrayals—a boss who speaks in a patronizing voice, a spouse who flirts with a friend, an airline that flies its plane dangerously close to another—also often leave little mark on conscious awareness.

Although I propose that not knowing is ubiquitous, I also propose that knowledge is multi-stranded, and that we can at the same time not know and know about a betrayal. Indeed, it is the human condition simultaneously to know and not to know about a given betrayal. The knowing is often the kind of knowledge or memory that cognitive psychologists call "implicit knowledge" or "implicit memory."

If I had "forgotten" that flight from St. Louis to Denver, the forgetting would have left me with little conscious knowledge of what happened. But it would likely have left me with other signs of learning and traces of the event. I might have found landing at Denver next time more frightening than I ever had before. Or I might have found myself "irrationally" trying to avoid the Denver airport.

The survivor of childhood abuse who "forgets" and does "not know" about the abuse similarly has memory and knowledge of the events that surface in other ways: specific phobias, learned behaviors, a self-perception of being a "bad girl" or "bad boy."

## Recovering from Betrayal Blindness: The Memory Debate

Some people come to realize that they have been betrayed a long time after the event. Sometimes this recovery from betrayal blindness happens when the person forms a new understanding of a remembered event. Other times it occurs in conjunction with recovering the memory of the events of the betrayal.

In a 1992 article in the *New York Times,* Daniel Goleman described one person's realization that he had been betrayed:

> Frank Fitzpatrick, a thirty-eight-year-old insurance adjuster in Cranston, R.I., began remembering having been sexually molested by a parish priest at age twelve.
>
> Mr. Fitzpatrick's retrieval of the repressed memories began, he said, when "I was feeling a great mental pain, even though my marriage and everything else in my life was going well." Puzzled, Mr. Fitzpatrick lay down on his bed, "trying to let myself feel what was going on."
>
> Mr. Fitzpatrick . . . slowly realized that the mental pain was due to a "betrayal of some kind," and remembered the sound of heavy breathing. "Then I realized I had been sexually abused by someone I loved," said Mr. Fitzpatrick. But it was not until two weeks later that he suddenly remembered the priest, the Rev. James R. Porter . . .

To forget and to remember are everyday aspects of human experience. Sometimes people gain awareness of events that they had previously not remembered. But sometimes the forgetting and remembering are dramatic enough to become the focus of inquiry and even controversy.

As I write this book, a war is being fought over the veracity of recovered memories of childhood sexual abuse. Although I comment on this controversy, this book is largely tangential to the Great Recovered Memory Debate. Although it addresses whether, why, and how recovered memories of real abuse occur, it is largely silent on whether, why, and how false memories may occur. Similarly, this book is also largely silent on the question so central to this debate: Are most contested memories based on real abuse? Instead of dwelling on contested memories,

I focus on the response of unawareness and amnesia to abuse and betrayal trauma. Although betrayal trauma theory and the false memory movement have origins in my own life experience (see the Afterword), I first presented my theory of betrayal trauma before the world or I had heard the term "false memory syndrome."

## Ross Cheit's Recovery from Betrayal Blindness

"Long-lost memories of sexual abuse can resurface. I know, because it happened to me. But I also know that I might not have believed that this was possible if [it] hadn't occurred to me. And that's what makes me nervous." Ross Cheit, Associate Professor of Political Science at Brown University, spoke these words in 1994, in his first public speech about these matters, at age thirty-eight, two years after recovering memories of being sexually abused in the late 1960s by William Farmer. Farmer had been the administrator of the San Francisco Boys Chorus summer camp, which Cheit had attended between the ages of ten and thirteen.

Professor Cheit then explained how surprising this realization was to him:

Two years ago, the topic of sexual abuse was something that I certainly knew nothing about. There had been one highly publicized case in California, this McMartin preschool case. I had heard of it. I didn't read the stories, and I certainly in no way associated myself with the topic. I was thirty-six years old . . . and I was busy working away as an assistant professor, teaching courses in sort of esoteric things that have nothing to do with human services, and really nothing to do with emotions. I was teaching courses on things like insurance and auto safety. And in early May 1992 . . . my local newspaper published its first stories about allegations of child molestation against former Catholic priest James Porter in Fall River, Massachusetts. I remember those front page stories well, because I had a sort of visceral reaction to them. I remember asking myself, why are these people bringing this up now?

And part of the question was, why are "they" bringing this up?

. . . And certainly, why are they doing it now? This is thirty years ago. Why are they doing this? In no way did I associate myself with these stories. And frankly, I thought the topic was somewhat disgusting. (1994a)

Despite Cheit's feeling in May 1992 that this distasteful topic of childhood sexual abuse was irrelevant to him, he experienced an astounding change in awareness of his own life just a few months later, in the middle of August, while on vacation with his wife:

We drove north through Maine to the Canadian province of New Brunswick. We were celebrating our tenth wedding anniversary. The day after our anniversary, we were at a little village on the coast of the Bay of Fundy . . . It was the last day that I would live without any awareness or remembrance of a nightly routine of sexual abuse committed upon me twenty-four years earlier by the camp administrator of a summer camp I attended . . . I woke up the morning of August 24th, 1992, with something akin to a bad taste in my mouth. It was like the residue of a dream, but it was stronger than that. I can't remember if I actually dreamed about this man, but I woke up thinking about him. I woke up thinking about a man I hadn't thought of in twenty-four years. He was a man I admired. He was a man who was more than twice my age at the time, and he was also at the time a student minister at the Methodist church. It was like he was in the room with me. I could picture him. I could hear his voice. I could remember him quite well. And it was very compelling. And I thought about him on and off for the next few days, and the days stretched into weeks before it really sank in.

But the earth did not shake that day. This was not some earth-shattering revelation. There was no epiphany. It was much more mundane than that. I was remembering somebody I hadn't thought of in a long time, and there was a combination of real affection and fondness for this man, and something very unsettling. What I remember, I would describe as "those things he used to do to me." But it was in no terms any clearer than that, and I didn't dwell on "those things he used to do to me." They were a bad memory. They were like remembering the time I stole something from the variety store and got caught. It was an embarrassing memory. It was certainly not the kind of thing I wanted to tell anybody about, not even my wife at first. And I was vaguely ashamed, although I'm sure that I didn't even use that word or those labels at the time. But I remember thinking, I let him do those things. And I was definitely silent about it. (1994a)

Ross Cheit ultimately prevailed in two lawsuits, one against William Farmer and one against the San Francisco Boys Chorus, for the abuse he suffered (Stanton 1995). With the help of a private investigator, Cheit located five additional victims of William Farmer and tape-recorded a confession by Farmer himself. Cheit's case of suddenly remembered sexual abuse is one of the most well documented cases currently available for public scrutiny.

Ross Cheit does not know exactly why his memories returned when they did. He identified several factors, however, that converged at this point in his life:

First, it was a particularly conducive stage in my life, I think . . . I was nearing middle age.

Second, it was the right time of year. It was not only the same month that I had always gone to camp. It was, as I would determine much later, within a few days of the exact anniversary of the last time I saw this man.

Third, my guard was down. I was on vacation. I've led a life of constant work since high school, getting all the degrees . . . and moving into the life of an assistant professor. And it was truly the first vacation I had taken with my wife in seven years. So the bustle of daily life had subsided. No newspapers, no telephone calls, no distractions.

Finally, and I think most compellingly, . . . I had recently learned that . . . a ten-year-old boy who is near and dear to me had joined a similar organization and was going to go to camp that summer. I didn't place particular importance on that when I heard it, but I knew that there was something about it I didn't like. And in fact, we were supposed to go to California for a vacation, and I would then have been able to see him at camp. And instead we ended up going to Canada.

Anyway, this bad taste persisted, and I kept thinking about that man and the things he did to me. (1994a)

As a boy in the San Francisco Chorus, why didn't Ross Cheit acknowledge that William Farmer was betraying him? Why didn't Cheit know that he had been abused? And why did he fail to consciously remember the abuse for a quarter-century?

Ross Cheit and I have discussed many aspects of his experiences. But before we ever spoke to each other we had independently identified *betrayal* as a key concept in forgetting sexual abuse. Cheit had not yet read my article on betrayal trauma (Freyd 1994) when he spoke about the central role of betrayal in his experience with Farmer. Referring to letters he had just read for the first time in twenty-five years, which he had written to his parents from camp in the 1960s, Cheit said:

> But the letters were just devastating, because the letters were the first time that I thought about these actions in terms of what this man meant to me in my life, in terms of a relationship rather than in terms of just actions.
>
> And I read these letters, and I realized how important he was to me. I thought he was a great guy. I really admired him.
>
> I read the letters. And the whole thing shifted, from just "those acts" to complete betrayal. And I broke down that night and cried in a way I had never cried before. And I was sobbing, saying the whole time, he was such a great guy.

Ross Cheit was betrayed by William Farmer, an adult in a position of authority. Ross Cheit had admired William Farmer. He had *trusted* him.

## Betrayal Trauma Theory

Betrayal is the violation of implicit or explicit trust. The closer and more necessary the relationship, the greater the degree of betrayal. Extensive betrayal is traumatic. Much of what is traumatic to human beings involves some degree of betrayal.

Betrayal trauma theory posits that under certain conditions, betrayals necessitate a "betrayal blindness" in which the betrayed person does not have conscious awareness, or memory, of the betrayal. A theory of psychological response to trauma, betrayal trauma builds from the belief that the degree to which a trauma involves betrayal by another person significantly influences the traumatized individual's cognitive encoding of the experience of trauma, the accessibility of the event to awareness, and the psychological as well as behavioral responses.

Self-interest would seem to demand that we be highly sensitive to betrayal and cheating. If, for instance, you discover that a grocery store cheats you by giving you less than you paid for, you are well advised to take note of this fact and either complain about the ill treatment or switch grocery stores. As a general rule, to the extent that you are able to choose with whom to engage in further social agreements, you would want to avoid those who had previously betrayed you. You would be well served to have an internal "cheater detector" providing you with information necessary to establish trustworthy social alliances (Cosmides 1989).

In certain kinds of abusive betrayals of children, however, escape is not a viable option. Here, the ability to detect betrayal may need to be stifled for the greater goal of survival. A child who distrusts his or her parents risks alienating the parents further, and thus becomes subject to more abuse and less love or care. In situations like these, it may be more advantageous to be blind to the betrayal.

A simple analogy can be found in the functioning of the human immune system. The immune system generally responds to infection with localized inflammation and fever, a systemic response. Inflammation and fever demand a great deal of energy, yet they are important to survival. However, there are situations in which these responses are more dangerous than helpful. If a hungry polar bear suddenly appears before a feverish explorer, for instance, the explorer's limited energy is better spent on running away than on coping with the fever. The usually healing responses of the immune system, which would cause the explorer to maintain fever, reduce activity, huddle shivering, feel sleepy, and be aware of pain, would all get in the way of fleeing from the polar bear. The innate fight-or-flight response takes over, ensuring that energy is directed to the brain and muscles. Thus, stress can suppress the immune system. What's more, in an emergency, analgesia—unawareness of pain—can occur as a lifesaving response.

Betrayal is like infection: often it is best to be aware of the problem and change one's plans accordingly. But there are situations in which it is actually dangerous to respond in this "usual" way to betrayal, just as there are situations in which it is actually dangerous to respond in the usual way to infection. In the case of betrayal, those situations occur when the person doing the betraying is someone the victim cannot afford *not* to trust. If the betrayed person followed the usual response pattern and did not trust the betrayer, he or she would only make the situation worse. Or so it would seem; a sad consequence of betrayal trauma is that sometimes—perhaps often—the victim could afford to know about the betrayal but does not know that such awareness is safe.

Betrayal trauma theory does not directly address the issue of veracity of recovered memories of abuse or trauma. Instead, it asks the basic question "If a child is abused and betrayed, what would we expect to happen to the information about that abuse and betrayal?" From a logical analysis of developmental pressures and cognitive architecture, we can expect cognitive information blockage under certain conditions (like sexual abuse by a parent), which will create various types of betrayal blindness and traumatic amnesia.

After he had read a prepublication copy of my article on betrayal trauma, Ross Cheit wrote to me about the centrality of betrayal to his experience:

I can't overemphasize the resonance between how you describe betrayal trauma and how I came to experience the underlying injury. I use the word "injury" advisedly. The concept of trauma never seemed right to me. It didn't fit my story. There were no threats. I never sensed danger. I didn't fear him. He was nice to me. Something didn't add up—and it slowly started bothering me more and more. A number of fairly common questions became as irritating as they seemed irrelevant: "Why didn't you tell anyone?" or "Why didn't you warn your friends?" and "So did he ever actually threaten you?" None of these questions fit. But your article quite accurately captures the nagging concern that did—essentially why didn't my cheater detector work? . . . I knew I had been had, so to speak, but I couldn't understand it. I couldn't explain it. Betrayal trauma does.

The nature and even existence of the phenomenon of forgetting traumatic events have sparked intense professional, legal, and public debate (see, for example, Enns et al. 1995; Loftus and Ketcham 1994; Terr 1994). The recent controversy has prompted the formation of international organizations promoting opposing points of view (Boodman 1994; Grant 1994). The debate pits those who believe in the essential reality of most recovered and repressed memories against those who question the validity of those beliefs.

In distinct contradiction to much of the popular media coverage of the current controversy, strong evidence shows that people can and do forget sexual abuse and other traumatic events. One problem in approaching this controversy and reviewing the empirical literature centers on *language*. What do we call the phenomenon of forgetting abuse: memory repression? dissociation? traumatic amnesia? These terms carry confusing and often daunting histories.

The imprecise and inconsistent terminology leads to critiques that focus on a certain limited definition of the phenomenon. For example, the popular use of the term "memory repression" in the current debate has prompted some critics to attack Freudian assumptions of "repression." In a November 17, 1994, article in *The New York Review of Books,* Frederick Crews wrote:

Once we recognize that a memory can disappear because of factors other than repression, even the best anecdotal evidence for that mechanism loses its punch. Consider, for example, the closely watched case of Ross Cheit, a Brown University professor who has recently proved beyond question that his suddenly recalled 1968 molestation by a music camp administrator was real. But had that abuse been repressed in the first place? In a phone conversation with me on September 7, 1994, Cheit declared that while he takes no position on the existence of repression, he is inclined to doubt that he abruptly and completely consigned his experience to oblivion. A more likely account is that the adult Cheit refocussed his faced but unrepressed experiences after he had read a book about pedophilia (as he did) and became morally exercised about it. While this, too, is guesswork, the fact that it can't be ruled out renders Cheit's case useless as a demonstration. (Crews 1994b, p. 55)

We know from looking at Cheit's case that Crews is confused about his facts: Cheit had forgotten his childhood abuse for approximately a quarter of a century and then remembered it rather suddenly as an adult. Crews's conceptual confusion is less transparent. He appears to be attacking a particular Freudian model in which memory repression is seen as distinctly different from other kinds of forgetting. Although Cheit remembered being sexually abused as a child after a quarter of a century of not remembering, Crews dismissed Cheit's case. Ross Cheit later objected to Crews's account in a letter published in *The New York Review of Books*: "I told Crews unequivocally that I had not thought of the perpetrator in more than twenty years" (Cheit 1994c, p. 76). Cheit also stated that the book on abuse had been purchased three months *after* he remembered the events.

Crews tried to explain why he considered Cheit's case "useless as a *demonstration* that repression exists" (italics in original) in a published response to Cheit's letter:

The reasons for that fact include the necessarily subjective and anecdotal character of every reported act of long-delayed remembering, even when, as in Cheit's case, the events at issue did occur. We cannot rule out the possibility that the moment of recall has been dramatically idealized or that information learned after that moment has gotten blended with it in subsequent retelling. Nor are there any agreed-upon markers that could clearly identify a given memory as having been repressed rather than merely neglected. (Crews 1994a, p. 77)

He also explained to Cheit (in a personal communication) that Cheit's case has nothing to do with the repressed memory debate and that the point Crews was trying to make in the article was that if repression theory is faulty, all the cases that call on that theory are in question.

There is a deep conceptual problem here. Freudian assumptions about repression—and interpretations of those assumptions—constitute a theory of a particular mental mechanism rather than an observable phenomenon. Accepting these Freudian assumptions about mechanisms is not logically necessary in order to accept as valid observations of amnesia in the face of abuse. In Chapter 3 I discuss some of the evidence supporting amnesia after trauma and abuse; in the remainder of this chapter I address the conceptual knots created by, and reflected in, the language surrounding traumatic amnesia. Evidence for amnesia should not be rejected because it does not seem to fit one particular set of assumptions of mechanisms or motivations for forgetting abuse.

## The Tangled Terminology of Forgetting

Is "memory repression" the same thing as "forgetting," "traumatic amnesia," or "dissociation?" It is not uncommon to find the concept of repression or memory repression characterized in such a way as to make it easy to shoot down. For instance, Elizabeth Loftus (1993) writes, "Repression is one of the most haunting concepts in psychology. Something shocking happens, and the mind pushes it into some inaccessible corner of the unconscious. Later, the memory may emerge into consciousness" (p. 518). With this sort of characterization of repression it is easy to dismiss the concept. In fact, however, believing in the reality of memory repression does not require a leap of faith. Instead, it follows naturally from a systematic analysis of the theoretical and empirical literature.

Memory repression can be defined as the failure to recall consciously something that is both significant and for which the inability to recall is apparently *motivated*. That motivation may be conscious or unconscious, and it may be internally or externally driven. "Traumatic amnesia" (the lack of conscious memory for a traumatic experience or part of a traumatic experience) is thus a result of memory repression. More broadly, repression can be defined as not only the failure to recall something from the past, but also the failure to be aware of current thoughts and feelings. At the most general level this broad definition of repression is consistent with what Sigmund Freud proposed in his essay "Repression," originally published in 1915: *"the essence of repression lies simply in the function of rejecting and keeping something out of consciousness"* (Freud 1963/1915, p. 105, italics in original). Thus, problematic "dissociation" (the lack of normal integration of thoughts, feelings, and experiences into the stream of consciousness and memory) can be equated with repression generally, a concept that, in its broadest use, includes not only memories but also current feelings and thoughts.

All of these concepts can be subsumed under the general term "knowledge isolation," though there are distinct types of knowledge isolation. For example, a distinction can be made between a lack of awareness of the past (which may be called memory repression or traumatic amnesia) and a lack of awareness of the current situation (which may be called repression of affect or dissociative state of consciousness). In the literature on trauma and on psychological defenses there is a common failure to distinguish between memory repression in the specific sense of failure to recall a past event and repression in the more general sense of a failure to be aware of some information that would normally be consciously accessible. This confusion of memory and consciousness is just one of a number of crucial confusions that plague the scholarship surrounding traumatic amnesia.

There are at least five areas of confusion about the meaning of repression: (1) profusion of terminology; (2) confusion of phenomena, motivations, and mechanisms; (3) confusion about phenomena; (4) confusion about motivation; and (5) confusion about mechanisms.

## Profusion of Terminology

Whatever we call it—repression, dissociation, psychological defense, denial, amnesia, unawareness, or betrayal blindness—the failure to know some significant and negative aspect of reality is an aspect of human experience that remains at once elusive and of central importance. As Freud wrote in *An Autobiographical Study,* "The theory of repression became the foundation-stone of our understanding of the neuroses . . . It is possible to take repression as a center and to bring all the elements of psychoanalytic theory into relation with it" (Freud 1953/1925, p. 30). The desire to forget significant and negative aspects of reality is most likely as old as human history; in the *Odyssey,* for example, Helen "threw into the wine which they were drinking a drug which takes away grief and passion and brings forgetfulness of all ills" (bk. IV, l. 78). Although Freud is most often credited with introducing the concept of repression into Western sensibility, others had used the term in a similar way before Freud. According to Matthew Erdelyi (1990), Johann Herbart "had used the concept as well as the term more than half a century before" (p. 1). And Bate (1955) cited Samuel Johnson's eighteenth-century use of the term "repression," arguing that Johnson anticipated psychoanalytic thought.

Probably because repression is such a central aspect of human experience, many terms are used to refer to not knowing about problematic aspects of reality. Freud alone used the following terms for repression (Erdelyi 1990, pp. 9–10):

after-pressure (after expulsion)
attention neglect/withdrawal
effortless and regular avoidance of the memory
avoidance of thought
banish from consciousness
censorship of consciousness
conscious rejection

debar the thoughts
defense
dissociation
exclusion from thought activity
fending off the incompatible idea
attempt at flight
inhibition of thought
intentional forgetting
intentional repression from conscious thought
keeping away from consciousness
keeping something out of consciousness
laborious suppression
not thinking of the unbearable idea
not to think about it anymore
preventing ———— from becoming conscious
pushing the unbearable idea away
repression, intentional repression
repudiation
resistance
splitting of the mind/ego
splitting-off of a group of ideas
suppression
to thrust ———— out of one's thoughts
withdrawal of cathexis (attention/processing resources)

In addition to these terms that Erdelyi noted Freud used, many others are commonly used in the current literature. For example:

amnesia
cognitive avoiding
denial
motivated forgetting
psychogenic amnesia
spacing out
suppression
traumatic amnesia
unawareness
warding off

## Confusion of Phenomena, Motivations, and Mechanisms

The profusion of terminology, while a problem in itself, may contribute to another problem: the phenomena, motivations, and mechanisms of forgetting or unawareness are confused with one another. As Karen Olio (1994a) pointed out: "The use of the term 'repressed' with its popular meaning 'to forget' creates confusion in a clinical context between the possible mechanisms (repression) and the existence of the phenomena itself (psychogenic amnesia)" (p. 4). Erdelyi (1985) also proposes a distinction between repression (the cause) and amnesia (the effect): "If repression always produces amnesia, then it is harmless enough to treat them interchangeably . . . However it is not clear that repression/cognitive avoidance necessarily produces forgetting for all classes of memory" (p. 16).

The problem does not end with the confusion of phenomenon and mechanism. Often a particular motivation is also blended into the concept. The putative motivation—to reject painful or disagreeable information—is so ingrained in the definition of repression as to make descriptions of repression indistinguishable from descriptions of motivation. Daniel Goleman (1985) wrote:

> The purpose of Freud's writing is to save the term "repression" for the keeping out of awareness of a single class of items—those that evoke psychological pain. The pain can be of many varieties: trauma, "intolerable ideas," unbearable feelings, anxiety, guilt, shame, and so on. Repression is the quintessential lacuna; it lessens mental pain by attenuating awareness, as does its close cousin, denial.
>
> The defense mechanisms . . . are recipes for the ways we keep secrets from ourselves. The defenses are diversionary, activated in tandem with painful information; their function is to buffer that pain by skewing attention. (pp. 112–113)

David Holmes (1990), often cited for his claim that "despite 60 years of research" there is at the present time "no controlled laboratory evidence supporting the concept of repression" (p. 96), defined repression as the involuntary "selective forgetting of materials that cause the individual pain" (p. 86). Holmes also hinted at anxiety as a necessary motivation in the third element in his definition: "repressed material is not lost but instead is stored in the unconscious and can be returned to consciousness if the anxiety that is associated with the memory is removed" (p. 86). While I agree that memory repression is best understood as forgetting that is motivated in some way, I find it problematic to assume any particular motivation in the definition of the concept of repression itself.

Faced with this encroachment of implicit motivation, some authors eschew "repression" in favor of a less laden term, such as "amnesia." However, using yet another term simply adds to the confusion. The term "repression" is so central to the literature and to folk psychology that we would do better to retain it, but be careful to use it without prematurely assuming particular motivations for the forgetting.

## Confusion about Phenomena

Is repression the same thing as unawareness? Is forgetting the same thing as amnesia? And is amnesia a kind of dissociation? There is disagreement about the nature of the phenomena of unawareness and amnesia, and about how the terms map onto the different phenomena.

A crucial issue is timing. Does the unawareness of the event occur instantaneously, or is it only afterward that the memory is banished from consciousness? This important distinction is often glossed over or ignored.

Some authors do distinguish an unawareness of current events from an inability to remember past events. Lenore Terr (1994), for instance, draws a distinction between "repression" and "dissociation" based on time. In her usage of the terms, repression is the subsequent burial of memories that were formed at the time of the event, whereas dissociation is the immediate blanking out of reality such that memories are not stored in the first place. She explains, "If repression is a burial of memory, dissociation is a sidewise slippage" (p. 85) and "To dissociate you have to step aside from feelings, thoughts, or the sense of connectedness. You have to partly turn off the psychological apparatus that fully perceives, registers, and stores memories. Or you may perceive the memories in one state and then fail to retrieve those memories until you are in that same state again. To repress, you have only to block retrieval of something already fully registered and stored. You are alert when you take in the stimuli that you later repress" (p. 70).

Terr illustrates this distinction with a case analysis of Patricia Bartlett, a woman who was betrayed and became amnesiac after finding her partner in flagrante delicto with another woman. In interviewing her, Terr discovered that Bartlett had suffered a horrible childhood trauma: as a young girl, she had watched her own mother burn to death. She had not remembered this fact until talking with Terr:

> Patricia did not remember the real story of her mother's death from the time it happened until the moment she stopped short in my office and whispered, "Wait." The act of telling me about her lifelong fear of bathwater and fires, and about her memories of incidents associated with those fears, forced the ugly memories forward in consciousness. (The name she had assumed as a reporter . . . , "Sally Burns," is interesting in this connection.) The memory Patricia retrieved about ten minutes before the ultimate remembrance of her mother's death—the recollection of seeing burned flannel soaking in the bathtub—also awakened her old hidden perceptions of singed cloth, hair, and flesh. Repressed memories surmounted Patricia's defensive barriers and spilled into consciousness. She saw the terrible sights she had put out of her conscious mind two decades before.
>
> Patricia Bartlett probably did not dissociate before or during the time her mother burned to death. It was so fast and so surprising that she may have completely taken in what happened and then repressed it. But she dissociated afterward, in the tub. In the same fashion, she may not have dissociated as she walked in on [her partner and the other woman]. There's a good chance she took in the scene and then repressed it. She dissociated afterward . . . That is why so much of Patricia's memory of the terrible events themselves remained available to her for retrieval, while the aftermath of each event became virtually lost to memory. (p. 93)

Yet another problem is the commonly held belief that the forgetting must be all or nothing. According to Karen Olio (1994a), "the popular media has promoted a simplistic caricature of traumatic memory, where continuous memory and delayed recall of traumatic events are portrayed as two different and mutually exclusive phenomena" (p. 4). Mary Harvey and Judith Herman (1994) contend that

> clinical experience suggests that adult survivors of childhood trauma arrive at their memories in a number of ways, with varying degrees of associated distress and uncertainty and, in some cases, after memory lapses of varying duration and extent. Among those patients who enter psychotherapy as a result of early abuse, three general patterns of traumatic recall are identified: (1) relatively continuous and complete recall of childhood abuse experiences coupled with changing interpretations (delayed understanding) of these experiences; (2) partial amnesia for abuse events, accompanied by a mixture of delayed recall and delayed understanding; (3) delayed recall following a period of profound and pervasive amnesia . . . Variations among them suggest that the phenomena underlying traumatic recall are continuous not dichotomous. (p. 295)

Harvey and Herman suggest that of the three patterns, the second pattern—partial amnesia—is the most common. A related confusion centers on what gets repressed or forgotten or never registered in the first place: all knowledge of an event or only parts of the knowledge, such as some feelings, thoughts, or conscious awareness.

While attending the 1994 annual meeting of the International Society for Traumatic Stress Studies (ISTSS), Laura S. Brown (1995) observed that "the recovered memory controversy was everywhere in the air" (p. 310):

> The proponents of the so-called "false memory" perspective have made a point of noting that trauma is not usually forgotten; they note the intrusive memories of Holocaust survivors, combat veterans, rape victims, all with the purpose of asserting that trauma is something recalled only too well . . . Given this presentation of

reality regarding trauma and memory, it might make sense to worry that the experts on those forms of supposedly always-remembered trauma would be critical of their colleagues who work with adult survivors of childhood abuse, the group of trauma survivors whose status as such has been so called into question by the "false memory" movement.

And yet, instead of this polarization, what emerged over the four days of the ISTSS meeting was a convergence of voices, from every corner of the field of traumatic stress studies, saying, "Wait a minute!" These voices reminded everyone that intrusive recall of trauma exists, side by side and in the same person, with post traumatic amnesias and memory deficits, peritraumatic dissociation, and post traumatic dissociative phenomena. (pp. 310–311)

Trauma survivors may have intrusive recall of the sounds of an event while simultaneously being unable to recall the sights, or vice versa. Or the feelings may be inescapably remembered over and over, without complete memory of the events that led to those feelings.

## Confusion about Motivation

Three primary reasons are traditionally given for the motivation of repression: avoidance of pain; avoidance of being overwhelmed; avoidance of unacceptable wishes. I propose a fourth, and primary, motivation: avoidance of information that threatens a necessary attachment. This motivation leads to some testable hypotheses, including the counterintuitive hypothesis that even "pleasant" events may be forgotten if they constitute betrayals that threaten necessary attachments.

Avoidance of pain is generally regarded as the most common motivation for repression. In his *Interpretation of Dreams* Freud stated, "This easy and regularly occurring deviation of the psychic process from the former painful memory presents to us the model and the first example of *psychic repression*" (Freud 1913, p. 476, italics original). Frieda Fromm-Reichmann (1950) wrote:

One more reason for the dissociation of childhood memories seems to stem from the fact that many frustrated, thwarted, unhappy parents compensate for the hardship of their own lives and the people who caused it by maltreating their young children, the only persons whom they can mistreat with impunity. If they deny the recall of unhappy aspects of infancy and childhood it may mean (to them) that they were not unhappy and also that they did not make their children unhappy. (p. 54)

Ralph R. Greenson (1967) explained, "Defense refers to processes which safeguard against danger and pain" (p. 77); Daniel Goleman (1985) wrote, "Painful moments or dangerous urges are repressed in order to ease the burden of mental anguish" (p. 113).

Avoidance of pain continues to be the most common motivation assumed for not remembering or not being aware of significant life events. There is clearly a phenomenological reality to pain avoidance through repression, as is captured by the many personal testimonies by survivors of abuse and trauma. Lillian Green (1992) conveyed the role of pain in forgetting, and pain in remembering: "To survive abuse inflicted by our families, we forget it and minimize it. We numb ourselves to the pain of it. Recovery from emotional, physical, or sexual abuse is a process of remembering and feeling" (p. 1).

But there may be other motivations for repression. In her 1992 book *Shattered Assumptions: Towards a New Psychology of Trauma*, Ronnie Janoff-Bulman presents her theory that trauma damages people by shattering fundamental assumptions of a benevolent world and a meaningful self. Trauma leads to denial and repression, she explains, in order to protect the self from this overwhelming new view of the world and the self.

[Denial] is a useful and valuable process that reflects the survivor's extraordinary psychological predicament postvictimization. For most people who view the world as benevolent and meaningful and themselves as worthy and effective, the initial impact of traumatic events is nothing short of overwhelming. Trauma-associated images and thoughts reside within the victim's inner world. They are powerful, intensely painful, and threaten to completely overwhelm the survivor. It is the process of denial that prevents a steady, unmodulated attack on the victim's cognitive-emotional world. Denial enables the survivor to more gradually face the realities of the victimization and incorporate the experience into his or her inner world. (p. 98)

The notion that the extremity of experience establishes the critical aspect of trauma lurks in the literature in a confusing way. For instance, Harrison Pope and James Hudson (1995), who contest the claim that repression has been demonstrated, argue that "a satisfactory test of the repression hypothesis must demonstrate amnesia for abuse sufficiently traumatic that no one would reasonably be expected to forget it" (p. 122). This notion of "sufficiently traumatic" may imply a kind of horror or unusualness or overwhelm as a necessary component of the trauma— although in Pope and Hudson's conceptualization this role of trauma, paradoxically, relates to its memorability yet is necessary for evidence of repression. "Sufficiently traumatic" may not well describe sexual abuse that is perpetrated by a parent over a long time, and that begins with nonabusive caresses and only very slowly progresses into sexual behavior. Indeed, it might be quite reasonable to expect someone to forget this sort of abuse.

Often the concepts of overwhelming information and pain are intermingled, as in this statement by Elizabeth Loftus and Katherine Ketcham (1994): "When we begin to look for memories we have lost, we enter a strange psychic realm called repression. The concept of repression presumes a certain power of the mind. Those who believe in repression have faith in the mind's ability to defend itself from emotionally overwhelming events by removing certain experiences and emotions from conscious awareness" (p. 7.)

This class of motivation for repression—that is, avoiding both overwhelming information and pain—may also include cases where the repression is theorized to protect the self or the psyche from overwhelming horrors. Terr explains that the psychological disorders that "follow from long-standing or repeated exposure to extreme external events" in childhood are related to the "massive defenses" ("massive denial, repression, dissociation, self-anesthesia, self-hypnosis, identification with the aggressor, and aggression turned against the self") that children use "to protect the psyche and to preserve the self" (1991, pp. 15–16).

Freud, who believed that avoidance of pain was a primary motivation of repression, also believed that it was motivated by the desire to protect against unacceptable wishes. He explained that "through repression the ego accomplished the exclusion from consciousness of the idea which was the carrier of the unwelcome impulse" (1936, p. 17) and that "the infantile ego, under the domination of the external world, disposes of undesirable instinctual demands by means of what are called repressions" (1949/1940, p. 118). Freud emphasized the conflict of instinct versus acceptable behavior, a sort of id-superego battle. The idea of avoidance of anxiety is mixed into this viewpoint. Also implicit here is the notion of unacceptable, uncivilized, obscene, or disgusting impulses.

In a certain sense, Freud's viewpoint is closer to mine, that the motivation behind repression is to protect against unacceptable behavior—but my emphasis is on the need to avoid the externalized, functional consequence of reducing attachment behavior in necessary relationships. I propose that the conflict is between knowing about a betrayal in the external world and maintaining a necessary system of belief in order to guide adaptive behavior.

Mardi Jon Horowitz acknowledges aspects of all of these motivations—avoidance of pain, avoidance of being overwhelmed, avoidance of unacceptable behavior. The "impulsive motive" to revisualize "traumatic perceptions," he writes, "is countered by a motive for repression: the images, like the perceptions, are potentially overwhelming and certainly unpleasant. Impulsive motives are repressed only when they cause some potential danger: they may seem too strong and hence potentially uncontrollable; they may conflict with other motives such as self-preservation, preservation of love by others, or moral standards" (1978, p. 193).

Each of the types of motivations Horowitz mentions—avoidance of pain, avoidance of being overwhelmed, avoidance of unacceptable impulses—might indeed lead to repression. But which motivations actually *do* lead to repression? The terminological muddle has obscured the very different possible motivations for repression, making it additionally difficult to achieve clarity about the reality of traumatic amnesia.

As I argue in detail in Chapter 4, the primary motivation of unawareness is one hinted at by Horowitz with the phrase "preservation of love by others." Horowitz, however, then focuses on the inhibition of impulsive motives as a motivation for repression, whereas I argue that the registration of external reality can be deeply affected by the need to preserve the love of others, especially if the others are parents or trusted caregivers.

## Confusion about Mechanisms

How is it possible that we can fail to know about a significant aspect of current reality or fail to remember a significant event from our own past? The current confusion about mechanisms commonly includes lack of clarity about key factors of time and effort: whether the motivation to repress must be conscious or unconscious; whether repression requires continuous expenditure of psychological energy over time; and whether the mechanisms leading to repression might be the failure of normal integrative processes rather than the active blocking of information.

The typical assumption about the mechanism for repression is that it is purposeful and clever. This is captured, for instance, by Loftus's description of repression: "Something shocking happens, and the mind pushes it into some inaccessible corner of the unconscious" (1993, p. 518). Freud also suggested that repression requires effort, yet he saw the timing differently: "An important element in the theory of repression is the view that repression is not an event that occurs once but that it requires a permanent expenditure of energy" (1936, p. 143). Yet, as I clarify in Chapter 5, this model of repression is just one of many possibilities for how information may be made unavailable to consciousness.

## Knowledge Isolation

Given the terminological and conceptual confusion, it is tempting to abandon the present terminology altogether. Since this is unrealistic, however, it may be useful to set aside the more problematic terms and formulate a single overarching concept: *knowledge isolation*. Once that is done, why, how, when, and from what knowledge is isolated can be determined, based on the resulting level of awareness of reality. Is the knowledge isolated at the time of the event? If so, is the limited material stored essentially unprocessed? Or is the knowledge instead blocked from consciousness after the event? Is the knowledge isolated following a desire to suppress awareness, or did it just seem to happen that something was not noticed or not forgotten? In Chapter 5 I discuss a variety of ways that knowledge about reality and significant events may be isolated from consciousness.

The concept of knowledge isolation encompasses the range of phenomena, motivations, and mechanisms implied by the varying uses of words like "repression," "amnesia," and "dissociation." This concept is useful specifically because it does not assume particular motivations, mechanisms, or resulting phenomena. These varying motivations, mechanisms, and phenomena may not be mutually exclusive. Indeed, I suspect that to some extent they all share a family resemblance that we then commonly call "repression," "dissociation," "amnesia," "unawareness," and the like. Freed from the theoretical baggage of existing terminology, and with the different components of knowledge isolation untangled, we are in a better position to formulate precise and testable statements about the phenomena, the motivations, and the mechanisms.

**3**

When she was in her forties, Elizabeth Loftus eloquently described the experience of remembering being sexually abused more than three decades earlier, at age six:

> The memory flew out at me, out of the blackness of the past, hitting me full force.
>
> . . . I saw Howard the baby-sitter who used to sit next to me on the sofa and rub my arm, using the back of his hand against the smooth skin, his fingers following the gentle curve from wrist to elbow and up for a second, then back down. Back and forth, a gentle curve, a sweet touch, soft, comforting, lulling. I remembered that Howard told me that babies came from eggs that hatched, and I remembered him telling me never to tell anybody about the things he told me, never to tell anyone about the way he touched my arm. "It's our secret," he whispered.
>
> One night after my younger brothers had gone to bed and after Howard had rubbed my arm for a while, he took my hand and led me into my parents' bedroom. He took his pants off, pulled my dress off over my head, and removed my underpants. He lay down on the bed and pulled me on top of him, positioning me so that our pelvises touched. His arms circled around me, I felt him pushing against me, and I knew something was wrong. Embarrassed and confused, I squirmed off him and ran out of the room. After that, there is only blackness in my memory, full and

total darkness with not a pinhole of light. Howard is simply gone, vanished, sucked away. My memory took him and destroyed him. (Loftus and Ketcham 1991, p. 149)

Why would, and how could, Elizabeth Loftus's memory "fly out" at her, "out of the blackness of the past"? And how could her memories take someone and "destroy" him, cause him to be "gone, vanished, sucked away"?

There is a great deal we do not know about response to psychological trauma, just as there is a great deal we do not know about the perpetration of trauma. One gap in our knowledge that fuels the current debate about the accuracy of recovered memories concerns the apparent paradox that traumatic memories are both the *least* forgettable of all memories (causing intrusive recollections and excruciatingly detailed remembrances) and the *most* forgettable of all memories (causing memory failure).

As Elizabeth Loftus went on to say about remembering her baby-sitter:

Ten hours later I was . . . exhausted but sleepless, too tired to pull myself back into the present or to dream about the future, too absorbed by that scene in my parents' bedroom when Howard the baby-sitter betrayed my trust, stole my innocence, and put an indelible impression, a bad, black memory into the place where only good, warm, happy memories should be. (Loftus and Ketcham 1991, pp. 151–152)

Elizabeth Loftus's description illustrates the paradox of traumatic memory: how the survivor can have a memory of the event that is "indelible" yet so blocked that it causes the perpetrator to "vanish," a memory that was forgotten yet flies "out of the blackness of the past."

## Contested Memory

Though this book is not about the accuracy of memory in disputed cases of abuse, I write in the midst of society's preoccupation with the accuracy question. This societal context demands attention. It exerts a tremendous force, not only on the way we think about memory of sexual abuse, but also about sexual abuse generally.

Yet although the contested memory debate demands attention, it should not take all our attention, lest it keep us from investigating more important questions about sexual abuse and memory.

My focus in this book is on understanding why and how memories of childhood sexual abuse can be unavailable to a survivor of abuse and how such memories can return. I begin with a child who is abused; I do not begin with a memory that is contested, nor do I begin with the question "Can a false memory be implanted?"

The phenomenon of forgetting sexual abuse is prevalent and well-documented. In making this argument I move into the territory of the contested memory debate, for many who question the accuracy of recovered memories deny the prevalence of forgetting actual abuse. Because of this, I should emphasize that betrayal trauma theory does not rest on a belief that the prevalence of the phenomenon of forgetting abuse is high; instead, it rests on the knowledge that this phenomenon is real, that its causes and mechanisms are not well understood, and that for those who experience it, the phenomenon is of profound importance.

It is also important to recognize that fabricated memories and recovered memories both exist (Schooler 1994). The popular media tend to tangle them into a snarl, so that evidence in support of the existence of memory distortion and error is used to invalidate a particular recovered memory. This is like saying that because we know some accusations of rape are false, a particular accusation of rape must be false. Individual contested memories deserve individual scrutiny.

In addition, empirical and theoretical questions demand to be posed separately. Can people recover memories for previously forgotten actual sexual abuse? If so, why, how, and how often does this happen? Can false memories for sexual abuse occur? If so, why, how, and how often? Assuming recovered and false memories are distinct, are there observable features that differentiate recovered from false memories? If so, what are they? If we assume a continuum in which memory is rarely perfectly accurate or completely false, what can we discover about the factors that influence the relationship between recovered memories and experienced events? Can people get "false memory syndrome"? What is it precisely? Why do they get it? How? How often does it occur? What are its parameters?

We also must ask about the perpetrator. Do false denials happen? If so, why? How? How often? Is there a false denial syndrome? If so, what are its parameters?

In this book, after establishing that the phenomenon of forgetting and later remembering abuse is real, I focus on just two of these questions: how and why do people forget childhood sexual and emotional abuse?

## Chronic Controversy

The current debate over trauma and memory is not new, despite how it may appear (see, for example, van der Hart and Friedman 1989; Herman 1992; Summit 1988). As Judith Herman wrote in her 1992 groundbreaking book *Trauma and Recovery:*

> The study of psychological trauma has a curious history—one of episodic amnesia. Periods of active investigation have alternated with periods of oblivion. Repeatedly in the past century, similar lines of inquiry have been taken up and abruptly abandoned, only to be rediscovered much later . . . Though the field has in fact an abundant and rich tradition, it has been periodically forgotten and must be periodically reclaimed.
> . . . The study of psychological trauma does not languish for lack of interest. Rather, the subject provokes such intense controversy that it periodically becomes anathema. [It] has repeatedly led into realms of the unthinkable and foundered on fundamental questions of belief. (p. 7)

Of all the traumas that provoke "such intense controversy that it periodically becomes anathema," childhood sexual abuse seems most incendiary. In an uncanny anticipation of the furor caused by the current memory debate, Roland Summit explained in 1988:

It is all of society, not just those immediately affected, that protects the secret of child sexual abuse. We have overlooked or outrageously trivialized this subject, not because it is peripheral to major social interests, but because it is so central that we have not yet dared to conceptualize its scope. Much as the individual victim is compelled into silence, self-punishment, dissociation, and identification with the aggressor, we as a society move thoughtlessly to deny sexual abuse and to conceal vast aggregates of pain and rage. Telltale outcroppings are resolutely covered over, fragmented, or mislabeled to protect our faith in a false concept of the status quo.

Paradox and impassioned prejudgments obscure any rational evaluation of child sexual abuse. Public and professional beliefs and counterbeliefs about this subject still resemble superstition more than science. Sexual abuse, which has gained such spectacular exposure in the past ten years, may be still so enshrouded in myth that we are able to catch only fleeting glimpses of reality. Each brief clearing of the fog brings out believers who claim fantastic insights, only to be scorned and forced to recant by those who insist that the believers have been bedazzled by an apparition, something false and dangerous. (p. 41)

The most famous example of the pattern of discovery and retraction of sexual abuse by professionals occurred a century ago when Freud proposed his "seduction theory." In an 1896 article about hysterical patients, "Heredity and the Aetiology of the Neuroses," Freud described the crux of his theory, which attributed hysterical symptoms to repressed memories of sexual abuse. The cause of hysteria, he wrote,

is indeed a memory relating to sexual life; but it is one which presents two characteristics of the first importance. The event of which the subject has retained an unconscious memory is *a precocious experience of sexual relations with actual excitement of the genitals, resulting from sexual abuse committed by another person;* and *the period of life* at which this fatal event takes place is *earliest youth*—the years up to the age of eight to ten, before the child has reached sexual maturity . . .

A *passive sexual experience before puberty:* this, then, is the specific aetiology of hysteria . . .

I will without delay add some factual details and some commentary to the result I have announced, in order to combat the skepticism with which I expect to meet. I have been able to carry out a complete psycho-analysis in thirteen cases of hysteria, three of that number being true combinations of hysteria and obsessional neurosis. (I do not speak of hysteria *with* obsessions.) In none of these cases was an event of the kind defined above missing. It was represented either by a brutal assault committed by an adult or by a seduction less rapid and less repulsive, but reaching the same conclusion. In seven out of the thirteen cases the intercourse was between children on both sides—sexual relations between a little girl and a boy a little older (most often her brother) who had himself been the victim of an earlier seduction. These relations sometimes continued for years, until the little guilty parties reached puberty; the boy would repeat the same practices with the little girl over and over again and without alteration—practices to which he himself had been subjected by some female servant or governess and which on account of their origin were often of a disgusting sort. In a few cases there was a combination of an assault and relations between children or a repetition of a brutal abuse. (Freud 1962/1896, p. 152; italics in original)

A year later Freud retracted the seduction theory. Recently a great deal of speculation has been presented about Freud's motives for his sudden retraction, including hypotheses about the power of the social forces in Europe at the time, Freud's family history and the possibility of an abusive father in his own childhood, and Freud's exhaustion from working with such difficult-to-treat patients (see Enns et al. 1995; Frasier 1994; Herman 1992; Masson 1984; Steinem 1994). Freud himself (1954) offered various reasons for rejecting the seduction theory, including his inability to fully treat his patients, the idea that so many fathers would be blamed for perverted acts (which seemed hardly possible), the problem of determining fact from fiction in memory, and the difficulty of ever knowing what really happens in infancy. As Carolyn Enns and her colleagues (1995) noted, "Many of these issues have been reiterated in the current literature, including the difficulties of working successfully with the long-term impact of sexual abuse, problems of reliably distinguishing reality and fantasy, and the fact that it may be impossible to recover all memories of the past" (p. 188). They also made a crucial observation: "None of Freud's arguments appeared to support the abandonment of a theory but identified complex issues that required additional exploration" (p. 188).

Kenneth Pope (1990) has observed that while psychology as a field is generally unsure of its own scientific epistemological basis, the "issue of what constitutes acceptable evidence is accentuated in the area of sexual abuse" (p. 231). One problem is that in order to study the effects of sexual abuse, the most researchers can do is carefully and systematically observe the phenomenon as it occurs naturally; ethical controlled experimentation is not possible. This does not make the study of sexual abuse necessarily less "scientific" (astronomy and paleontology are examples of sciences that also must use methods of observation of natural phenomena), but it does make it less rigorously experimental. Pope (1990), in a pointed analogy, noted that the tobacco industry criticized on similar grounds the evidence supporting the claim that smoking is harmful, citing the fact that smokers are not randomly selected, but self-selected.

"It is crucial," Pope cautioned, "that we maintain an active awareness of the degree to which individual or collective defensiveness may be biasing our evaluations of whether certain actions actually cause harm" (p. 231). This collective defensiveness may add to the harm of the original actions, as well as create a climate in which those harmful actions will be repeated on future generations. Lynn Schirmer, a survivor of sexual abuse, recently put it this way: "All this questioning around the validity of memories seems to have added weight onto the non-believing side . . . I can tell you . . . that after [encountering some of the disbelief], I feel as if no one will ever believe me again. Pedophiles rejoice, you are off the hook, as long as you're not caught in the act and your victims grow up before it is safe to tell."

## Doubting the Prevalence of Sexual Abuse

We do not know how prevalent childhood sexual abuse is. The most widely cited figures come from Diana Russell's (1986) community sample of 930 women. She found that before reaching eighteen years of age, 16% of females were sexually abused by a family member, 31% by a non-family member, and 38% by either or both family and non-family members. Similar results were reported by Lois Timnick in the *Los Angeles Times* (Timnick 1985a): 27% of female and 16% of male respondents, in a national random sample of 1,252 males and 1,374 females contacted by telephone, reported sexual abuse during childhood. David Finkelhor (1979) surveyed 540 female and 266 male college students. He found that 19% of females and 9% of males reported forced sexual contact before age eighteen.

In 1953 Kinsey wrote that one in four women reported childhood sexual abuse (Kinsey et al. 1953). Even conservative estimates from current studies indicate that sexual abuse is widespread (see Peters, Wyatt, and Finkelhor 1986 for a review of prevalence studies). Pope and Hudson (1995) point out that "using the conservative estimate that 10% of women and 5% of men have endured serious childhood sexual abuse" (p. 121) would suggest that 14 million adults in the United States are survivors of childhood sexual abuse.

Despite the many studies showing high rates of childhood sexual abuse (see Figure 3.1), a great deal of disbelief prevails. In 1991 I presented a summary of the Russell results to my department colleagues as part of a colloquium presentation. To my consternation, one of my colleagues began to rub his face anxiously as I presented the findings; he continued this behavior for the remaining forty-five minutes of my lecture. Later, I told him that he had seemed disturbed by my talk and asked him if there had been a problem in what I had said. He replied forcefully that he did not believe the Russell findings, that it was simply "impossible" that such a high proportion of women were sexually abused. My colleague's disbelief may well have stemmed from his reading of the clinical literature from before the 1970s, in which incest and rape were typically presented as very rare. For example, Samuel Weinberg (1955) indicated that there are 1 or 2 cases of incest per year for each million U.S. citizens; D. James Henderson (1975) cited a similarly low rate of between 1.1 and 1.9 per million; these estimates are off by 5 orders of magnitude.

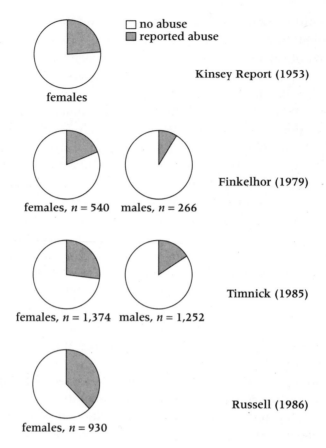

no abuse
reported abuse

Kinsey Report (1953)

females

Finkelhor (1979)

females, *n* = 540   males, *n* = 266

Timnick (1985)

females, *n* = 1,374  males, *n* = 1,252

Russell (1986)

females, *n* = 930

*Figure 3.1*   Prevalence rates of childhood sexual abuse from four samples.

Disbelief may also reflect the difficulty most of us have in thinking that adults—especially good-looking, middle-class adults—would be motivated to engage in sexual behavior with children. In a newsletter published by the False Memory Syndrome Foundation (FMSF), an organization that promulgates the idea that most recovered memories of childhood sexual abuse are false, the following was presented in answer to the question "How do we know we are not representing pedophiles?": "We are a good looking bunch of people: graying hair, well-dressed, healthy, smiling . . . Just about every person who has attended is someone you would likely find interesting and want to count as a friend" (p. 1). In a similar vein, as evidence of the falsity of accusations of abuse, an FMSF board member was quoted in an article in the *San Francisco Examiner.*

> "Nobody wants to have anal intercourse with a two-year-old except someone who is insane," said Dr. Paul McHugh, chief of psychiatry at Johns Hopkins University . . . "But now I'm seeing all these men with fine records, stable lives, marriages intact, their children with fine school records, and they are being accused of the most horrible and violent acts." (Salter 1993, p. A-18)

## Doubting the Harm of Sexual Abuse

Another sort of doubt that plagues the field is that sexual abuse causes harm (Ramey 1979; J. Henderson 1983). For instance, Kinsey and his colleagues seemed to minimize the negative consequences of sexual abuse: "It is difficult to understand why a child, except for its cultural conditioning, should be disturbed at having its genitalia touched, or disturbed at seeing the genitalia of other persons, or disturbed at even more specific sex contacts" (Kinsey et al. 1953, p. 121). Similarly, Domeena Renshaw, in her 1982 book *Incest: Understanding and Treatment,* wrote: "Our contemporary struggle to understand and eliminate child abuse has mistakenly launched an overzealous crusade to regard all incest as criminal child abuse. In a minority of cases, rape or coercive noncoital incest presents a crisis of both physical and sexual abuse. But incest may be tender, affectionate, consensual, non-abusive, and noncoital" (p. 73). This book later suggests: "To incest participants who may read this book and who may identify with or relate to segments on any page, I would like to say, You are not alone. You have experienced another kind of love which has been condemned in our society. It may have puzzled and distressed you, but you have had strength and courage to live with quiet dignity. You have learned as you grew that life presents ambiguities and differences" (p. 160).

In an interview conducted in Amsterdam in June 1991 and published as "Interview: Hollida Wakefield and Ralph Underwager" in the winter volume of *Paidika: The Journal of Paedophilia,* Ralph Underwager, who was involved in the creation of the

FMSF and served on its advisory board until this interview was circulated, was asked, "Is choosing paedophilia for you a responsible choice for the individual?" He responded:

> Certainly it is responsible. What I have been struck by as I have come to know more about and understand people who choose paedophilia is that they let themselves be too much defined by other people. That is usually an essentially negative definition. Paedophiles spend a lot of time and energy defending their choice. I don't think that a paedophile needs to do that. Paedophiles can boldly and courageously affirm what they choose. They can say that what they want is to find the best way to love. I am also a theologian and as a theologian I believe it is God's will that there be closeness and intimacy, unity of the flesh, between people. A paedophile can say: "This closeness is possible for me within the choices I have made." (Underwager quoted in Geraci 1993, pp. 3–4)

Later on in the interview, Hollida Wakefield, a member (as of this writing) of the advisory board of the FMSF, said: "It would be nice if someone could get some kind of big research grant to do a longitudinal study of, let's say, a hundred twelve-year-old boys in relationships with loving paedophiles. Whoever was doing the study would have to follow them at five-year intervals for twenty years. This is impossible in the U.S. right now. We're talking a long time in the future" (p. 12).

Of course it is a fair question to ask: Does adult-child sexual conduct harm the child? A plethora of studies suggests that, in the majority of victims, it does (see, for instance, Briere 1984; Browne and Finkelhor 1986; Enns et al. 1995; Herman 1992; McLeer et al. 1988; National Victims Center 1992; Rowan and Foy 1993). Histories of childhood sexual abuse are especially common in clinical populations (see, for example, Bryer et al. 1987; Chu and Dill 1990; Goodwin et al. 1988). In addition, many findings relate incest and other forms of childhood sexual abuse to psychogenic amnesia and other dissociative symptoms (for example, Braun 1990; Putnam 1989; Putnam et al. 1986; Strick and Wilcoxon 1991; Terr 1988, 1990; van der Kolk and van der Hart 1989).

The coexistence of a history of childhood sexual abuse and

adult distress, however, does not prove that the abuse *caused* the distress. In many families in which sexual abuse has occurred there are other family problems (parental alcoholism, emotional abuse, marital discord) that are also harmful to children. Genetic factors may also enter into the equation, perhaps by affecting the degree of the individual's vulnerability and resilience. A striking range of outcomes is observed for childhood abuse survivors: some children and adults show many symptoms of distress, while a minority of children and adults seem to emerge relatively unharmed (see Kendall-Tacket, Williams, and Finkelhor 1993). Nonetheless, the majority of survivors of sexual abuse report one or more periods of intense pain, loss of trust, loss of self-esteem, and other serious reactions, either at the time of the abuse or later (see, for example, Romans et al. 1995). The testimony is clear: childhood sexual abuse is harmful.

Minimizing the likelihood of sexual abuse or doubting its harm may result in a vicious circle: sexual abuse that is being perpetrated is denied even as it occurs. This helps to create an environment that implicitly permits the abuse of children. There is, for example, the case of the Reverend James Porter. As the *Boston Globe* reported in 1992:

> Church officials have said that at various times they witnessed Porter's assaults or were told of them by children or parents, yet they still allowed him easy access to children as a supervisor of altar boys and through involvement in church-sponsored youth activities . . .
>
> In retrospect, the inaction is striking in light of how often and how pointedly church authorities were made aware of the possibility of molestation.
>
> "I look back now and think how fortunate I am that I didn't get creamed . . . by a parent, by the law," Porter said in a tape-recorded conversation when Fitzpatrick confronted him in 1990. (July 2, 1992, p. 26)

## Forgetting Sexual Abuse

Doubt about whether sexual abuse can be forgotten is at the heart of the current controversy. Can people forget such things?

Despite difficulties with research in this area, a great deal of empirical evidence for forgetting traumatic events has been recorded. Psychogenic amnesia has been documented for a variety of traumatic experiences (see van der Hart and Nijenhuis 1995; van der Kolk 1987; Terr 1994), including veterans' amnesia for their combat experiences (Archibald and Tuddenham 1965; Brende 1987; J. L. Henderson and Moore 1944; McFall et al. 1991). Bruno Bettelheim (1960) described forgetting his experiences in Nazi concentration camps: "Anything that had to do with present hardships was so distressing that one wished to repress it, to forget it. Only what was unrelated to present suffering was emotionally neutral and could hence be remembered" (p. 197).

More recently researchers have documented amnesia for childhood sexual abuse. John Briere and Jon Conte (1993) reported results from a large study in which over 59% of adults reporting sexual abuse also reported amnesia for the abuse at some point. Shirley Feldman-Summers and Kenneth Pope (1994) reported that approximately 24% of a national sample of psychologists indicated that they had experienced sexual and/or physical abuse in childhood; of those abuse survivors approximately 40% reported a period when they had forgotten some or all of the abuse.

Elizabeth Loftus, Sara Polonsky, and Mindy Fullilove (1994) reported that 54% of women in an outpatient substance abuse treatment group reported a history of childhood sexual abuse; of these, 19% reported that they had forgotten the abuse for a period of time and that later the memory returned. An additional 12% reported a period of partial forgetting. Thus 31% of the participants in this study reported some disruption in their memory for the sexual abuse.

The studies by Briere and Conte (1993), Feldman-Summers and Pope (1994), and Loftus, Polonsky, and Fullilove (1994) are *retrospective*—that is, adults were asked about their childhood abuse histories and about the persistence of their memory for that abuse. Depending on the form of the question and the population studied, the rates of reported amnesia appear to vary from moderate to high (see Figure 3.2).

There is also an important *prospective* study of amnesia for

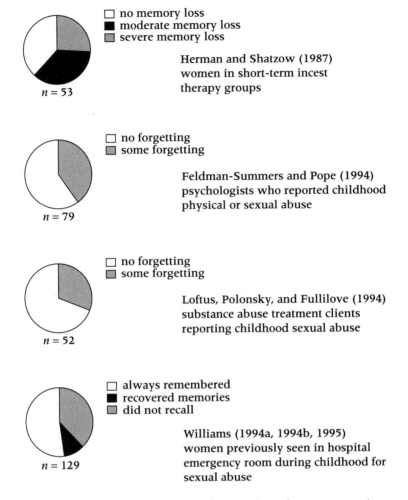

no memory loss
moderate memory loss
severe memory loss

Herman and Shatzow (1987)
women in short-term incest
therapy groups

$n = 53$

no forgetting
some forgetting

Feldman-Summers and Pope (1994)
psychologists who reported childhood
physical or sexual abuse

$n = 79$

no forgetting
some forgetting

Loftus, Polonsky, and Fullilove (1994)
substance abuse treatment clients
reporting childhood sexual abuse

$n = 52$

always remembered
recovered memories
did not recall

Williams (1994a, 1994b, 1995)
women previously seen in hospital
emergency room during childhood for
sexual abuse

$n = 129$

*Figure 3.2* Rates of forgetting sexual abuse from three retrospective studies and one prospective study.

childhood sexual abuse by Linda Meyer Williams (1994a, 1994b, 1995). From 1973 through 1975, 206 girls (aged ten months to twelve years) were examined in the hospital emergency room of a major northeastern city as the result of reports of sexual abuse. Then, in 1990 and 1991, 136 of these victims of sexual abuse were located and interviewed. From this group Williams was able to analyze the memories of a subsample of 129 of these women.

Williams compared the women's memories of their childhood experiences with the childhood sexual abuse documented as a result of the hospital admission. The women were eighteen to thirty-one years old at the time of the interviews. They were interviewed privately by a trained interviewer. The typical interview took three hours. The women were asked a series of questions about their experiences with sexual contact during childhood. The interview procedure was designed in such a way that the women might feel comfortable making such disclosures (see also Femina, Yeager, and Lewis 1990). Forty-nine of these women (38% of the sample) did not report the abuse that had led to their hospital admission as children, nor did they report any other abuse by the same offender.

Williams (1994a, 1994b) anticipated and responded to many questions about her methodology, analyses, and conclusions. In anticipation of the criticism that failure to report is not evidence of failure to recall, she conducted additional analyses to test alternative explanations for her results. For instance, to test the hypothesis that women who did not report the abuse were simply reluctant to talk about very personal matters, she devised a way to measure their willingness to divulge personal information. Those who did not recall the abuse were no less likely to tell the interviewer about confidential or potentially embarrassing information about their sexual history than those who did recall abuse. In separate analyses Williams rejected alternative explanations based on infantile amnesia (although she did find that age was related to amnesia, amnesia rates were still quite high even for the group who were eleven and twelve years old at the time of the abuse) and the possibility that the sexual abuse was simply not significant enough to be remembered. In addition Williams was able to respond to the assertion that sexual abuse was not recalled because it never occurred; she analyzed the 23 cases that met the highest standard for validity and found that for those cases the no-recall rate was even higher (52%) than for the group as a whole.

Williams's study will continue to invite both criticism and acclaim. Replications and extensions of this study are certainly needed, given the import of the findings. In the meantime the data Williams has collected strongly support the claim that women who are sexually abused in childhood do not always remember that abuse as adults.

Williams (1994b, 1995) also investigated recovered memories. She found that of the women who did recall the abuse that was documented in their 1970s records, approximately one in six reported some previous period when they had forgotten it. That is, approximately 10% of her total sample reported recovered memories.

This suggests that close to half of the women in Williams's study—women with documented sexual abuse histories—could not remember the abuse at the time of the interview or some time before that (see Figure 3.2). In other words, this study suggests that for victims of childhood sexual abuse, *forgetting the abuse is not unusual*. Williams suggests that victims of never-discussed, never-documented abuse may be even more likely to forget the abuse than survivors of documented abuse.

When current accounts of the abuse and the records from the 1970s were compared, Williams found that the women with recovered memories had no more discrepancies in their accounts than did those women who reported that they always remembered the abuse. Williams concluded, "Some women, it appears, do reliably recover memories of child sexual abuse" (1994b, p. 1184). But she also found that the women with recovered memories of documented events tended to be skeptical of their memories, referring to them as possibly just "dreams."

While always remembering a traumatic experience (hypermnesia) and not being able to remember it at all (amnesia) seem at first glance to be mutually exclusive phenomena, in fact the two responses exist simultaneously. Mary Harvey and Judith Herman (1994) have suggested that partial amnesia for abuse events accompanied by a mixture of delayed recall and delayed understanding is the most common pattern observed clinically among survivors of childhood sexual abuse. In keeping with this, Laura S. Brown (1995b) observed that the notion of the "real" trauma survivor "who always remembers gave way to the empirically derived data on actual trauma survivors who suffer from alternating experiences of hypermnesia and amnesia" (p. 311).

Judith Herman and Emily Schatzow (1987) investigated the

veracity of recovered memories and the persistence of memory of sexual abuse among a group of 53 women who participated in short-term therapy groups for incest survivors. They found that 20 of the patients (38%) had always remembered the abuse, 19 (36%) had moderate memory loss, and 14 (26%) had severe memory loss. The 62% overall amnesia rate in this study was very high; interestingly, the vast majority of women in this group (75%) were abused by their fathers or stepfathers, and as I shall discuss in Chapter 6, abuse by a parent is a primary risk factor for amnesia.

In retrospective studies, we cannot rule out the possibility that those who report always remembering abuse have in fact forgotten some parts of the abuse but did not recover the memories and thus could not report the memory failure. Similarly, we cannot be sure of the accuracy of the memories; it is possible some of the recovered memories are false. Herman and Schatzow reported that 39 patients (74%) were able to obtain confirmation of the sexual abuse from another source. Another five (9%) "reported statements from other family members indicating a strong likelihood that they had also been abused, but did not confirm their suspicions by direct questioning" (p. 10). Six patients (11%) made no attempt to obtain corroborating evidence from other sources, and three (6%) were unable to obtain any corroboration in spite of attempting to do so. There is as yet no agreed-upon definition of corroboration in studies such as this; critics might question the reliability of the corroboration just as they question the reliability of the recovered memories.

Pope and Hudson (1995) are critical of Williams's conclusion that lack of reporting is evidence of amnesia, and they are critical of the conclusion in retrospective studies such as Loftus et al. (1994) and Herman and Schatzow (1987) that the abuse reported actually occurred. Pope and Hudson recommend that future studies build upon Williams's methodology, but extend it in various ways. They suggest for instance that one "seek a group of individuals unequivocally documented to have been traumatized" (p. 125). One serious conceptual issue here, however, is the possibility that the very factors that make documentation of trauma (especially "unequivocal" documentation) difficult also affect the probability of recall of the abuse. If this is the case—if, for instance, incest perpetrated by parents in relatively functional families is both the most likely sort of abuse to be forgotten *and* the most likely sort of abuse never to be documented—then we have a problem.

## The Prevalence of Forgetting Sexual Abuse

In February 1993 the American Psychological Association (APA) formed the Working Group on Investigation of Memories of Childhood Abuse to review the research literature on delayed memories for childhood abuse. In November 1994 the six-member Working Group released its first public report, the "Interim Report of the APA Working Group on Investigation of Memories of Childhood Abuse" (henceforth called Interim Report). The report had four basic conclusions:

- Most people who are sexually abused as children remember all or part of what happened to them.
- Abuse that has been forgotten for a long time can be remembered. The mechanism (or mechanisms) that allow such delayed recall to occur is not currently well understood.
- Convincing pseudomemories for events that never occurred can be constructed. The mechanism (or mechanisms) that allows these pseudomemories to occur is not currently well understood.
- There are gaps in our knowledge about the processes that lead to accurate or inaccurate recollection of childhood sexual abuse.

The Interim Report is an admirable achievement. That its authors were able to achieve consensus on so many issues is remarkable when one considers the fact that the six-member panel was made up of psychologists who had very different perspectives on the memory debate. Most of their conclusions are correct. However, the first of the four, that most people who are sexually abused as children remember all or part of what happened to them, may be misinterpreted.

This statement does not claim anything about rates of forgetting abuse; it claims only that most people remember all *or part* of the abuse. Therefore, it can be said, and most likely is true, that most people who were abused forget part of the abuse *and* that most people who were abused always remember part of the abuse. For example, if 20% of abused people have a complete memory of the abuse throughout their lives, 20% of abused people have almost no memory of the abuse for a period in their lives, and 60% of abused people forget some but not all of the abuse for a period in their lives, one could say that 80% of abused people remember all or part of their abuse *and* that 80% forget all or part of their abuse.

The problem is that the statement is too vague to evaluate empirically. "Part of" could mean anything from remembering vague feelings of violation, to remembering the details of a room in which a rape occurred, to remembering abusive events but without conscious realization of abuse, to remembering most of an abusive event but forgetting a few details. Yet the statement is likely to be interpreted by many readers to mean that recovering memories of childhood abuse is rare. In an article on the APA's report, for example, the December 13, 1994, issue of *Newsday* concluded, "While the issues are far from settled, a report issued last month by the American Psychological Association suggests that the phenomenon of recovered or repressed memories is a rare one. 'Most people who were sexually abused as children remember part or all of what happened to them,' said Judith L. Alpert, a psychologist in New York City who co-chaired the six-member panel." This interpretation is inconsistent with the data, as presented, for example, in Figure 3.2. It is clear from these data that the phenomenon of forgetting abuse is not "rare."

At all levels—political, forensic, and social—the belief that forgetting sexual abuse is rare may be dangerous: it may lead some to question the credibility of those who claim to have forgotten and remembered abuse. In fact, there is no evidence that people who do recover memories—no matter how rare the phenomenon is—are less likely to be telling the truth. Feldman-Summers and Pope (1994) report that the rates of corroboration for abuse memories are unrelated to whether there had ever been a period of forgetting. Similarly, Herman and Shatzow (1987) report high levels of corroboration for previously amnesic patients who had recovered memories of sexual abuse. Even if it were true that the phenomenon of recovered or repressed memories is rare, we must be careful in evaluating individual cases. When people claim to have forgotten all of their abuse, they may in some cases later discover that they had always remembered some events that were abusive, but because of internal evaluations and labeling had not acknowledged them as such. Perhaps this is the point that Judith Alpert had in mind in her *Newsday* quote—but if so, the point obviously got lost. When parents claim that they are accused by adult children who suddenly regained memories, this does not mean that the children had forgotten the abuse; it means only that the parents are claiming that they did. For instance, Lee Davidson (1994) wrote about her own memories of sexual abuse and her parents' insistence that she suffers from False Memory Syndrome (FMS), "The assertion that I suffer FMS is bizarre to say the least because I have never based any of my accusations on previously repressed memories. I have always remembered what my mother did" (p. 13). Davidson explained that while she remembered the events of the abuse, she had not interpreted them as abusive until she was in therapy: "My main problem was accepting the fact that what Mom had done to me was abusive. I grew up first believing these things happened to all children—and later assumed they happened because I was such a bad child" (p. 16).

There are reasons to suppose that incestuous abuse is forgotten at a higher rate than other sexual abuse, and there is some preliminary empirical evidence that supports this claim (see Chapter 6). However, we are missing crucial data about both the rates of incestuous abuse overall and the rates of amnesia within the category of incestuous abuse. What percentage of sexually abused children were abused by a parent figure? What percentage of victims of sexual abuse by a parent figure had a period of forgetting the abuse? Depending on the answers to these questions, forgetting sexual abuse might be found to be common. Suppose that 80% of individuals who were sexually abused were abused by a parent. And suppose that 75% of individuals abused by a parent have had a period of forgetting most of or all of the abuse, while 25% of individuals abused by a non-parent have had a period of forgetting most or all of the abuse. That would mean that 65% of all sexually abused individuals would have had a period of forgetting their abuse.

How would we get the data to answer to these questions? We could attempt to answer the first question—what are the rates of incestuous abuse in the population?—by looking at documented cases of sexual abuse and then calculating what percentage of the cases involved a parent figure as perpetrator. However, we have reasons to doubt that cases of parent-figure sexual abuse are documented at the same rate as other cases of sexual abuse.

In theory we could best answer the second question through prospective study; that is, we would want to identify a representative group of sexually abused children in which the abuse was documented and then evaluate subsequent memory and amnesia rates as a function of the relationship of the perpetrator. However, to the extent that abuse by parents is less likely to be documented, it is probably not possible for us to get a sample in which the victims of parental abuse are adequately represented. Furthermore, those cases of parental abuse in the sample that do turn up are likely to be atypical, because the factors that lead to documentation would not be randomly distributed. There is thus theoretically a severe problem of reporting bias that contaminates samples of documented abuse. Nonetheless, at least one prospective study (Williams 1995) supports the claim that rates for amnesia are higher for incest survivors than for other sexual abuse survivors. I review this finding in Chapter 6.

Instead of pursuing a prospective study, we could attempt to answer the second question through retrospective study by asking adults about their history of remembering and forgetting abuse. In fact, this has been done, and the results of the majority of recent studies show a higher amnesia rate for incestuous abuse than for other sexual abuse, despite the claim by one of the APA panel members, Elizabeth Loftus, and her colleagues that "whether a woman remembers her abuse throughout her whole life or forgets then regains the memory is unrelated to a number of important factors, such as whether the abuse was violent or incestuous" (Loftus, Polonsky, and Fullilove 1994, pp. 79–80). In contrast to this claim, in Chapter 6 I review the empirical evidence and present a theoretical explanation for a relationship between incestuous abuse and amnesia.

## Delayed Disclosure and Self-Doubt

A number of issues are tangled within the debate about the accuracy of recovered memories. One tangle concerns the evidentiary status of delayed disclosure and expressed self-doubt about the reality of the disclosures. When adults disclose abuse decades after the events occurred, the disclosures are sometimes met with disbelief because of the delay: *If the abuse happened, why didn't she tell someone about it at the time of the event?* This sort of disbelief is often exacerbated when the adult survivor claims that some or all of her memories for the abuse were only recently recovered: *If the abuse happened, why didn't she remember it for all that time?*

Many survivors convey enormous doubt about the reality of their own abuse memories, whether the memories were continuous or not. As Jody Davies and Mary Frawley (1994) describe it:

Where such memories begin as nonexistent or vague—and only emerge in clear form for the first time during therapy—the patient's confidence in the reliability of such memories is subject to the most intense doubting. This could be expected. Of enormous interest, however, is the fact that, even when patients begin treatment with vivid incest memories, a sense of chronic doubting and questions about the accuracy of these recollections almost inevitably plague the therapeutic process. Chronic doubts about what did and did not happen, along with a persistent inability to trust one's perceptions of reality, are perhaps the most permanent and ultimately damaging long-term effects of childhood sexual abuse. Such doubts make it extremely difficult for the patient to arrive at a point where she can come to believe in her own history. It would be hard to exaggerate the pain an incest survivor feels as she struggles to regain confidence in the working integrity of her own mind or the intense pressure that such doubting induces in the analysts to either confirm or disconfirm the patient's questions about the reality of abuse. (p. 109)

Without special knowledge of the natural response to child-hood sexual abuse, it would make sense to infer from this sort of self-doubt that the memories of abuse are not true. In fact, however, this self-doubt about reality is common among abuse survivors. As Linda Meyer Williams noted, even women with documented abuse histories doubt their memories, wondering if they are "just dreams."

Davies and Frawley note that the self-doubt about reality expressed by a sexual abuse survivor is inextricably bound to the nature of the childhood abuse itself. They explain that the "imperative" in childhood for the abuse survivor "to subordinate her own perceptions of reality to those of an overwhelming and invasive other represents one of the most insidiously damaging effects of childhood abuse" (p. 103). This childhood imperative then has implications for the adult survivor's ability to know reality:

> The world of the adult survivor of childhood sexual abuse is a fragmented, discontinuous, and often frightening reality that sub-sumes a multitude of contradictory experiences, frequently elud-ing logical cohesion and organization. Caught in the cross currents of partisan perspectives, torn apart by the inability to integrate mutually incompatible experiences of reality, and driven by the opposing needs to both obfuscate actual experience and yet be hypervigilant to the ever-present dangers of repeated abuse, the adult survivor of childhood sexual abuse often feels out of control and crazy. (pp. 103–104)

This evidentiary doubt that often follows delayed disclosures and expressed self-doubt in adult survivors has a parallel in the phenenomena of the believability of current child victims of sexual abuse.

### Lessons from the Child Sexual Abuse Accommodation Syndrome

In an editorial in the October 3, 1994, issue of the *New Yorker*, Lawrence Wright wrote, "A psychiatrist named Roland Summit explained to the jury [in the Kelly Michaels case] that when children deny that sexual abuses happened the denial can be evidence that the abuses actually did occur. The name he gave to this Catch-22 logic was the Child Sexual Abuse Accommodation Syndrome" (p. 6).

Wright's statement in the *New Yorker* was mistaken.

Summit (1983) had developed the Child Sexual Abuse Accommodation Syndrome (CSAAS) from clinical observation. It describes the dilemma faced by children who have been abused when they attempt to communicate their experience to potential caregivers. They sometimes hesitate to disclose the abuse, and even retract disclosures. The reasons for this relate to a child's limited options for coping in the face of prevailing adult indifference and disbelief. "The course of processing traumatization during sexual abuse is therefore compromised not only by the intrinsic victim-perpetrator interaction but by the isolation and psychological orphaning unwittingly imposed on the child by noncomprehending observers" (Summit, Miller, and Veltkamp, in press, p. 4).

The CSAAS includes five stages of accommodation: (1) secrecy; (2) helplessness; (3) accommodation and entrapment; (4) delayed, conflicted, and unconvincing disclosure; and (5) retraction. Summit's primary contribution with his statement of the syndrome was to counteract commonly held myths that sexually abused children would tell about the sexual abuse without delay and with consistency. His intention was to restore the credibility of children whose natural reactions to sexual abuse are often used as reason to disbelieve them.

Summit's clinical observations of secrecy are supported by various kinds of evidence. For instance, Finklehor (1979) found that the majority of college students reporting sexual abuse in his study also reported that they had told no one about the abuse as children. A large study by the *Los Angeles Times* found that only 42% of the adults who reported childhood sexual abuse had told anyone within a year of the abuse, and one in three had told no one until the researchers asked about the abuse (Timnick 1985a).

The observation of delayed disclosure is supported by a study by Teena Sorensen and Barbara Snow (1991), who examined 116 cases of confirmed child sexual abuse. The children in this study were referred to treatment because of sexual abuse. The cases were confirmed by a confession or legal pleas in criminal or juvenile court by the offender (80% of the cases), or a conviction in criminal court for one or more of the alleged offenses (14% of the cases), or medical evidence highly consistent with sexual abuse (6%). Sorensen and Snow observed that when disclosure occurs, many children refrain from telling the whole story, revealing a little at a time to "test the water" and see how adults react: "Disclosure of child sexual abuse is best described by this research as a process, not an event. The common presumption that most abused children are capable of immediate active disclosure by providing a coherent, detailed account in an initial investigative interview is not supported by these findings, which suggest that only 11% of the subjects were in active disclosure at the time of the initial interview" (p. 11).

Sorensen and Snow noted that the disclosure process often moved from denial, to tentative disclosure, to active disclosure, and then sometimes recantation followed by reaffirmation. The authors reported that the tentative disclosure stage "presented particular concern . . . because the children frequently appeared confused, inaccurate, and uncertain, often vacillating from acknowledgment to denial." They found that only 11% of the children in their sample were able to provide a disclosure of sexual abuse without denying or behaving tentatively. Examples of tentative disclosures, according to Sorensen and Snow, included forgetting ("I forgot"); distancing ("It happened to Joe"); minimizing ("It only happened once"); empowerment ("He tried to touch me but I hit him and ran away"); dissociation ("When he puts his hands there, I go to the pink forest"); discounting ("I was only kidding").

Sorensen and Snow found that children who are victims of confirmed child sexual abuse sometimes recant their allegations after disclosure: "In approximately 22% of the cases, children recanted their allegations" (p. 11). Similar rates of recanting have been reported by other investigators (for example, Crewdson 1988; Faller 1988). Sorensen and Snow found that "of the children who recanted their allegations, 93% later reaffirmed the original complaint of abuse" (p. 14). They observed that their results pointed to the "importance of viewing disclosure as a process with phases that, like developmental tasks, can be resolved. Similarly, if the phase is viewed as an isolated event that ends or limits the extent of the child's support and contact with the system, then the child may become fixed at one phase and be unable to resolve it or progress" (p. 14). This observation about the damage to children could pertain also to the potential damage to adult survivors, who confront a society unable to understand the confusing and inconsistent process of delayed disclosure.

Despite empirical support for Summit's observations about the way children communicate their abuse experiences, the CSAAS continues to be extremely controversial. In 1992 Summit published an article entitled "Abuse of the Child Sexual Abuse Accommodation Syndrome," in which he documented the myths and misconstructions the CSAAS has been subjected to. In that article, Summit explained that the CSAAS is a "clinical observation that has become both elevated as gospel and denounced as dangerous pseudoscience. The polarization that inflames every issue of sexual abuse has been kindled further here by the exploitation of a clinical concept as ammunition for battles in court. The excess heat has been generated by false claims advanced by prosecutors as well as a primary effort by defense interests to strip the paper of any worth or relevance" (p. 153).

In response to the *New Yorker* editorial by Wright, Summit wrote that he had been wholly uninvolved with the particular case in question (and thus said nothing to the jury). He also noted, "The Child Sexual Abuse Accommodation Syndrome makes no claim to provide evidence of children's truth. And it would be fatuous to argue that denial is really confirmation in disguise. I have never said such a thing anywhere." He went on:

While the CSAAS is not the holy grail of child abuse, and I am not the most distinguished mentor in the field, the paper and I have come to share something of an iconic significance in the history of child sex abuse awareness. The more the CSAAS can be trivialized and demeaned, and the more its author can be discredited, the greater is the impact of iconoclastic propaganda. And the goals of that effort are not justice nor fairness nor progress; they are instead to turn back the clock to a more blissful ignorance, when complaints of abuse were less cause for concern.

The *New Yorker* did not publish Summit's letter, but it did publish a short retraction by Wright in a subsequent issue.

## Child Victims and Adult Survivors

Society's response to child victims and adult survivors of sexual abuse is often uncannily similar (Armstrong 1994). Lawrence Wright, the author of the *New Yorker* editorial that inaccurately characterized the CSAAS and Roland Summit's behavior, is also the author of the two-part series "Remembering Satan," published by the *New Yorker* in 1993 (Wright 1993a, 1993b), which focuses on the Ingram case. Later revised and published as a book (Wright 1994b), Wright's reporting of the case has had a great deal of impact on public opinion, convincing many that false memories of abuse are likely.

In 1988 Paul Ingram, a deputy sheriff in Olympia, Washington, confessed to sexually abusing his two daughters. After extended and repeated questioning, Ingram claimed to remember committing increasingly bizarre and horrific crimes. Charges based on these later confessions (which have been widely criticized for having been inappropriately obtained) were eventually dropped. Ingram pleaded guilty to the original charges, and he was sentenced to prison. He later recanted all his confessions. Appeal courts, however, have ruled that the initial confession of sexual abuse was properly obtained (Herman 1994).

Judith Herman (1994) described being interviewed by Wright as he was preparing his *New Yorker* articles:

> Wright acknowledged that the facts of the [Ingram] case were subject to more than one interpretation. But his mind was made up: some of the crimes that Ingram and his daughters described were so horrendous that he simply could not believe they might have occurred. Furthermore, Wright reasoned, if any of the allegations in this case were false, then all must be false, and if they were false in this case, then they must be false in numerous other cases. To Wright, the Ingram case represented an archetype, a modern-day equivalent of the Salem witch trials. (p. 43)

Herman noted that Wright went on to claim in the *New Yorker* that "thousands of people throughout the country have been accused on the basis of recovered memories" and that "certainly many [of the memories] are false." But when Herman asked Wright how many cases of false accusation he had actually documented, Wright responded, "One" (quoted by Herman, p. 43).

Jonathan Schooler (1994) has argued convincingly that current evidence suggests that both recovered memories of actual events *and* fabricated memories, especially in the presence of "a persuasive individual in a position of authority" (p. 452), are real psychological phenomena. A therapist, like a parent, may be a "a persuasive individual in a position of authority." A common theme in popular articles about the contested memory debate is that overzealous and untrained therapists implant memories of sexual abuse into their clients' minds. Although many people recover memories of childhood sexual abuse and other traumas without the intervention of a therapist, it is true that many other people do remember abuse only after initiating psychotherapy. Could these recovered memories in fact be "false memories" implanted by a therapist? If therapists can implant memories through suggestion, does this happen often? Little hard evidence currently exists to aid in answering these questions.

There are several good reasons why real memories of abuse may arise in the context of therapy. Therapy may provide the first opportunity for a person to feel safe enough to remember the abuse; the therapist may be the first person to ask the client about abuse; and the client may have sought therapy because of memories just beginning to emerge, which are causing emotional crisis without explicit understanding of the source of the crisis.

Nonetheless, some therapists may indeed be causing false memories. We do not know how often this may occur. It would seem that the ease of implanting a false memory would vary depending on how closely that memory overlaps actually experienced events (Freyd and Gleaves, 1996). Preliminary support of this hypothesis is provided by Kathy Pezdek (1995). Pezdek attempted to plant false memories of events from childhood that were either familiar (being lost in a shopping mall) or unfamiliar (having an enema). Pezdek found that 3 of the 20 participants "remembered" the false familiar event, but none "remembered" the false unfamiliar event.

As a young woman Jill Christman recovered memories of childhood sexual abuse (Christman, in press). She remembered this abuse while in therapy with a suggestive and otherwise problematic therapist. During the period in which Christman began to remember abuse she was taking Prozac, which had been prescribed by her therapist. The memories came to her in a confusing and inchoate way. She experienced great doubt about them. As the memories came to her, she began to believe that she and another child had been abused *together*. This seems hardly plausible. Yet Christman was able to locate the other victim, who had always remembered the abuse and who confirmed Christman's memories. Despite bizarre circumstances (two children abused together) and memories that were initially doubted, recovered in the context of questionable therapy, Christman found corroboration for the abuse she recovered.

But without the eyewitness corroboration, how many would have believed Christman's memories? Without the corroboration, it would have been tempting to think that the therapist had implanted the memories into the mind of a young woman. In this rare case, the memories were corroborated. Most survivors of childhood sexual abuse receive no corroboration, as there are usually no eyewitnesses other than the single victim and the perpetrator, and the perpetrator usually denies the accusation.

Clients who endure bad therapy may nonetheless come to know the truth of their life; unfortunately, that truth may be discounted because of the poor therapy. Even clients of good therapists may be disbelieved and the therapists criticized simply because some find the outcome of the therapy distasteful or because the therapists are unwilling to pressure their clients to suppress the truth of their own lives.

## Language Is Power

Language is a powerful factor in the current contested memory controversy. Such terms as "false memory syndrome" and "recovered memory therapy" convey scientific and scholarly authority, yet they have been coined in the context of the debate, not in the context of scientific, medical, or clinical research or practice. It is instructive to attend to the terms used in this debate, and to the effects those terms have on our ability to conceptualize the issues.

One phenomenon worth paying particular attention to is what I call first-naming: the alleged victims of abuse are typically referred to in articles and scientific conferences by their first names, whereas the alleged falsely accused parents are typically referred to by their last names.

I originally observed first-naming in a somewhat different context. I noticed that my female colleagues and I were more likely to be addressed by undergraduate students and staff by our first names than were our male colleagues of similar age and status. Others have made similar observations about the role of first-naming in power relationships (see, for example, Goffman 1967; Brown 1965; Henley 1977; Lakoff 1976). Nancy Henley (1977), for instance, writes, "Along the status dimension, status difference is indicated by nonreciprocal usage: the lower-status speaker uses terms of respect, such as titles and the formal pronouns. The higher-status speaker addresses the lower-status one informally, for example, by first name . . . Thus the employer is Mr. Gordon, and the employees, Frank and Mary; the teacher is Professor Black, and the students Joan and Bobby" (p. 68).

Women in the public eye are more likely than men to be known by their first name (Lakoff 1976; Henley 1977). Psychiatrists and psychologists, even feminist theorists writing about the need to empower therapy clients, typically refer to their clients by their first name but refer to their colleagues by full or last name. This first-naming is the pattern despite the fact that the clients are typically given pseudonyms. Why call the client "Cathy" instead of "Ms. Jones" or "Dr. Smith"?

Similar patterns of language usage are applied to women and to members of racial and ethnic minorities. As Henley (1977) writes: "In the south in years past (and perhaps in some areas today), every white person of any age had the privilege of addressing any black, of any age, by first name, and receiving a polite form in return" (p. 68). Blacks were "boys," not men owed the respect of a full name. Women of all races are still often called "girls." When black men are called "boys" or women of all races called "girls," the adult is labeled a child, with the lack of respect that goes with it.

A similar use of language occurs in the contested memory debate; adult women claiming childhood abuse may be repeatedly identified as "the daughter." For instance, in an article published in the London *Guardian,* Beatrix Campbell (1995) wrote about various cases of contested memories that have gained public attention in Great Britain. Although her article was not antagonistic to the possibility of recovered memories, a section of her article is titled "The Daughter." By referring to an adult woman with recovered memories as "the daughter," Campbell might have unintentionally undermined the woman's credibility by evoking images of a child. Clearly, in articles such as Campbell's, family relationships need to be specified, but there are many alternatives to using just that one label for someone.

Authors, commentators, and scientists can choose to avoid first-naming adults who allege a history of abuse. This will help give adult survivors a degree of adult agency in the way in which they are depicted. Avoiding daughterizing is more difficult: How does one write or speak about something that is inherently about relationships while choosing language that does not play into the existing power structure? For example, how do we describe family relationships when we write about adult survivors of childhood sexual abuse? On the one hand we may want to capture the power imbalance implicit in an incest family by using the terms "father," "mother," "daughter," and "son." At the same time, however, we should evaluate whether our language is in fact daughterizing the adults in such a way as to reduce their credibility by playing into social stereotypes of children. With care, I believe it is possible to use language in a way that avoids contributing to power imbalances, while still allowing us to communicate with accuracy. For instance, introducing an adult first in terms of adult accomplishments before applying the label "daughter" will go a long way toward counteracting the potentially infantalizing effect of the label.

Another term that is particularly manipulative in the contested memory debate is "witch-hunt." It is often said that those who promote belief in the veracity of recovered memories or allegations of childhood sexual abuse are swept up in a hysteria analogous to that of the Salem witch-hunts (see, for example, Baker 1992; Ganaway 1993; Gardner 1991; Loftus 1995; McHugh 1992;

Victor 1991). The false memory movement commonly refers to its opposition as engaged in a witch-hunt. Yet, as Ross Cheit (1994a) has said:

> For all this talk about us being a nation at war with child abuse, and for all the media hype about witch-hunts and false allegations—and don't ever let anyone use the word witch-hunts about this; there were no witches—the fact remains that in 1994, it is extremely difficult to come forward with allegations of sexual abuse. And the external forces of denial are almost overwhelming.
>
> If a case as verified as mine meets with denial, I dread to think about the experience of people who don't have the kind of corroboration that I do. And I really worry that we're getting close to a point where it's going to be impossible to prosecute child molesters, because we don't believe children, and now we don't believe adults.

## WHY FORGET?

**4**

A young woman told author Louise Armstrong about her child-hood relationship with her father, a prominent lawyer:

> The times are hazy. But Daddy had always come by to kiss us good-night. At some point I woke up and realized he was sitting on the side of my bed and had pushed my nightgown up and was just touching me, more or less all over. I foxed sleeping and after a while he left. These visits grew more frequent and longer. He always came in long after I was supposed to be asleep and never spoke. I was always awake when he arrived although I was pretending to be asleep (I wonder now if he knew). These encounters were obviously clandestine, and there were a whole other set of visits, right at bedtime, that were less actively physical, but in some ways more pressured. At these points, Daddy would ask me to do something for him and would be displeased if I balked. In some ways they bothered me more than the other visits, because I was awake and he knew it and I felt therefore responsible. (p. 23)

This account was published in 1978 in Louise Armstrong's now-classic book, *Kiss Daddy Goodnight: A Speak-Out on Incest.* In the book, Armstrong described her own always-remembered childhood sexual abuse. She did not expect that other survivors would have forgotten and then remembered the abuse, but when she sought out abuse survivors in order to report their experiences, Armstrong, like others before and after her, discovered the phenomenon of forgetting sexual abuse. As the young woman quoted above, speaking years before the current controversy about memory, went on to say:

> Until about a year ago I had no awareness that any of it had happened. I had completely removed it from any form of consciousness. Until that point I had not come near to having a relationship even as close as a best friend. Two years ago I began seeing the college psychiatrist (generalized dissatisfaction with the way I was leading my life). A year later I came perilously near being close to somebody and was greeted with a rush of memories—flashes of scenes, disconnected and disconcerting. (pp. 23–24)

What would have motivated this young woman to forget her childhood sexual abuse? As discussed in Chapter 2, the most common reasons given are avoidance of pain, overwhelming information, or terror. As Daniel Goleman (1985) put it: "Repression is the quintessential lacuna; it lessens mental pain by attenuating awareness, as does its close cousin, denial. The defense mechanisms . . . are recipes for the ways we keep secrets from ourselves. The defenses are diversionary, activated in tandem with painful information; their function is to buffer that pain by skewing attention . . . Painful moments or dangerous urges are repressed in order to ease the burden of mental anguish" (pp. 112–113).

Elizabeth Loftus and Katherine Ketcham (1994) assume a similar motivation for repression: "The concept of repression presumes a certain power of the mind. Those who believe in repression have faith in the mind's ability to defend itself from emotionally overwhelming events by removing certain experiences and emotions from conscious awareness" (p. 7). For some people amnesia for sexual abuse—including its presumed motivations—seems so counterintuitive that they disregard the empirical evidence that it exists, evidence reviewed in the last chapter. In this chapter, I focus on *why* people forget abuse; the phenomenon and the motivation are two separate issues.

Disregarding evidence that people forget childhood sexual abuse on the grounds that it seems impossible that they would do so is analogous to disregarding evidence that childhood sexual abuse is widespread on the grounds that it seems impossible that a sizable number of people would be motivated to behave sexually with a young child, or to refusing to believe that the Holocaust occurred on the grounds that it seems impossible that a sizable number of middle-class physicians would have agreed to participate in murder as Nazi doctors.

Perhaps those who find forgetting sexual abuse counterintuitive believe that the more traumatic, dramatic, or extreme an experience, the more likely it is that that experience will be remembered. This idea, that traumatic events are the least likely to be forgotten, can be so seductive that it can not only lead people to conclude erroneously that forgetting sexual abuse is rare or nonexistent (Henderson 1975), it apparently can also inspire a kind of idiosyncratic logic, such as: "to prove repression, abuse must be sufficiently traumatic that any normal child would be expected to remember the events" (Charlton 1995, p. 15; see also Pope and Hudson 1995)—in other words, in order to be proven, repression must be a bizarre response.

Implicit in this viewpoint is the assumption that sexual abuse is memorable because it is so unusual or so extraordinary. However, in the case of a child who has been sexually abused by a parent from early childhood, and in such a way that the abuse grew gradually from apparently loving behaviors, the abuse may be neither unusual nor extraordinary.

Ironically, an unwillingness to believe that sexual abuse can be forgotten on the grounds that the experience is deeply memorable is similar to the notion that pain and terror are *reasons for* forgetting sexual abuse. In both cases the true nature of childhood sexual abuse and the fundamental reason for forgetting it are overlooked. To explain why people sometimes forget childhood sexual abuse I will consider three issues: the purpose of pain, the role of attachment in human survival, and the significance of detecting—or not detecting—betrayal.

## Betrayal Is the Key

Betrayal trauma theory proposes that the traumas that are most likely to be forgotten are not necessarily the most painful, terrifying, or overwhelming ones (although they may have those qualities), but the traumas in which betrayal is a fundamental component. This proposition points to the central role of social relationships in traumas that are forgotten.

Interpersonal traumas, such as domestic abuse and child abuse, are clearly examples of social traumas that possess components of betrayal, especially in cases where the perpetrator is a trusted and intimate person in the life of the victim. The more the victim is dependent on the perpetrator—the more power the perpetrator has over the victim in a trusted and intimate relationship—the more the crime is one of betrayal. This betrayal by a trusted caregiver is the core factor in determining amnesia for a trauma.

Jonathan Shay (1994), in his book *Achilles in Vietnam: Combat Trauma and the Undoing of Character,* wrote that the key concept to understanding the damage done to a soldier is betrayal. Shay argues that an army is a moral construction and that soldiers trust army authority figures as powerful personal authority figures, just as these soldiers trusted their parents as powerful personal authority figures. "The moral power of an army is so great that it can motivate men to get up out of a trench and step into enemy machine-gun fire," (p. 6) Shay observed. A soldier may be as controlled by and dependent on the army as a small child is controlled by and dependent on his or her parents. A soldier's survival may well depend on allegiance to the army, and on the loyalty to his leader and the other soldiers a soldier is inspired to feel. Thus, according to Shay, "when a leader destroys the legitimacy of the army's moral order by betraying 'what's right,' he inflicts manifold injuries on his men" (p. 6).

Humans can be exquisitely sensitive detectors of betrayal or cheating. But they can also be remarkably blind to betrayal or cheating that may seem obvious to an outside observer.

Consider two fictitious scenarios: that of Wesley and Myles and of Reg and Wil.

Wesley is a busy executive who has for the past three years paid $50 per week to J. L. for housecleaning services. J. L. was an excellent housecleaner, spending four to five hours to clean the house thoroughly while Wesley was at work. Suddenly, however, J. L. had to move to another city and could no longer clean Wesley's house. J. L. suggested to Wesley that he hire J. L.'s neighbor Myles instead. Wesley agrees to hire Myles to clean his house and offers to pay him $50. However, after a few weeks Wesley notices that his house is not as clean as it had been when J. L. was the housecleaner. Then Wesley discovers that his gold dress watch is missing from the top of his highboy, where he thought he had left it. In fact, unbeknownst to Wesley, Myles has stolen the watch and some other items. Wesley comes home early one day and discovers that Myles has already left after only two hours of cleaning. Wesley feels a rush of anger toward Myles. Suddenly he does not trust Myles and feels that Myles has cheated him. Wesley scours his house to see if his other valuable objects are where he has left them. He feels cheated and makes plans to fire Myles after confronting him about the missing items and the absence from work.

Reg is a busy executive who has, for the past three years, paid $50 per week to J. L. for housecleaning services. J. L. was an excellent housecleaner, spending four to five hours to clean the house thoroughly while Reg was at work. Suddenly, however, J. L. had to move to another city and could no longer clean Reg's house. Around that time, Reg's boss tells Reg that his son Wil is looking for a job housecleaning. Reg agrees to hire Wil to clean his house and offers to pay him $50. However, after a few weeks Reg notices that his house is not as clean as it had been when J. L. was the housecleaner. Then Reg discovers that his gold dress watch is missing from the top of his highboy, where he thought he had left it. In fact, unbeknownst to Reg, Wil has stolen the watch and some other items. Reg comes home early one day and discovers that Wil has already left after only two hours of cleaning. Reg is puzzled at first, but then decides that Wil must have had an emergency that called him away from his work. Reg does not think about the gold watch or Wil and sits down to read the Sunday paper, which he had not had the time to read before.

Wesley and Reg responded very differently to the same information. One explanation for their responses would be to assume that Wesley and Reg are very different sorts of people: Wesley, suspicious and paranoid; and Reg, optimistic and mellow. I contend, however, that two people like Wesley and Reg could be similar in personality and disposition and still display divergent awareness and behavior when faced with the possibility of a cheating employee. The crucial issue is the consequence of awareness of cheating. In Wesley's case, Myles is an employee and nothing else; if Wesley fires Myles there is little chance for harmful repercussions to Wesley, and instead an opportunity to hire a more trustworthy person in his place. In Reg's case, Wil is his boss's son. If Reg were to become aware of Wil's cheating, Reg would face a major conflict that might result in his alienating his boss and losing his job. Reg could be aware of Wil's cheating and still decide not to act on that information in order to avoid alienating his boss. However, the nature of the emotional response to cheating is such that it is very difficult to be aware of being cheated and not behave in ways that display some of that awareness. Awareness of cheating typically produces strong feelings of anger, frustration, and a desire to avoid the cheater. These emotional reactions are difficult to conceal. Blindness to the cheating protects Reg from displaying these natural responses toward Wil.

In other words, Wesley is aware of Myles's betrayal because it is adaptive for him to be aware of it, and Reg is blind to Wil's betrayal because it is more adaptive for him to be blind to the betrayal than aware of it. The variable here is the nature of the relationship between the cheated person and the cheater. In Wesley's case, Wesley holds the power in the relationship. In Reg's case his power is compromised by the fact that Wil's father is Reg's boss.

While Reg might risk alienating his boss and even losing his job were he to be aware of Wil's betrayal, a child who is being betrayed by a parent is in a much more precarious situation. While Reg may be able to notice Wil's betrayal and pretend he does not, a young child is ill equipped to manage such a facade. While Reg has choices of alternative employment, a child may have no choice in alternative caregivers. For a child, the risk of full awareness of betrayal by a parent or caregiver may be, or may seem to be, a matter of life and death.

## The Functions of Pain and the Blocking of Pain

Why do people block pain? One would think that getting rid of pain is an end in and of itself. This intuition is expressed often. Over a hundred years ago, the Scottish missionary and explorer of Africa, David Livingstone, was attacked by a lion that crushed his shoulder. Livingstone described what happened:

> I heard a shout. Starting, and looking half round, I saw the lion just in the act of springing upon me. I was upon a little height; he caught my shoulder as he sprang, and we both came to the ground below together. Growling horribly close to my ear, he shook me as a terrier dog does a rat. The shock produced a stupor similar to that which seems to be felt by a mouse after the first shake of the cat. It caused a sort of dreaminess, in which there was no sense of pain nor feeling of terror, though quite conscious of all that was happening. It was like what patients partially under the influence of chloroform describe, who see all the operation, but feel not the knife. This singular condition was not the result of any mental process. The shake annihilated fear, and allowed no sense of horror in looking round at the beast. This peculiar state is probably produced in all animals killed by the carnivora; and if so, is a merciful provision by our benevolent Creator for lessening the pain of death. (1857, p. 12)

Livingstone interpreted his escape from pain as a divine gift. Escaping pain was the goal.

The idea that we are driven to get rid of pain for the purpose of getting rid of pain has some truth to it—we *are* motivated to get rid of pain—but it ignores why we are so responsive to pain in the first place: pain is a motivator for changing our behavior in order to survive. If we are hungry, we eat. If we are cold, we cover ourselves. If we are tired, we sleep. If our foot hurts, we stop walking. In each of these cases, we take an action that brings an end to the pain, and that is of fundamental importance to our survival in direct ways. We need food, warmth, rest, and the opportunity to heal wounds. We get rid of pain in order to stay alive.

But what about those times when we do not feel physical pain that would normally be felt? Why would we block pain?

As Livingstone reported, we have an impressive system of natural analgesia, sometimes referred to as the "stress response" (Maier, Watkins, and Fleshner 1994). Laboratory experiments with animals have shown that stress can induce analgesia:

An important part of an organism's response to emergency situations is a reduction in sensitivity to pain. In meeting the behavioral demands prompted by exposure to stressful situations, such as those involving predation, defense, dominance, or adaptation to an extreme environmental demand, an organism's normal reactions to pain could prove disadvantageous. Pain normally promotes a set of reflex withdrawals, escape, rest, and other recuperative behaviors. During the stressful encounter these reactions to pain might be suppressed automatically in favor of more adaptive behavior. (Kelly 1985, pp. 340–341)

Animals can get rid of pain through analgesia, but what about humans? Kelly (1985) noted that "soldiers wounded in battle and athletes injured in sports sometimes report that they do not feel pain. Perhaps, as in the laboratory, stress induces analgesia only in the most extreme or life-threatening situations" (p. 342). Kelly also observed that human physical pain can be altered by behavioral interventions and even psychological states:

Pain is a protective experience that we share with almost all animals. Because there is such an urgent and primitive quality about the array of sensations that we call painful (for example, pricking, burning, aching, stinging, and soreness), it is difficult to appreciate that the neural activity associated with pain, like that of other sensory systems, can be modulated by a wide range of behavioral experiences. Pain can be altered by drugs, acupuncture, and surgery, but it can also be altered by the joy of childbirth, the fear of a dentist, by stress, hypnosis, and many other forms of stimulation and ritual. The extraordinary plasticity of human pain suggests that neural mechanisms must exist that either modulate transmission in primary pain pathways or modify the organism's emotional reaction to pain . . . Both types of modulatory activity occur in the nervous system. (1985, p. 331)

Dissociation during trauma and traumatic amnesia (or "repression") are commonly understood to be psychological defenses against psychological pain, as if removing pain is a logical end goal. Yet, in an evolutionary or functional sense, it would not be adaptive to have an animal spontaneously experience pain, either physical or psychological, and then go to great lengths to get rid of the pain merely to be rid of it. Instead, it is more logical to assume that pain exists to motivate changes in behavior. Natural systems for blocking pain would be adaptive only if the behavioral consequences of pain in a particular situation are themselves maladaptive (Kelly 1986; Levinthal 1988). In other words, an animal is surely motivated to avoid and alleviate pain, but behind that motivation is an evolutionary goal directly related to survival.

Suppose Deanna breaks a leg on a skiing accident while traveling with a companion. The pain is so severe that Deanna is unlikely to want to move at all, and she is certainly unlikely to stand up and walk. Instead she waits while her companion goes to get a rescue team. On the other hand, if Beverly has a similar accident while traveling alone, there is a good chance that she will spontaneously block perception of the leg pain and get up and try to hobble to safety. In the first case, the pain is protecting Deanna from sustaining the further damage that may be caused by walking on a broken leg. In the second case, the blockage of pain is allowing Beverly to escape the life-threatening situation of being trapped alone in the snow. Presumably Beverly abhors pain as much as does Deanna, but only Beverly's circumstance is likely to create the spontaneous blockage of pain.

Deanna's pain carries information: in essence her pain says, "Do not walk on my leg; do not cause further damage!" Beverly's blockage of pain suppresses that information; her nervous system automatically risks damage to her leg in order to ensure her immediate survival. Survival may similarly depend upon blocking purely mental information and the corresponding psychic pain. According to this perspective, memory repression, dissociation, and related defenses are not functions we have to reduce psychic pain per se. Instead, those phenomena function to control social cognition and thus to control social behavior. At times, the mind may use psychic pain in order to invoke defenses, but the functional utility of defenses is not for the end result of merely avoiding pain; there must be a survival advantage in invoking the numbing of pain and simultaneously blocking information. Indeed, in the long run it is arguable that psychological defenses do not reduce psychic pain at all, just as it is more likely that Beverly will experience leg pain (because of the further harm inflicted by walking on a damaged leg) than will Deanna. But in the short run such knowledge isolation may be necessary for survival.

## Attachment

If betrayal by a trusted caregiver is the key to predicting amnesia for abuse, attachment is the key to understanding why amnesia is adaptive in instances of such betrayals.

In 1959 Harry Harlow published his classic article "Love in Infant Monkeys" in *Scientific American*. Harlow separated newborn monkeys from their mothers and put them into cages containing artificial "mothers." In one experiment the infants had a choice of mothers. One was made of wire with a rubber nipple that provided milk for the infant; the other had no nipple but was made of soft cloth. The infants chose to spend most of their time with the cloth mother, and when they were frightened they chose the cloth mothers and clung to them. Harlow argued from this that monkeys were motivated more by a need for comfort than by a need for food.

Harlow also studied the effects of removing all social stimuli from birth. After a year of such isolation, the monkeys were clearly disturbed. When normal monkeys were introduced to the isolated monkeys, the isolated monkeys withdrew to a corner or rocked back and forth for hours. If a normal monkey approached an isolated monkey, the isolated monkey would sometimes bite itself until the normal monkey would leave it alone. The isolated monkey's problems continued into adulthood. The males were generally unable or unwilling to initiate sexual activity with a potential partner. When previously isolated females were made pregnant through artificial insemination they were not able to care for their infants properly, generally ignoring the infants, or even abusing or killing them when the infants sent distress signals.

More recently, Stephen Suomi and Harry Harlow (1972) dis-

covered that some of the damage caused by early social depri-
vation in monkeys can be reversed by putting the separated
monkeys with younger nurtured monkeys. When the previously
isolated monkeys were permitted to live with these "monkey
therapists" for three or four years, the previously isolated monkeys began to appear normal. However, monkeys who were
initially deprived, even after apparently having recovered, easily
regressed when experiencing stress (Novak and Harlow 1979).
Similarly, so-called recovered monkeys are more susceptible
than normal monkeys to drug and alcohol abuse when presented
with the opportunity to consume such substances (van der Kolk
1987). These studies with infant monkeys, our biological relatives, have clear implications for the human requirement for
social contact and attachment in infancy and childhood. John
Bowlby (1969; 1988) drew attention to the fundamental role of
attachment in humans after he observed the damage done to
orphans who were separated from their parents. The physical
and mental survival of human infants and children is widely
recognized as dependent on a successful attachment between the
child and the caregiver. Under healthy conditions during the first
year of a human's life, while caregivers and infants are responding to each other, the infant and the caregiver develop an affectionate, intimate, reciprocal, and enduring relationship.

Melanie Klein (1975), Otto Kernberg (1976), Heinz Kohut
(1983), and object-relations theorists developed psychoanalytic
theory beyond Freudian psychoanalytic theory by pointing to
the crucial importance of early attachments between infants and
their love objects, who they assumed to be the infant's primary
caregivers, especially the mother. Primary caregivers meet the
infant's physical needs, providing protection, recognition, and
acceptance. According to object relations theorists, these relationships have an enormous impact on personality development.
From them the infant develops a sense of self, security, and
identity. If the relationship is adequate the infant forms a secure
bond to the mother or other caregivers, then gradually separates,
finally developing the ability to relate to other people as an
independent and secure person (Ainsworth 1989). If the relationship is inadequate, the child will have difficulties with self-

esteem, trust, or commitment, and may have more serious personality disorders (Eagle 1984).

Linda Burton (1995) described her beliefs about the appearance of children who are deprived of "good mothering":

> [They] tend to look disheveled and have signs of poor personal hygiene. Nobody takes them to the photographer for cute pictures, and nobody buys them car seats. More often than not, mistreated children appear frightened, vacant, withdrawn, aggressively hostile or nonresponsive. Occasionally, they show signs of malnourishment and/or other physical abuse. They look, for the most part, like the kids who have checked out the world and found it to be a very scary place. (p. 1C)

Burton captures the devastation that occurs when the caretaking and attachment system breaks down. Although children may be mistreated and *not* appear this way, for those children for whom mistreatment and its consequences are so transparent, their immediate survival is greatly at risk.

Because attachment is of overwhelming significance, a complex system of emotional, cognitive, and behavioral components is operative during the child's development. The system ensures attachment: children love their caregivers, and that love motivates the children to display affection toward their caregivers, which in turn elicits love, nurturing, and protection from the caregivers.

## The Psychology of Detecting Betrayal

What happens when a child, charged by life to become attached to and elicit attachment from a caregiver, is betrayed by that very caregiver?

Leda Cosmides (1989) has postulated that humans have a naturally evolved mental mechanism devoted to detecting cheaters. Cosmides and John Tooby (1992) explain that in human evolution the ability to reason rapidly and accurately about social contracts would have been important for survival and reproductive fitness. They argue that detecting violators of social contracts—detecting cheaters—would have been a mental ability of especially high value. Cosmides and Tooby also contend that general-purpose logical reasoning abilities would not be as well-suited for detecting violations of social contracts as would specific mental mechanisms designed to detect cheaters. They give an example:

> Suppose you and I agree to the following exchange: "If you give me your watch then I'll give you $20." You would have violated our agreement—you would have cheated me—if you had taken my $20 but not given me your watch. But according to the rules of inference of the propositional calculus, the only way this rule can be violated is by your giving me your watch but my not giving you $20. If the only mental rules my mind contained were the rules of inference of the propositional calculus, then I would not be able to tell when you had cheated me. (pp. 179–180)

In a series of experiments Cosmides (1985; 1989; Cosmides and Tooby 1992) tested the hypothesis that humans are specifically able to detect cheaters, yet are not equally able to reason about similar problems that do not involve cheating. Cosmides used the Wason Selection Task, a method of measuring human reasoning ability, as her experimental paradigm for this research. In the Wason Selection Task a subject is asked to see whether a conditional hypothesis of the form *if p then q* has been violated by any one of four scenarios. The scenarios are represented by cards, as displayed in Figure 4.1. Most people perform poorly on the Wason Selection Task (which requires searching for disconfirming evidence) when the problem does not involve social contracts, as is the case in the first example in Figure 4.1. In contrast, they tend to do well when the situation involves a violation of a social contract (such as detecting cheaters), as in the drinking age problem illustrated in the bottom half of Figure 4.1. In her experiments Cosmides excluded familiarity of the particular social contract by creating situations that involved fictitious cultures, benefits, and costs (for example, "If you eat duiker meat, then you have found an ostrich eggshell" or "If a man eats cassava root, then he must have a tattoo on his face"). She compared scenarios that made these rules into social contracts with scenarios that made these rules purely descriptive. Cosmides found that subjects correctly detected the rule viola-

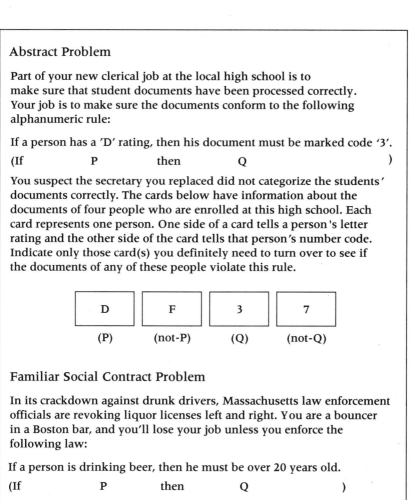

## Abstract Problem

Part of your new clerical job at the local high school is to make sure that student documents have been processed correctly. Your job is to make sure the documents conform to the following alphanumeric rule:

If a person has a 'D' rating, then his document must be marked code '3'.
(If        P        then        Q        )

You suspect the secretary you replaced did not categorize the students' documents correctly. The cards below have information about the documents of four people who are enrolled at this high school. Each card represents one person. One side of a card tells a person's letter rating and the other side of the card tells that person's number code. Indicate only those card(s) you definitely need to turn over to see if the documents of any of these people violate this rule.

| D | F | 3 | 7 |
|:-:|:-:|:-:|:-:|
| (P) | (not-P) | (Q) | (not-Q) |

## Familiar Social Contract Problem

In its crackdown against drunk drivers, Massachusetts law enforcement officials are revoking liquor licenses left and right. You are a bouncer in a Boston bar, and you'll lose your job unless you enforce the following law:

If a person is drinking beer, then he must be over 20 years old.
(If        P        then        Q        )

The cards below have information about four people sitting at a table in your bar. Each card represents one person. One side of a card tells what a person is drinking and the other side of the card tells that person's age. Indicate only those card(s) you definitely need to turn over to see if any of these people are breaking the law.

| drinking beer | drinking cola | 25 years old | 16 years old |
|:-:|:-:|:-:|:-:|
| (P) | (not-P) | (Q) | (not-Q) |

*Figure 4.1* The effect of content on the Wason Selection Task (based on Cosmides 1989; the drinking age problem adapted from Griggs and Cox 1982). The logical structure of these two tasks is identical; they differ only in content. The correct solution in each case is *P and not-Q*. Although less than 25% of college students choose both these cards for the abstract problem in the top half of the figure, about 75% do for the familiar social contract problem (Cosmides and Tooby 1992).

tions that corresponded to detecting cheaters between 70% and 75% of the time, but that they correctly detected the rule violations that corresponded to detecting descriptive rules between only 21% and 25% of the time (1989, Experiments 1 and 2). Cosmides and Tooby (1992) showed that these results are not obtained when the logic of the task is to detect people being altruistic; the enhanced ability that people have to reason about social-contract problems in the Wason Selection Task appears to be limited to cases in which they are detecting cheaters.

Cosmides and Tooby interpret these results as supportive of their framework of evolutionary psychology. For our purposes, the implications these findings have for the significance of detecting betrayal are what is significant. Furthermore, whether we acquire this ability to detect cheaters through nature or nurture, we seem to show evidence of it early in life. As anyone who has spent much time with a young child can attest, the cry "That's not fair!" is both often heard and accurate.

That we would be good at detecting cheaters makes sense; under many conditions, it is to our advantage to be highly attuned to betrayals. To the extent that we are able to choose with whom to engage in further social agreements, we want to avoid those who have previously betrayed us. Presumably this is why the thought "I've been cheated" or even the suspicion "I think I've been cheated" arouses powerful negative feelings. These negative feelings presumably motivate future avoidance of cheaters.

### Pain, Attachment, Betrayal, Amnesia

We are exquisitely sensitive to cheating when we can choose to avoid the cheater. Being sensitive to betrayal brings pain, and the pain can be great. When the betrayer is someone on whom we are dependent, the very mechanisms that normally protect us—a sensitivity to cheating and the pain that motivates us to change things so that we will no longer be in danger—become a problem. We must block the awareness of the betrayal, forget it, in order to ensure that we behave in ways that maintain the relationship on which we are dependent.

Some traumas, such as natural disasters, car accidents, or combat, may cause immediate terror and may lead to conditions typical of posttraumatic stress disorder (PTSD), such as increased arousal (agitation and hypervigilance), generalized numbing (depression and avoidance), and intrusive cognitions (unwanted and disruptive thoughts) (Horowitz 1986; Krystal 1990; McNally 1992). Profound amnesia (as opposed to other symptoms of PTSD) is a likely result in cases involving a betrayal of trust that produces conflict between external reality and social dependence. (This prediction is explored in more detail in Chapter 6.) Of course, a particular event, such as combat (Shay 1994), may be simultaneously a betrayal and a terrifying experience. Rape is such an event: the victim's life may be immediately threatened while she or he is psychologically betrayed (Spiegel 1989).

Childhood sexual abuse is especially likely to be seen eventually by the victim as a betrayal (Bunge 1993; Dominelli 1989; Finkelhor and Browne 1985; Miller 1984). Further, evidence shows that the most devastating psychological effects of childhood sexual abuse occur when the victims are abused by a trusted person who was known to them (Feinauer 1989).

If a child experiencing sexual abuse were to process the betrayal in the normal way, he or she would recognize the betrayal and be motivated to stop interacting with the betrayer. Instead, the child must ignore the betrayal. If the betrayer is a primary caregiver, it is essential that the child not stop behaving in a way that inspires attachment. For the child to withdraw from a caregiver he or she is dependent on could be life-threatening. Thus the trauma of childhood sexual abuse, by its very nature, requires that information about the abuse be blocked from the mental mechanisms that control attachment and attachment behavior. The information that gets blocked may be partial (for instance, emotional responses only), but in many cases the information that gets blocked leads to more profound amnesia.

In other words, in order to survive in cases of core betrayals (abuse by a trusted caregiver on a dependent victim) some amount of information blockage is likely to be required. The probability of amnesia is a function of the degree of betrayal, although other factors also contribute to the likelihood of amnesia (as I discuss in Chapter 6).

Marilyn Van Derbur Atler was crowned Miss America in 1958.

In 1991 she wrote about remembering the incest she had suffered at night for thirteen years:

> My father sexually violated me in my bedroom from the time I was five until I was eighteen and left home for college . . . I had no conscious knowledge of what had happened at night until I was twenty-four . . . I don't remember how or when I split my mind. I do know that the terror of the night caused me at some age, probably between five and six, to dissociate into the day and the night child. The day child knew nothing of the night child's existence. (p. 80)

Marilyn Van Derbur Atler's recovered memories of sexual abuse were corroborated by her sister, Gwendolyn Mitchell, who had always remembered being abused. Why did Marilyn forget the abuse and Gwendolyn remember it? Although amnesia is an adaptive mechanism for coping with the betrayal that is sexual abuse by a trusted caregiver, it is not the only way of coping. But some degree of information blockage is necessary. According to Lenore Terr (1994), who interviewed Gwendolyn Mitchell and studied the cases of both Marilyn Van Derbur Atler and her sister, both women as girls had elaborate systems of defense in which the information about the abuse was directed away from central consciousness. While Gwendolyn Mitchell remembered the fact that she was abused, she apparently did not remember everything; for example, she does not remember penetration, though there is some reason to believe she was taken to an abortionist by her father. According to Terr, Gwendolyn Mitchell coped with the abuse by dissociating herself from it so as to not experience it, and by using fantasy to make up for parents who were actually abusive and distant.

Did Marilyn Van Derbur Atler's coping mechanism—complete amnesia for the abuse—produce a greater attachment between her and her father than existed between Gwendolyn and her father? According to reporter Linden Gross (1994), Marilyn felt no anger toward her father while growing up because she had no conscious knowledge of what he was doing to her. I asked her to compare her and her sister's relationship with their father when they were children. Marilyn told me that her sister Gwen was beaten (personal communication, May 16, 1995).

Then, when Marilyn was seven years old and Gwen was thirteen and ready to start ninth grade as an honor student, she was sent away to a boarding school. Marilyn reported: "I had never heard of a boarding school. I just knew she was sent away . . . Seeing Gwen beaten and sent away, let me know as a child that defying is not the way to go! This may not have been a conscious thought but there is no doubt I got the message of what would happen if I defied." This report suggests that Marilyn's strategy of being totally unaware of her nighttime violations was supportive of her maintaining her parents' support and nurturance in the day-time. Marilyn was not beaten and she was not sent away. In the long run, however, Marilyn paid a very high price for her un-awareness in childhood, as an adult suffering inexplicable pa-ralysis and other problems.

Lillian Green (1992) also reflected on the costs of knowing and not knowing about her own abuse. She quoted her mother's response to being told about her brother's sexually abusive acts: "I'm sorry we can't be a family. You can't visit on the holidays. We can't share things. There are bad feelings. I hoped therapy would help you" (p. 170). Knowing about the abuse in this case meant emotional abandonment from her family. As Green ex-plained:

> As children in abusive families, we tried to minimize the abuse and earn the caretaking we needed by complying with our par-ents' demands, both spoken and non-verbal. To satisfy them, we assumed the characteristics we thought they wanted us to have, characteristics which became our roles. To avoid abuse and ne-glect, we suppressed or disguised what didn't fit these roles. Parts of us went underground, disconnecting from our external selves, and remaining undeveloped. Splitting ourselves in hidden pieces enabled us to survive, but cost us dearly. (p. 131)

Perpetrators can take advantage, and even enhance the like-lihood, of the natural inclination victims of childhood sexual abuse have to forget the abuse. Eric Lister (1982) considers "forced silence" to be a neglected dimension of the trauma. Writ-ing about the commonly spoken command that the victim re-main silent about the abuse, Lister says, "This prohibition of communication, enforced by some implicit or explicit threat, constitutes a secondary trauma of enormous import and has been ignored in the literature" (p. 872).

Perpetrators do not need to threaten their victims, even implicitly, although threats are in many cases used to ensure silence. Some perpetrators encourage silence by communicating that the event is a shared secret or by inducing a kind of trance in the young victim.

On the February 2, 1995, Public Broadcasting Corporation television show *The MacNeil/Lehrer News Hour* Ross Cheit described his memories of abuse by an authority figure whom Ross the boy had trusted completely:

> I woke up thinking about Bill Farmer. It was a kind of sinking feeling in my stomach of, oh, God, right, how he used to come into my cabin at night and do these things to me . . . I could picture this all the first day. I could picture him sitting on my bed, talking to me about sort of how my day had gone, talking quietly, and he'd start, he'd put his hand on my chest and start kind of stroking my chest as he talked to me. He'd just be kind of, you know, rubbing my chest. And he'd talk, and eventually he'd start reaching his hands, and his hand would start moving down my chest. And I can still feel the feeling of having my stomach muscles tense up, and Bill saying, "Relax, relax."

Considering the role of betrayal, and the perpetrator's reinforcement of a child's natural response of not knowing about the betrayal by a trusted caregiver, the resulting amnesia makes a great deal of sense.

## WAYS OF FORGETTING

# 5

Frank Fitzpatrick, the man who initiated the investigation of the Reverend James R. Porter based on his recovered memories of childhood sexual abuse, described the process of recalling previously forgotten assaults:

> I came to the realization in late summer of 1989 that in general my life was quite good but that my feelings did not reflect this reality . . . It dawned on me one day that the emotional pain I felt must have a cause of which I was unaware . . . I made a conscious decision to let myself feel the emotional pain more fully, to try to figure out from where it came. I was alone in the house. I lay down on my bed, closed my eyes, and let myself feel. Emotion and sounds were the things to flood back on that first occasion. I felt an immense, monstrous betrayal by someone that I loved. I relived the part of the sexual assault that had occurred when my eyes were shut. There were sounds of rhythmic, heavy, sexual breathing in my ears and some kind of crumpling sound. The feelings of being sexually assaulted were clear and unmistakable. I was not in therapy, and had not been for two years. I had never heard of such a thing as repressed memories of sexual assault, but I was experiencing their return. (1994, pp. 4–5)

How could Frank Fitzpatrick—or Ross Cheit or Marilyn Van Derbur Atler or any person—experience repeated childhood betrayal and abuse, fail to remember the events for years, and yet eventually, as an adult, be able to recover those memories? For this forgetting and remembering to occur, the mental processing that allows for continuous, consciously accessible memory was disrupted, although other, limited memory processing continued. For forgetting and remembering to occur, information about the event has to get into the nervous system in some form, be inaccessible at some time, yet be accessible at another time. Thus, somewhere in the brain processing must be disrupted or at least dissociated from its usual integrated flow. This disruption or dissociation of information flow can be understood in the context of cognitive psychology and cognitive science.

In this chapter I propose that current understanding of the cognitive processes of attention, perception, and memory affords ways of understanding how betrayal traumas can be forgotten and later remembered. I begin by considering the phenomenology of unawareness, forgetting, and remembering. I then discuss the research, conceptualization, and knowledge of cognitive psychology. Finally I suggest ways that the knowledge of cognitive processes can be employed to make sense of the phenomenon of forgetting and remembering sexual abuse.

## The Phenomenology of Unawareness, Forgetting, and Remembering

To know some aspects of a given reality and to not know other aspects of that same reality is to be human. I know that the person to whom I'm speaking is angry; I may not know what he is angry about. I know that the food I am eating tastes good; I may not know that it is also carcinogenic.

We know things we cannot articulate, and we know things we do not even know we know. *To know* is not unitary. We know how to do things that we do not know how to explain—riding a bicycle, for example. We have intuitions and insights that are inexplicable at the moment. We may *feel* that someone is lying to us by their voice or expression but be unable to specify the clues we are using to arrive at our conclusion. We may show through our behavior that we have experienced particular events but have no conscious awareness of the learning experience (my sons mimic my husband's table manners without knowing it).

We may perform tasks without knowing how we did them, amazing ourselves at our abilities—or our unawareness of our abilities.

Paying conscious attention to a skill that we usually perform automatically can be very disruptive. When I was a graduate student in psychology, I once heard a lecture on the mental processes involved in controlling finger and hand motion during touch-typing. I became fascinated with the topic for a few weeks, and found myself attempting to monitor and analyze my own typing behavior. To my alarm, I found myself not being able to type as accurately or quickly as I had before. My ability to type was disrupted by my paying conscious attention to the skill. (Don't try this yourself if you have a writing deadline to complete.)

Read the sentence below (from Reed 1988, p. 49). Then read it again, counting the number of *f*'s.

FINISHED FILES ARE THE
RESULT OF YEARS OF SCIENTIFIC
STUDY COMBINED WITH THE
EXPERIENCE OF MANY YEARS

How many *f*'s did you find? There are a total of six. If you counted fewer than six, try again. Most people find this a difficult task. It is easy to fail to be aware of something (in this case, the *f* in the word *of*).

Try reading the following sentence:

I
LOVE
PARIS IN THE
THE SPRINGTIME

Did you notice anything wrong with that sentence? Many people fail to read the sentence accurately. Read the sentence backwards, word by word, and you will probably notice that there are two *the*'s. Such errors of omission are common, and usually harmless.

Perception is a constructive process. We do not take sensory input and record it without distortion. We select information to admit into our nervous system; the information is filtered by our sensory organs such that some information is excluded; we then analyze, transform, and interpret that information. Some of it comes into conscious awareness; other parts of it remain outside our awareness. We are thus not passive receivers of external information; instead, we are active processors of it. Memory is no more comprehensive than perception, and it is arguably less comprehensive, if by "less" we mean a discrepancy between external and internal reality. Memory is limited by perception, and is further limited by distortions caused in the storage and retrieval of information.

Nonetheless, there are many reasons to believe that our perceptual and memory systems are essentially in tune with external reality. If you misread the sentence above as "The president is angry" or "I love Rome in the springtime" or "I love Paris in the wintertime" you might be making a mistake that would prove costly, but misreading the sentence as "I love Paris in the springtime" is, under most conditions, probably quite adaptive. Small errors of perception may be common and adaptive, but to hallucinate—to see something that is in fact not there—is both dangerous and unusual. To be wildly inaccurate in one's perception or memory can put one's ability to survive at risk. It is reasonable to assume, therefore, that most of the time perception and memory are roughly accurate: details may be in error, and material may be lost to awareness, but we perceive and remember the essential truth of critical aspects of the external world. As Brewin, Andrews, and Gotlib (1993) found in their consideration of individuals' retrospective accounts of their own past, empirical evidence suggests that there is a "basic integrity to autobiographical memory" (p. 94).

This does not mean that perception and memory are always accurate, just that it is reasonable to assume that for humans to be functional, some minimum degree of accuracy about important aspects of the environment is to be expected. Indeed, for people who do not have that minimal accuracy—that is, psychotics—life itself is endangered. There are times, however, when one's perception and memory may be inaccurate, and when this happens, the inaccuracy usually takes the form of errors of omission, things not perceived or remembered.

In short, we do not passively perceive or remember reality,

and we do not receive all of it all of the time. But most of the time we take in a sufficient amount accurately enough to function.

## Forgetting

Forgetting and remembering are part of the human experience. As Elizabeth Loftus put it in her book *Memory*, "Forgetting is a common experience for all of us" (1980, p. 65). There are many ways to forget and many ways to remember. One factor related to forgetting is the initial encoding of information. In some cases of "forgetting," the material to be remembered was never encoded fully to begin with. In other cases, the material was well encoded yet later is not available to consciousness. Loftus explains: "Forgetting occurs in many ways and undoubtedly for many reasons. One reason we forget is that we never stored the information we want to remember in the first place. Because we didn't pay enough attention to it, it was lost from our memory system in a matter of seconds. But even in cases where we seemingly have learned something quite well, we are sometimes unable to remember it later" (1980, p. 66). If an event was well encoded in the first place and only later became difficult to remember, one might think that under the correct circumstances the memory might be eventually recovered. However, if the material was truly lost from one's memory system in a matter of seconds, it is hard to see how someone could ever recover a memory of the event. Between the two extremes, where most instances lie, are many possible scenarios of *partial initial encoding* that can lead to the forgetting and later remembering of events. If the material to be learned or the event to be recalled is initially only partially encoded, subsequent memory recovery may be possible, but that subsequent memory recovery will have a different flavor than that of recovered events that were previously better encoded.

## Remembering What Was Forgotten

All of us have forgotten someone's name, the location of an important object in one's house or office, or something explicitly studied for an examination, only to have the memory pop back into consciousness later. Most of us have also experienced the recollection of childhood events not thought of for years. Sometimes we can identify the memory trigger, or cue, that caused the recollection: a particular odor similar to one from childhood, a visit to a childhood locale. Other times the memories come back for no discernible reason. Most of the time these childhood memories do not shock us, as they are not at odds with what we have always believed about our childhood. If the smell of carnation-scented soap suddenly reminds you of a time you were with your grandmother as a young child, you may be aware that you have not thought about that time in years, maybe not since it happened. As long as the event or scene you are remembering is benign, or at least in keeping with what you otherwise know, you are unlikely to find the return of the memory particularly noteworthy.

In a conversation with my then nine-year-old son, he asked me if I would pay him the five cents' deposit on the empty soda can he was carrying. I laughed and said, "No, thanks," pointing out that I had purchased the soda in the first place. A moment later, I was flooded with images from my childhood. I vividly remembered collecting empty soda bottles in a small town in Rhode Island while I was visiting my grandmother. I remembered the glass bottles jangling on the wagon I was pulling. I remembered Carol, the girl next door, walking next to me down the street with the wagon. For a moment I felt I was there, a young girl, walking down the street. Then I remembered more: Carol and I fishing on a pier, building a tent on the porch with sheets; and a strange elderly woman who lived on an upper floor of my grandmother's house. The memories flooded back, rich and mostly pleasurable: Carol's kitchen, her brother's sailboat, the path down to the beach . . . I don't believe I had thought about some of these things for decades. The details returned with distinct but difficult-to-articulate feelings, best described simply as "how it felt back then." After these memories returned I tried to date them. How old was I? I mused. I was allowed to walk around town and the fishing pier and the beach without adults; that suggests I was perhaps nine or ten years old. But I felt a lot younger than that. Strange, I thought, that the details are so rich but I cannot determine my age.

The return of these memories did not require that I make a major adjustment to my overall beliefs about my childhood, and the memories did not cause me pain (and my telling them to others is unlikely to inspire distress or denial on the part of the listener), but the process was otherwise similar to the return of less pleasant memories. In this case, the process began with the simple trigger of my son's comment about getting money for the return of a soda can (coupled, perhaps, with the particular look on his face that reminded me of my own delicious feeling of anticipating a handful of coins in return for the bottles on the wagon). The memories returned with such vivid sensory and affective detail that I briefly felt I was reliving a moment from my childhood. I then reinterpreted the memories in terms of my current understanding: I thought of activities, people, and places I had not thought of in many years, and aspects of the memories I was not sure about, such as my age at the time.

Experimental psychologists have investigated the return of memories, typically after much less time than thirty years (see, for example, Ballard 1913; A. S. Brown 1976; Erdelyi and Becker 1974; Wheeler 1995). One early demonstration of the spontaneous return of "memories" was provided by Pavlov (1927), who conditioned dogs to salivate at the sound of a metronome by providing them with food when they heard the metronome. At first, when the reinforcement (the food) was withdrawn, the dogs' salivation at the sound of the metronome decreased. After that, however, the salivation increased over time. In Pavlov's experiments, the dogs salivated on hearing the metronome because they associated the sound of the metronome—the cue—with food. This sort of "memory" is of course different in many ways from a human's conscious episodic narrative memory of an event. I discuss the different types of memories in a later section of this chapter. For now, the point is that forgetting and remembering are common in both animals and humans.

### Dissociation

Have you ever suddenly snapped to attention while driving, only to discover that you have driven for miles with no conscious awareness? Or maybe you have driven absent-mindedly to the wrong location, perhaps an old residence or workplace you have not visited for some time. Or perhaps you've gone to turn on the oven but found it's already preheated. Surely at some point you, like other human beings, have done something complex without being aware of it. This is a form of divided mental control, or dissociation—a lack of integration between mental activity and conscious awareness.

As Ernest Hilgard wrote:

> The unity of consciousness is illusory. Man does more than one thing at a time—all the time—and the conscious representation of these actions is never complete. His awareness can shift from one aspect of whatever is currently happening inside his body or impinging on him from without, or events that are remembered or imagined. Furthermore, as an active agent, he is always making decisions and formulating or implementing plans, and he likes to believe that he exerts control over what he is doing; often, however, he may be deceived about the causes of his behavior. (1986, p. 1)

Hilgard mentions the ubiquity of automatic processing, in which activities occur outside of consciousness. In the 1880s Pierre Janet, a French philosopher and psychologist, introduced his dissociation theory. Janet, in an impressive anticipation of modern cognitive psychology and neuroanatomy, conceptualized the human mind as comprised of separate subsystems able to operate independently and automatically. Janet believed that psychiatric patients with hysteria were displaying normal human independent systems, but in a more extreme form. He theorized that in these patients integrative activities were diminished, "causing the development of symptoms that appear as magnifications of the activity designed to preserve and reproduce the past" (van der Hart and Friedman 1989, p. 5). In addition, Janet discovered that most of these patients suffered from dissociated traumatic memories.

Today the word "dissociation" is often used in connection with disorders of thinking or behavior. For example, Bernstein and Putnam define dissociation as "a lack of normal integration of thoughts, feelings, and experiences into the stream of consciousness and memory" (1986, p. 727). The *Diagnostic and Statistical*

*Manual of Mental Disorders,* Fourth Edition (*DSM* IV), published by the American Psychiatric Association (1994), recognizes five dissociative disorders: dissociative amnesia (inability to recall aspects of personal life history), dissociative fugue (sudden travel away from one's home along with the inability to recall one's past and confusion about one's identity), depersonalization disorder (persistent feelings of being detached from one's self and the environment), dissociative identity disorder (previously termed "multiple personality disorder," characterized by the existence of two or more personalities that are capable of controlling the individual's behavior), and "dissociative disorder not otherwise specified" (dissociative symptoms not classified by the other disorders). The American Psychiatric Association states, "The essential feature of the dissociative disorders is a disruption in the usually integrated functions of consciousness, memory, identity, or perception of the environment. The disturbance may be sudden or gradual, transient or chronic" (American Psychiatric Association 1994, p. 477). In addition, the existence of dissociative pathology is now recognized as contributing to posttraumatic stress disorder (PTSD).

According to the *DSM* IV, amnesia (forgetting autobiographical information) is a common and significant symptom associated with dissociative disorders. For instance, an aspect of dissociative identity disorder is an "inability to recall important personal information that is too extensive to be explained by ordinary forgetfulness" (p. 487), and an aspect of posttraumatic stress disorder is an "inability to recall an important aspect of the trauma" (p. 428). There is also a diagnosis of dissociative amnesia: "an inability to recall important personal information, usually of a traumatic or stressful nature, that is too extensive to be explained by ordinary forgetfulness" (p. 477).

As Pierre Janet first observed a century ago, excesses in dissociation leading to amnesia and dissociative symptoms seem to be highly associated with the endurance of trauma. The relationship between dissociative disorders and trauma has been documented in many empirical studies using a variety of measurement instruments (see, for example, DiTomasso and Routh 1993; Chu and Dill 1990; Sanders and Giolas 1991; Miller, McCluskey-Fawcett, and Irving 1993; van der Kolk, Perry, and

Herman 1991). But Janet was also correct to emphasize that some degree of dissociation is always present in normally functioning humans, and that excess dissociation is simply an exaggeration of normal ways of thinking and controlling behavior. Dissociation is thus both a normal aspect of human experience and, in the extreme, a symptom of disorder. However, even when classed as a disorder, dissociation is arguably a reasonable response to an unreasonable situation. When being betrayed by a caregiver a child needs to dissociate the information about the betrayal from mechanisms that control attachment-forming and attachment-maintaining behavior. This dissociative response is adaptive, not pathological. It may lead to problems later on, and it may cause disruptions of awareness and memory, but it serves to sustain the child and ensure a degree of nurturing.

In addition, some forms of dissociation may be induced by culture. In the late 1970s I lived in Japan for eight months. For the first few months I lived in a traditional Japanese house built with paper interior walls. To my American sensibilities, these walls provided about as much privacy as a sheet draped across the room. I was amazed to discover, however, that my Japanese friends and neighbors seemed to be truly unaware of what were to my ears very audible voices and sounds from a nearby room. As I explored Japan, I discovered that personal physical space was often severely limited. People were pushed together in Tokyo subway cars and shared small rooms. Yet privacy seemed in no short supply. The Japanese were socialized not to be aware of sounds and sights and bodily feelings that I found salient.

In our own culture we are similarly socialized to be aware of some aspects of reality and not others. For instance, we seem to be much more conscious of communications that occur through verbal channels than nonverbal ones. Carol Gilligan (1991) suggests that as girls go through adolescence they learn to deemphasize their bodily sensations. She suggests that adults in our culture tend to feel that their identity is located primarily inside their skull. This would suggest a kind of culturally induced dissociation of incoming information.

Forms of human socialization may affect our ability to dissociate aspects of reality. Indeed, becoming socialized to a culture may be partly dependent on one's falling into a kind of culture-appropriate "trance" in which one assimilates the norms and expectations of the members of the group or the culture. Such a state occurs in both small and large social organizations, in families and in nations, and the behavior may seem disturbing when viewed by an outsider or when it is extreme, as when "normal" German citizens engaged in heinous acts under Hitler, or when cult members commit mass suicide. But to dissociate aspects of reality from awareness, to be in some degree of trance, may be inescapably human.

## Cognitive Mechanisms

I, like others, used to think that memory was a coherent, single system (Figure 5.1). My introduction to theories of memory in courses on cognitive psychology reinforced this impression. I was taught that memory was like an enormous library, with items in memory akin to books in that library. Each item had to be *encoded* (purchased and catalogued), then *stored* (put away somewhere in the stacks), and then finally *retrieved* (checked out).

The encoding-storage-retrieval theory was in fact a bit more complicated, with distinctions made between short-term and long-term memory, and with associative links between items in memory, but fundamentally, the idea was that memory could be conceptualized as a *thing*. Furthermore, at least in its early formulation, this theory saw memory as different from other functions of the nervous system, such as perception, emotion, and motor behavior.

Now, thanks to advances made in cognitive psychology and neuroscience, we know that memory is far from being a monolithic system, separate from other mental functions. It is, rather, a component of a multitude of systems that serve other mental functions. The human brain is multifaceted, capable of many kinds of learning: perceptual learning, motor learning, emotional learning, etc. And for each kind of learning there is necessarily memory. Thus, there may be as many different memory systems as there are different capabilities of the human mind.

Memory is anything and everything that involves learning in our nervous system. Joaquin Fuster recently wrote, "Memory is

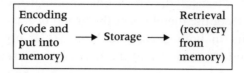

*Figure 5.1*  Traditional model of memory.

a functional property, among others, of each and all of the areas of the cerebral cortex, and thus of all cortical systems . . . Furthermore, as the cortex engages in representing and acting on the world, memory in one form or another is an integral part of its operations" (1995, p. 1). The sort of memory that we are conscious of when we purposely try to recall a fact is but a tiny fraction of the memories that we use in dealing with our daily lives.

This conception of memory involves not just variety, but also simultaneity. According to the prevailing viewpoint in cognitive science, we have in place many separate mental modules, or cognitive mechanisms (presumably themselves composed of millions of interconnected neurons), capable of processing incoming information in parallel and organized into even larger mental processing clusters (see Figure 5.2). While there is likely to be some connectivity between modules, the connectivity between modules is presumably much less than that within modules (Fodor 1983; Hinton and Anderson 1981; Rumelhart, McClelland, and PDP Research Group 1986). Often, different modules process the same event in different ways. For instance, if you are hungry and see some food on a precipice, your information-processing modules that compute strategies for acquiring food may produce strong signals for you to move toward the food. At the same time, your information-processing modules that compute strategies for secure movement may produce strong signals for you to avoid the precipice, thus creating an approach-avoidance dilemma.

Another example of parallel processing may be familiar to anyone who has ever attempted a reduced-calorie diet. Imagine this scenario: You are on a diet. Your friend offers you a piece of chocolate cake. You may simultaneously salivate, wish for the

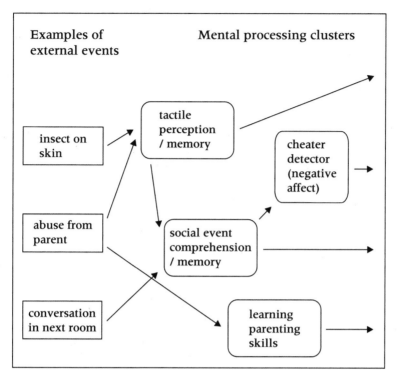

*Figure 5.2* A schematic model of cognitive processing of information as it enters the nervous system. Multiple modules process events in parallel. In reality what are represented here as "clusters" may in fact be complex systems of interconnected processing involving many modules; this figure is highly schematized and is intended only to illustrate the concept of multiple aspects of ongoing reality processed simultaneously by multiple mental mechanisms.

cake, perhaps reach for it, say "No, thank you" to your friend, and wonder to yourself if this one piece of cake might be okay for you to eat after all. You are likely to experience some degree of internal conflict: you are aware of the fact that you are having competing reactions to the cake. You might not, however, be conscious of the fact that you are salivating. Everyday encounters with the world present us with numerous situations that have the potential to provoke conflicting reactions, but we are aware of them only some of the time. In many cases not only do multiple mental mechanisms evaluate the same event for different qualities, but other mechanisms simultaneously make decisions about behavioral responses without our conscious awareness.

A given memory is often dependent on a specific set of mental mechanisms, as opposed to being more general or all-purpose (Squire 1992). For instance, memory for riding a bicycle is heavily tied to mechanisms that control motor behavior. Positron emission tomography (PET), a brain imaging technique, provides additional evidence that information stored in memory is selectively yoked to relevant mental mechanisms. Using PET scans, Alex Martin and his colleagues at the National Institute of Mental Health showed that the areas of the brain that mediate perception of color are activated in a memory task that involves accessing the color of an object, and areas of the brain that mediate perception of motion are activated in a memory task that involves accessing the motion of an object. They suggest that their data indicate that "object knowledge is organized as a distributed system in which the attributes of an object are stored close to the regions of the cortex that mediate perception of those attributes" (Martin et al. 1995, p. 102).

Different mental modules can be at work simultaneously, as when we drive a car and engage in a conversation. This fact about human behavior can be understood in terms of Ernest Hilgard's (1986) notion of divided control, or neo-dissociationism. This sort of dissociation is not pathological. Indeed, automatic processing, which is involved in such simultaneous activities as driving a car while talking, requires divided control structures. Of course, the combination of multiple mental mechanisms, automatic processing, and divided control structures occurs for social information processing, too. Multiple, or simultaneous, processing is at work in situations such as a person saying in an obviously angry voice "I'm not angry" and sincerely meaning both the words and the tone of anger.

*Selective Attention*

The ability to selectively attend to incoming information in an appropriate way and especially the ability to selectively admit information into consciousness are necessary for proper functioning. Children with attention deficit disorder, for instance, have difficulties functioning because they are distracted by too much stimulation. Even when information is not entering consciousness, we can still be processing some of it (Treisman 1960). For instance, if you are at a cocktail party, listening to one conversation and ignoring another, under certain conditions you may suddenly become aware of the previously unattended conversation, such as when your name is used or the conversation turns to something that has special significance for you.

A classic demonstration of intrusive information and automatic processing in attempts at selective attention—that is, our inability to completely exclude the unattended stimulus from entering the nervous system—is the Stroop effect, named for its creator, J. Ridley Stroop (1935). Participants are asked to name the ink color of words printed in different colors. In one case the words are color names ("blue" or "yellow") that are congruent with the ink colors (the word "blue" is printed in blue ink). In another case the words are color names that are not congruent with the ink colors (for example, the word "blue" is printed in yellow ink, while the word "yellow" is printed in red ink). In a third case the words are neutral terms ("keys" or "bedroom") and the ink colors are randomly assigned to the different words. Participants find it much more difficult to name the ink color when the words are incongruent with the ink colors than when the words are congruent with the ink colors, or when the words are neutral. People are unable to avoid processing the meaning of the words they read.

Figure 5.3 shows a modified version of the Stroop task that does not involve color. For each boxed-in list, try saying out loud how many characters are on each line. (For example, the first line of each boxed list has two characters.) You will probably discover that the task is more difficult to perform with the lines of digits than with the lines of letters.

Figure 5.4 shows the results from a Stroop experiment that was part of a larger project investigating cognitive mechanisms of dissociative experiences (Freyd et al. in preparation). It shows the average time a group of 154 subjects took to name the ink colors of eight items on a list of conflicting color words and a list of strings of X's. Participants took longer to name the ink

| aa | 33 |
| bbbb | 1111 |
| c | 2 |
| ddd | 555 |
| eeeee | 66666 |
| f f | 44 |
| ggg | 222 |
| hhhh | 8888 |
| i | 9 |
| jjjjj | 77777 |

*Figure 5.3*  Stimulus materials from a modified version of the Stroop task.

colors when the items were conflicting color words than when they were just neutral X's.

Edna Foa (Foa et al. 1991), Richard McNally (Kaspi, McNally, and Amir 1995; McNally, English, and Lipke 1993; McNally et al. 1990), and their colleagues have developed an emotional Stroop task to investigate the processing of threat-related information in traumatized populations. In this research, participants are asked to name the ink colors of threat-related words or terms (such as "body bag" for Vietnam veterans or "rape" for rape victims) and of neutral or other control words. The results indicate that the threat-related words, when specific to the trauma, create more interference in color naming than do neutral words.

The standard Stroop experiment provides a measure of selective attention and its limitations. When participants name ink colors instead of reading the printed word, they are selectively attending to the color. The fact that it takes participants longer to name ink colors when the word meanings conflict with the ink colors (or, in the case of the emotional Stoop paradigm just described, when the word meanings call attention away from the ink colors) shows that selective attention is not all or none. Thus, two aspects of attention are important to understanding the cognitive processing of trauma. First, we have the ability to focus on and become aware of just one part of reality. Second and separately, we are simultaneously likely to process to some degree unattended aspects of reality.

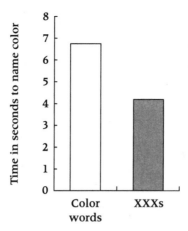

*Figure 5.4* Stroop experiment results for 154 subjects.

## Varieties of Memory

Cognitive scientists usually distinguish different kinds of memory and knowledge. One distinction is between declarative knowledge and procedural knowledge (Squire 1992). Roughly, *declarative knowledge* is knowing *what* (the facts one knows) and *procedural knowledge* is knowing *how* (the skills one has). These types of knowledge are often dissociated, as in knowing how to ride a bicycle but having little declarative knowledge about that skill. According to Matthew Erdelyi (1990), it appears that declarative knowledge is more likely to be repressed than procedural, kinesthetic, and sensory information.

A related distinction is between explicit and implicit memory. Until recently most research in memory focused on *explicit memory,* in which subjects were asked to deliberately remember something. Both tests of recall (for example, "Name the seven dwarfs") and tests of recognition (for example, "Indicate which names belong to the seven dwarfs: 'Dopey'; 'Sleepy'; 'Shy'") are explicit tests of memory; they require conscious remembering. In contrast, *implicit memory* is measured through tasks in which no conscious, effortful memory is requested. An example of a test of implicit memory is a perceptual priming task, in which a participant is asked to recognize a word that is flashed on a screen very briefly. The question is whether words the participant has been previously and recently exposed to influence performance in this task. Usually participants are more likely to recognize a briefly flashed word if it has just recently been presented to them, even if they are not conscious of its having been presented previously. For example, because a few sentences back you read the word "deliberately," you would probably be better able to recognize that word if it were flashed briefly than if you had not recently read it—even if you were not aware of having read it. In other words, an implicit memory may be entirely dissociated from an explicit one.

Recently a great deal of interest has focused on implicit memory and the unintentional recollection and influence of prior experiences (see Schacter 1992; Squire 1992). Neuropsychological evidence suggests anatomical underpinnings for these sorts of knowing. For instance, brain lesions that affect the hippocampus and adjacent cortical areas are associated with moderate to severe disruptions of explicit memory, but seem to cause relatively little disruption to implicit memory (Squire 1992). Recent research suggests that conscious recall (explicit memory) and unconscious influences (implicit memory) are indeed dissociated at the cognitive level (see Jacoby and Kelly 1992). Even verbal material can be shown to be remembered implicitly, but not explicitly, under certain conditions.

The distinctions in types of memory—even the terminology—are currently in flux. As of this writing, the terms *explicit* and *implicit* generally refer to a distinction between ways in which memories are accessed, while the terms *declarative* and *procedural* generally distinguish the kinds of information stored. Declarative knowledge is often associated with explicit memory, while procedural knowledge (including sensory and emotional memories) is associated with implicit memory. Some researchers (for example, van der Kolk 1994; Squire 1992) treat these two distinctions as arising from the same basic dichotomy in memory systems, whereas others (for example, Roediger 1990) argue that these two sets of distinctions are orthogonal. I believe that there are valid empirical and theoretical reasons for both approaches, and that much additional evidence is needed in order to arrive at a definitive answer. In this book, I generally follow the approach of Squire (1992), as I wish to emphasize the difference between the sorts of memories we usually focus on (both explicit and declarative) from the others. In the long run, however, I suspect that the more detailed distinctions will prove to be meaningful, and that precise memory distinctions will be necessary in order to understand different individuals' detailed patterns of forgetting and remembering. For now, however, assume that there are two kinds of memory: one is explicit, declarative, episodic, and verbalizable; the other is implicit and/or procedural—in short, encompasses everything that the first kind of memory does not.

One way to study implicit memory in the laboratory takes advantage of what is known as the stem-completion task. As part of a Stroop experiment, my colleagues and I (Freyd et al. in preparation) gave 154 college student participants the following list of words, which were printed in different colors of ink:

| | |
|---|---|
| k i t c h e n | p l a n e t |
| b e d | s k y |
| b a t h | m i s t |
| t e l e v i s i o n | a i r p l a n e |
| c e l l a r | r a i n b o w |
| g a r a g e | h o r i z o n |
| h a l l | s t a r |
| b e d r o o m | r a i n |

We asked the participants to name the ink color of each word. Later we asked the participants to attend to some, but not all, of the words from this list by asking them to rate how much they liked each word. After that, we asked them to attempt to remember the words from the original list (the one above). (You can try a variation of this experiment yourself. Count the number of words in the list above; try to avoid reading them. Then try to write down the words from that list without looking back at them.) Participants had very poor explicit memory for the words that they were not asked to attend to later—that is, the ones they were not asked to rate (just as you probably had a hard time writing down the words in the list generally, because you were not asked to read, or attend to, them).

Finally, we asked participants to complete each word in the following list by filling in each blank with a letter (to try it yourself, fill in the blanks with the first word that comes to mind):

g a r _ _ _
b a _ _
s _ _
b e _
s _ _
b e _
h o _ _ _ _ _
p l a _ _ _
m i _ _
h a l _

There are many possible responses to each item. The following list gives some examples; the first word in each line is a word from the earlier list of words the participants had been given:

garage, garden, gargle, garlic
bath, ball, bark, bank
sky, sun, sob, sip
bed, bet, bee, beg
horizon, holiday, hormone, holster
planet, plasma, plague, plates
mist, mill, mint, mind
hall, half, halt, halo

A typical result, using tasks such as this, is that participants have a bias to select a word they have been exposed to (as compared to words they have not recently been exposed to) even when they do not consciously remember the word. This tendency points to the existence of implicit memory, and experiments such as this can be used to measure such memory. If you tried this experiment yourself, you may have firsthand evidence that implicit and explicit memory can be shockingly dissociated.

Sharon Zeitlin and Richard McNally (1991) investigated memory in Vietnam combat veterans with and without posttraumatic stress disorder (PTSD), comparing implicit and explicit memory for combat words and other types of words. They found that only PTSD patients exhibited an implicit memory bias for combat words. This finding suggested to Zeitlin and McNally that such implicit memory bias "may underlie the 'reexperiencing' symptoms characteristic of PTSD" such as intrusive thoughts and nightmares (p. 451).

Bessel van der Kolk (1994) has emphasized the distinction between explicit and implicit memories in his analysis of traumatic memories. Van der Kolk argues that there is mounting evidence from psychobiological studies that some traumatic events leave memory traces that are lacking in narrative interpretation, and that are in essence implicit memories only. (Van der Kolk uses the terms "explicit" and "implicit" to encompass declarative and procedural knowledge respectively.)

Van der Kolk points out that in 1889 Janet distinguished between the active, constructive, and reconstructive nature of explicit (declarative) memory for normal events and implicit (procedural) memory for trauma. Janet wrote: "certain happenings . . . leave indelible and distressing memories—memories to which the sufferer continually returns, and by which he is tormented by day and by night." (Janet 1919/1925, as quoted by van der Kolk 1994, p. 258). Van der Kolk notes, "Clinicians and researchers dealing with traumatized patients have repeatedly observed that the sensory experiences and visual images related to the trauma seem not to fade over time and appear to be less subject to distortion than ordinary experiences" (p. 258).

Van der Kolk also notes that traumatized people show significant state-dependence in their recall of traumatic memories. When current conditions resemble conditions they experienced at the time of the trauma, people are likely to become aroused, have flashbacks to the trauma, and show signs of panic. According to van der Kolk, "Contemporary biological researchers have shown that medications that stimulate autonomic arousal may precipitate visual images and affect states associated with previous traumatic experiences in people with PTSD but not in control subjects . . . In our own laboratory approximately 20% of PTSD subjects responded with a flashback of a traumatic experience when they were presented with acoustic startle stimuli" (1994, p. 259).

Based on biological evidence (including hormone studies, brain lesion studies, and brain scans), van der Kolk relates the nature of traumatic memories to neuroanatomical dissociations

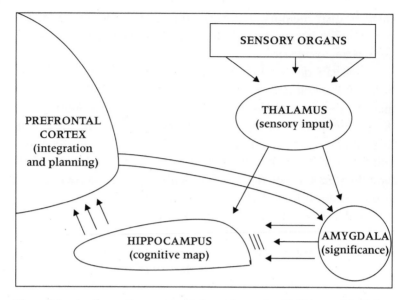

*Figure 5.5*   A schematic representation of van der Kolk's model of the effects of emotional arousal on declarative memory. The brain regions known as the thalamus, amygdala, and hippocampus are each involved in the integration and interpretation of incoming sensory information. According to this model, the thalamus projects sensory information to both the amygdala and hippocampus. Determination of emotional significance is mediated by the amygdala, and the creation of declarative memories is mediated by the hippocampus. Van der Kolk suggests that while moderate or high activation of the amygdala enhances memorability, thus ensuring good memory for mildly stressful experiences, excessive stimulation of the amygdala interferes with hippocampal functioning, inhibiting episodic interpretation for traumatic experiences. Van der Kolk suggests that memories for traumatic experiences are then stored in sensorimotor modalities, such as somatic sensations and visual images, which he considers relatively indelible, as compared with the more reconstructive and thus changeable nature of episodic memory.

between the hippocampus and amygdala. Figure 5.5 displays van der Kolk's conceptualization of the divergent pathways of traumatic and nontraumatic memories. An important consequence of van der Kolk's argument, if he is correct, is that laboratory studies on nontraumatic memory make poor models for traumatic memories. If different anatomical systems are activated in the two cases, it may be impossible to generalize from one case to the other. Van der Kolk suggests that one reason why traumatic memories may be difficult to consciously recall in a narrative, episodic form is that they were never stored in such a form in the first place. Further, he suggests that in some ways traumatic memories may be more accurate than nontraumatic memories, because of the nature of the memory stores for the two different sorts of memories. Traumatic memories, according to this viewpoint, are not reconstructed narratives as are most memories, but the reactivation of undistorted sensory and affective traces.

Van der Kolk's theories and research in this area are extremely important. However, at this point it is not possible to say whether traumatic memories are overall more or less accurate than nontraumatic memories. We need studies in which recall accuracy for documented traumatic and nontraumatic events is carefully controlled or measured. Such studies would have to be attentive to factors such as the complexity of the event, the age of the participant at the time of the event, and so on. Further, I am not convinced that all instances of betrayal traumas, including childhood sexual abuse, take place under the sort of highly terrorizing or fearful conditions van der Kolk hypothesizes are necessary in order to create traumatic memories. Some betrayals may be dissociated from consciousness or repressed because of the danger the information holds for other important functions, such as social behavior (discussed in Chapter 4), though they may not be "traumatic" in the sense of being highly fear-inducing. In addition, some instances of sexual abuse may not be recognized as traumatic until after the fact, and only then are they pushed out of consciousness or forgotten. There are also more everyday betrayals, such as marital infidelity, of which those betrayed seem to be able to remain unaware despite the fact that retrospectively they may acknowledge that the evidence was in front of them all along (such situations will be discussed further in Chapter 7). These everyday betrayals, for which those who experience them seem capable of a kind of amnesia and then memory recovery, do not fit the sort of fear-inducing traumas on which van der Kolk bases his theory.

Still, van der Kolk has provided us with one convincing explanation of why some traumatic memories are not available to consciousness for some people. At the same time, alternative motivations for forgetting are possible and even likely. There are lots of ways to forget, and lots of ways to remember.

One possible point of convergence between van der Kolk's emphasis on emotional arousal and fear in determining traumatic memories and my emphasis on betrayal in dependent relationships has to do with van der Kolk's notion of dual systems of knowledge and my concept of the abused person's knowing about the abusive caregiver. It is possible, for instance, that even in cases where amnesia for sexual abuse is strong, at an unconscious level the abused person fears the abuser, and this fear motivates certain behavior, such as avoidance of the situations believed to trigger the abuse. Thus people who have forgotten abuse may find themselves afraid of certain people or situations without understanding the basis of their fear. As Frederick Buechner described this situation in his novel *The Wizard's Tide:* "And because he didn't connect the scared feeling with what really scared him . . . all sorts of things scared him that didn't bother other people at all" (1990, p. 57).

Recent research provides a neuroanatomical model of the underlying dissociation of these different kinds of knowing. Antoine Bechara and his colleagues (Bechara et al. 1995) recently demonstrated a striking dissociation between declarative knowledge on the one hand and conditioned learning on the other. They presented brain-lesioned patients with colored slides, some of which were paired with a loud boat horn. In an experiment like this, normal participants become conditioned to the slides that are paired with the loud horn, as measured by changes in skin conductance. Normal participants also learn the declarative facts about which slides were paired with the loud boat horn. Bechara's group found that a patient with damage to the hippocampus, a part of the brain critically involved in the formation of declarative knowledge, failed to acquire the declarative facts about which slides were paired with the loud boat horn but did acquire the conditioned response. In contrast, a patient with damage to the amygdala, a part of the brain involved in determining the significance of events, did not acquire conditioned autonomic responses to stimuli but did acquire the declarative facts about the pairings.

*Declarative Memory*

Within the category of declarative knowledge, distinctions have been made between episodic and semantic knowledge (see Tulving 1983). *Episodic memory* is the knowledge of specific, time-dated events one has experienced. *Semantic memory* is knowledge that is not time-dated, as in our knowledge of the English vocabulary. Nelson (1993) further distinguishes between "generic event memory," "episodic memory," and "autobiographical memory." Generic event memory does not include a precise time and place, but instead is memory for a familiar event, such as driving to work; episodic memory includes information about time and place; autobiographical memory is part of one's "life story." Nelson argues that autobiographical memory is unique in that it depends on a linguistic representation and, since language encoding is not available to very young children, "infantile amnesia" results.

Episodic memory for events is subject to change over time. Frederick Bartlett (1932) demonstrated the reconstructive nature of memory for stories and line drawings. In his elegant, groundbreaking experiments, participants were asked to reproduce narratives and schematic (impoverished and ambiguous) line drawings. As participants reproduced these stories and drawings over and over, the products slowly transformed. Often the transformations rendered the information more in accord with the schemas of the participants' culture. Bartlett thus demonstrated the highly interpreted and reconstructive nature of these sorts of memories. An important point to keep in mind, however, is that the material he had participants remember was almost entirely declarative; there were no lived-through events with associated implicit memories to ground the reality of the memory. One possible explanation for the errors participants made is that they transformed the material to be more in line with their pre-existing knowledge, enabling the information to be more easily shared with others (Freyd 1983)—a virtue for material such as verbal narrative or schematic line drawings, which depends on social agreement for its meaning.

A series of studies by Elizabeth Loftus has suggested that memory is reconstructive for richer material than that used by

Bartlett. In Loftus's studies participants are given misinforma-
tion through subtle suggestion (Loftus 1980). One way this is
achieved is by asking leading questions such as "Did you see the
broken headlight?" This question implies that there was a headlight to be seen. An alternative question is "Did you see a broken
headlight?" Loftus has found that when subjects are asked questions after watching a film of an auto accident, for example,
participants asked about *the* headlight are more likely to report
that a headlight was present in the film whether or not it actually
was than are participants asked about *a* headlight. These clever
experiments show that people are suggestible about details for
events.

A more recent experiment by Loftus (Loftus and Ketcham
1994) suggests that a whole narrative can be implanted into
memory such that some people come to believe they lived
through an event they never experienced. In this now famous
"shopping mall" experiment some subjects came to believe that
they were lost in a shopping mall as a small child when report-
edly they had not in fact been lost. This study has been criticized
on a number of grounds, including the possibility that all children have some emotional experience of getting lost, or almost
lost, at least briefly. If so, the memories could be considered not
wholly false. In the best known case example, Loftus's subject
"Chris" was convinced of the shopping mall story after being
told that his older brother and mother both remembered the
event well. If this demonstration proves to hold up under replication it suggests both that therapists can induce false memories and, even more directly, that older family members play a
powerful role in defining reality for dependent younger family
members.

Different mental modules use different internal codes (Pavio
1990). For instance, codes for linguistic information may be quite
different from codes for visual motion information. Different
sorts of procedural or sensory memory are likely to be themselves dissociated. For instance, memory for visual information
is different from memory for auditory or emotional information.
Although these types of memory will normally have *associative
links* to allow integrated event perception, they are distinct neural

entities. Numerous experimental results in cognitive psychology offer strong support for multiple mental codes.

These distinctions in memory and mental coding may relate to the different operating characteristics of mental modules. A single real-world event can be perceived and represented by multiple mental mechanisms, and the information represented in multiple codes. For instance, a person typically may encode declarative episodic information about the event (the kind of information that one might later be able to verbalize). At the same time that person may also be encoding sensory memories, such as auditory, visual, and tactile memories, with each memory created in its own internal code by virtue of the processing units involved. In nontraumatic memories, at least, these different memory codes are associated in various ways through hippocampal processing (Squire 1992).

*Context-dependent Memory*

Both external contexts (for example, location) and internal contexts (for example, mood) can influence retrieval of information (see Bower 1981, 1987; Eich 1989, 1995; Smith 1995). If the retrieval context is matched to the initial learning context, memory is often improved over cases where the context is not well matched. In one study, members of a university diving club were asked to learn lists of words while they were on the shore or underwater. Then they were tested for their ability to recall the words, either on shore or underwater. Those who had learned the lists underwater performed better when tested underwater and those who had learned the words on shore performed better when tested on shore (Godden and Baddeley 1975). Although some researchers have had trouble replicating the effect, recent studies indicate that it is indeed a real phenomenon (see Eich 1995 and Smith 1995).

Context-dependent memory, and mood-congruency effects, have been interpreted in terms of associative links with affective states—that is, the internal state provides associative links to stored information. An alternative view is that mood states regulate the dominance of cognitive modules, and thus the dominance of certain memory stores. Perhaps large-scale affective states such as depression exist *primarily* to control the dominance of cognitive modules. When depressed, for example, we may reduce the dominance of modules that control opportunistic behavior for the overall goal of conserving energy.

Context-dependent memory effects may help explain why long-forgotten memories may return at particular times. Many adults who experience the return of memories of childhood sexual abuse identify the presence of a child of a certain age in their current life as a trigger for the memories (as Ross Cheit experienced; see Chapter 1). The context that the child provides may be more than a simple visual cue; it may result also from empathetic processes in the adult that serve to recreate some of the perspectives, emotions, and thoughts of a child of a certain age in the adult's mind. These triggers, combined with a desire to protect the child from harm, may be sufficient to evoke implicit memories of abuse or to release the inhibition of explicit memories. In a letter of May 7, 1995, Marilyn Van Derbur Atler linked the return of additional memories of sexual abuse to the age of her child:

> The memories of thirteen years of incest (5 to 18) were recovered when I was 24. When I was 39, my body went into physical paralysis and I was hospitalized three times. The doctors could find no physical cause for the paralysis. (The spells continued until I was 51.) It took us three years to understand the reasons for the paralysis—our daughter, Jennifer, was turning 5—the age when the violations began. Her age began bringing up feelings as another part of me used every ounce of energy to repress the feelings.
>
> At age 45 (when Jennifer was entering puberty) my life shut down completely for six long years. It is not unusual for a child to trigger memories and feelings.

### Perception and Memory

Repression and dissociation are often seen as two separate defenses. One way they are distinguished is in terms of time: Dissociation is a real-time defense in which consciousness is not fully engaged on the event at hand; repression is an after-the-fact defense in which memory for the event is in some way impaired. But Ernest Hilgard (1986) and others have proposed that repression is best understood as amnesia resulting from dissociation. What makes definitions difficult is that both repression and dissociation involve various degrees of information blockage—from the exclusion of affect only to the almost total exclusion of episodic declarative knowledge—and that there is no clear demarcation between the two. While the temporal distinction is important (that is, when the information blockage takes place), it is not an either-or issue. Information can be blocked at any time from the onset of an event to the attempted recall of it. Similarly, different kinds and amounts of information can be blocked, from selective blockage of emotional response through more massive blocking.

Ivor Browne (1990) has argued that when we experience complex events, our experience extends beyond the temporal limits of the event itself. For instance, if on Friday your best friend announces her intention to move to Japan for three years, you might be processing that information rather steadily most of Saturday and Sunday, and only by Monday might you have integrated the information. Browne suggests that traumatic events are repressed when the mind halts the usual processing that ordinarily continues over time.

An important implication of Browne's idea is that perception and memory are closer to being the same thing than is usually assumed. I define memory as a function of mental mechanisms, including perceptual mechanisms—not a separate brain system. Most of my own experiments have investigated the role of time in mental representations of the world (see, for example, Freyd 1987; 1993a). I have shown that when we perceive an event we also automatically anticipate the future—and that that anticipation is part of our perception, part of our representation of the external world. My empirical work has focused on the blurring of perception, memory, and anticipation for small time periods—fractions of a second. Processing of more complex events involves the blurring of immediate experience with prolonged mental processing over longer time periods.

Browne's (1990) suggestion is consistent with Nelson's (1993) proposal that autobiographical memory depends on a time-consuming encoding process of recounting events in a representational format that is shareable with others. Browne's suggestion may also be consistent with the neuropsychological finding that the hippocampus has a specific time-dependent role in integrating explicit memories (Squire 1992). Perhaps this time-consuming function of the hippocampus is inhibited after betrayal traumas, producing a sort of traumatic amnesia that leaves intact implicit memories for the event.

Laura S. Brown (1995a) has suggested the term "unfrozen memories" for recovered memories. This term seems especially apt when we think about the various roles of time in memory. Intact "normal" memories for rich events are created over a period of time, during which the event itself is being perceived and understood. The perception and the memory of the event include internalization of temporal aspects of the event. When a memory of a forgotten event is recovered, these temporal processes may indeed be "unfrozen." If the event was not processed to the usual extent, at that point the processing may resume. And if the memory for the event is returned to active working memory, stored memories of aspects of the event may well unfold in real time, creating a powerful sense of being back in the original event.

*Shareability*

Shareability is a theory that I initially proposed (Freyd 1983; 1993) to explain the discrepancy between mental processing that is highly analog and continuous on the one hand, and mental processing that is apparently discrete and categorical on the other. This theory considers the consequences of the fact that humans depend heavily on the sharing of information. In essence, it proposes that through the process of information sharing we recode internal material to be discrete—stable across space and time—and hence more easily communicable. Thus, shared information may be qualitatively different from private information. Further, the very purpose of consciousness may be related to the social sharing of information: a mental coding format that allows information to be shared.

Perhaps episodic memory is the shareable trace we lay down for future communications. This shareable trace may allow a kind of communication within the individual mind, just as it does between different minds (Freyd 1983) by providing a format that is accessible to, and interconnected with, multiple modules. If so, human consciousness may be simultaneously about integration of the self (James 1890) and communication between individuals (Nelson 1993). Interestingly, in a case study employing cognitive science measures of a patient with multiple personality disorder, Mary Jo Nissen and her colleagues (1988) found that "the degree of compartmentalization of knowledge in this patient appears to depend on the extent to which that knowledge is interpreted in ways that are unique to a personality as well as the extent to which processes operating at the time of retrieval are strongly personality-dependent" (p. 131). This suggests that consciousness plays a crucial role in personality— that is, self-integration.

I believe that at least some of the properties we observe in knowledge structures emerge during the sharing process and do not directly reflect inherent constraints on individual minds. This theoretical position is at odds with the viewpoint now dominating most of linguistics and cognitive psychology that observed structure directly reveals innate or learned constraints of the human mind. The shareability theory does not deny that ultimately these constraints have their roots in the individual mind, but it claims that there are emergent properties qualitatively unique to the process of information sharing.

Shared information becomes more categorical than it is when originally represented in the individual mind. This touches on a fundamental problem in psychology: What is the basis of categorization? The accepted position is that the need and the ability to categorize information stem from the individual (for example, see Pinker and Bloom 1990). The theory of shareability takes an alternative position: that in some situations categorization takes place only because information is shared (although shareability might also have led, through natural selection, to some innate categorization mechanisms too; see Freyd 1983; 1990). It occurs because of the greatly reduced channels of information flow between two or more separate minds, compared to the representational capacities of the individual mind, combined with the strong pressure to minimize information loss.

Suppose, for instance, that a group of rafters attempts to share information about the currents in a river, for which only some rafters have direct perceptual experience. If each individual's representation of the information includes fine-grained, but idiosyncratic, information about the river currents, initially there will be enormous potential for information distortion when sharing this information over a group of people. However, over time and as an increasing number of individuals share the information, a small set of values along initially continuous dimensions will emerge as anchors within the shared structure, perhaps partly based on mutual knowledge accessed through analogy or metaphor (Freyd 1983). The sharing process thus behaves like a discrete filter that is relatively stable across time and space. Similarly, tacit agreement on a small number of categories along potentially continuous dimensions minimizes information loss. In other words, the fine-grained or continuous information is traded for stability over time and space. Thus the river rafters develop a language of position and action—naming various rocks, developing codes for describing the extremity of the rapids—that gives them stability of information but loses the nuances registered in the individual minds of the rafters.

According to the shareability theory, private knowledge is often represented with dimensions that capture the continuous structure of the real world, but shared knowledge is constrained by properties that emerge in communication, such as the limitations of the communication medium and the pressure to minimize information loss. Thus, in shared knowledge underlying continua are partitioned into discrete categories. For instance, although the continuity of a temporal dimension is basic to representations serving much of cognitive processing, the continuity property may be limited to only some cognitive modules. It might make sense to quantize the temporal dimension in conscious representations, assuming that the representations serving consciousness have evolved to be most shareable (given that we are a social species). It may even be that continuity is limited to the module in which the representation resides; that is, it may be that continuous information is not shareable from module to module within the individual mind. In other words, module-to-module communication might lead to a kind of shareability within the mind (Freyd 1983).

The possibility that continuity and discrete categories both exist because of the contrast between nonshared and shared mental processing units (whether we consider the units to be individual brains or individual modules within a brain) may shed some light on the discrete or continuous nature of mental representation. Currently, the mixed empirical evidence has fueled many debates, including some current controversy surrounding connectionist versus symbolic models of cognition (for example, see Pinker and Prince 1988). Perhaps mental representations are continuous within an individual brain or individual brain module, but at larger levels of interaction and analysis, shareability has the effect of partitioning that continuity into discrete categories.

The concept of shareability suggests that analyzable constraints emerge when knowledge is shared. Such constraints are likely to have a large effect on mental representations with dynamic information (such as fine-grained knowledge of river currents), for such information is continuous, and shareability will force underlying continua to be represented as categories. The existence of qualitatively different sorts of mental representations may account on the one hand for our ability to represent a great deal of the complexity and continuity of the real world when necessary for perception and action and, on the other, for our ability to represent the world with sufficient economy and simplicity when we need to communicate our knowledge of it.

Shareability theory suggests that memory for never-discussed events is likely to be qualitatively different from memory for events that have been discussed. This difference will be greater when the sensory, continuous memories for the events were not recoded internally in anticipation of verbal sharing. Thus, if an event is experienced but never recoded into shareable formats, it is more likely to be stored in codes that are continuous, sensory, and dynamic.

### Motivated Forgetting, Memory Inhibition, and Memory Recovery

The typical explanation in cognitive psychology for why forgetting occurs does not assume that forgetting is motivated. Instead, the traditional focus has been on decay and interference as reasons for forgetting.

*Decay* is the passive and gradual erosion of information, operative in short-term and sensory memory. If information is not actively maintained, it dissipates rapidly. For instance, if you have just looked up a telephone number but fail to write down or mentally "rehearse" that number, your ability to remember the number is likely to decrease fairly rapidly.

The evidence for decay in long-term memory is less clear. Instead, it appears that *interference* can account for most decay-like loss of information in long-term memory. Interference has classically been divided into two categories: proactive and retroactive. Proactive interference occurs when memories and existing knowledge interfere with the creation of new memories. If you have a friend whom you have known for years as Jim and he informs you that he now wants you to call him James, you may have difficulty learning the new name, because the older one is creating proactive interference. Retroactive interference occurs when newly acquired information interferes with the retrieval of old information. If you study Japanese as a foreign language, for instance, you may discover that your previous ability with Spanish as a second language decreases as you learn the new language. Indeed, you may experience both proactive and retroactive interference: you may find yourself speaking words from both languages when attempting to converse in either one. Without any interference at all, it is possible that memories do not decay over time.

Experimental psychologists have periodically been interested in *motivated forgetting*. Freud (1923) argued that we forget most of our earliest memories because of the conflictual nature of the material. Similarly, Robert Henderson (1985) suggested that under certain conditions it is adaptive for animals to forget fearful events. It is generally noted that human beings have a bias toward positive memories; this may lead us to feel nostalgic for times when we might not actually have been very happy. Elizabeth Loftus observed, "People who return from a vacation often tend to remember the happy times and forget the sad times. People who gamble are prone to remember the times they won and to forget the times they lost" (1980, p. 71). Loftus's observation is supported by systematic observation. Waldfogel (1948) discovered that adults are more likely to forget unpleasant childhood memories than pleasant ones. Wagenaar (1986) found a similar effect when he studied autobiographical memory. He kept a detailed record of daily events over a six-year period. Later he was able to recall more than half of the positive events but only one-third of the negative events. In a study of adults' early childhood memories, Kihlstrom and Harackiewicz (1982) noted that "unpleasant and traumatic memories were especially susceptible to change, shifting toward the neutral and/or trivial on the second trial—suggesting selectivity in the service of avoidance" (p. 146).

William James (1890) noted that forgetting even neutral information may be adaptive: "If we remembered everything, we should on most occasions be as ill off as if we remembered nothing" (p. 68). Elizabeth Bjork and Robert Bjork (1988) and others have pointed out that without forgetting our memory systems would be so full of clutter and outdated information as to be useless; yet it is both useful and adaptive to keep some trace of old information that can, under certain circumstances, be readily retrieved. This view suggests that adaptive forgetting is a matter of inhibiting information as opposed to discarding it entirely.

Bjork and his colleagues (Bjork and Bjork 1988, 1992; Bjork 1989; Geiselman, Bjork, and Fishman 1983) have investigated the role of inhibitory processes in a cognitive psychology laboratory paradigm referred to as "directed forgetting." In this paradigm, subjects are instructed to forget material after they have learned it, and memory for that material is subsequently impaired. In a related line of research, Michael Anderson and his colleagues (Anderson and Bjork 1994; Anderson, Bjork, and Bjork 1994; Anderson and Spellman 1995) have demonstrated the existence of mechanisms that cause direct inhibition of previously well-encoded material. Even well-encoded materials may be forgotten under controlled conditions. The mechanisms of forgetting in these cases may be related to certain kinds of amnesia, such as post-hypnotic amnesia (see Geiselman, Bjork, and Fishman 1983; Kihlstrom 1983) or naturally occurring "fugues," in which a person suddenly forgets his or her own history, often following a traumatic event (see Hilgard 1986; Terr 1994).

Although often our ability to remember things decreases with time, some laboratory experiments demonstrate that retention for material can improve over time. Alan Brown (1976) reviewed the literature on recovery of memory and argued that evidence supports the reality of such spontaneous recovery. When participants take repeated tests for the same information, memory improvement ("hypermnesia" or "reminiscence") often occurs (see Ballard 1913; A. S. Brown 1976; Erdelyi and Becker 1974; Payne 1987). Hypermnesia is especially pronounced for memory of pictures, or memory instructions for words that emphasize mental imagery (Payne 1987).

Mark Wheeler (1995) has demonstrated spontaneous memory recovery in experiments using a variety of study materials, including pictures and words. Participants were presented with materials to learn. In some conditions the participants had to learn additional materials that were likely to cause retroactive interference for the first set of materials. Wheeler discovered that participants' memory for the first set of materials improved with a longer delay before testing, demonstrating spontaneous recovery of material without repeated testing. According to Wheeler, "The absolute recovery is important, not only because it is counterintuitive but also because it demonstrates that the target material was not permanently forgotten; rather it was only temporarily nonproduceable" (p. 183). He speculates that the spontaneous recovery results from the release of retrieval inhibition.

These laboratory studies, using nontraumatic, nonemotional stimuli, demonstrate that people can forget well-learned material and can later recover memories of that material.

## A Cognitive Perspective on Forgetting and Remembering Abuse

The concepts considered so far in this chapter—the ubiquity of unawareness, forgetting, remembering, dissociation, and the cognitive mechanisms of attention and memory—can be drawn upon to understand amnesia and memory recovery for childhood sexual abuse and other betrayal traumas.

The cognitive mechanisms that underlie this blockage of information are dissociations between normally connected, or integrated, aspects of processing and memory. These cognitive dissociations can lead to the more global phenomenology and symptomology of clinical dissociation (such as dissociative identity disorder, formerly multiple personality disorder).

A continuum of possible forms of dissociation underlies this overall phenomenology. At one end of the continuum are dissociations occurring early in the process that prevent information from being encoded and stored as episodic, or narrative memory. These traumatic amnesias use mechanisms of selective attention to keep out information and can be understood in terms of low-level failures of memory integration. Multiple modules process events in parallel. Therefore, for dissociation to occur it is not necessary for the traumatic information to be entirely blocked from entering the nervous system (see Figure 5.6). The information needs only to be blocked from entering mechanisms that control attachment behavior. In some cases this may be achieved by dissociating affective information from declarative or episodic knowledge. However, as our control of social interactions often involves consciousness, it is often adaptive for the information to be blocked from consciousness as well. This blockage may depend on mechanisms of selective attention, in which information can be blocked from consciousness despite some degree of unconscious processing. A recent study by Cloitre and others (1996) suggests that women with a history of childhood abuse are particularly skilled at selectively following instructions to remember, leading the authors to speculate that a strategy for coping with abuse "may be enhanced remembering of designated events (e.g., information not associated with abuse) rather than forgetting of traumatic events." Consistent blockage of information about abuse could presumably lead to profound amnesia.

Although information may be blocked from entering conscious awareness and/or declarative memory stores, sensory traces, or procedural memories, may well be laid for traumatic events.

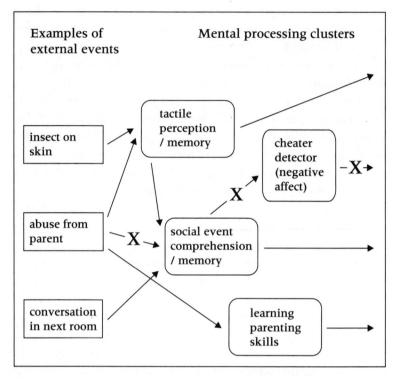

*Figure 5.6* A revised schematic model of cognitive processing of information as it enters the nervous system, showing examples of information blockage (the X's).

The information may be processed for learning certain adaptive strategies, which later in life may lead to highly maladaptive behaviors. For instance, if mechanisms exist in early childhood for learning parenting skills (as primate and human data suggest they do), these mechanisms may operate at full potential during abusive events, though information may be blocked from reaching the mechanisms that control social behavior and representation.

Another way dissociation and amnesia may occur is in the mind's blocking not the initial entry of information, but the repeated processing of that information through feedback loops of various kinds. Figure 5.7 shows a highly simplified version of possible feedback loops that could be blocked. To the extent that episodic memory of complex events depends on cognitive

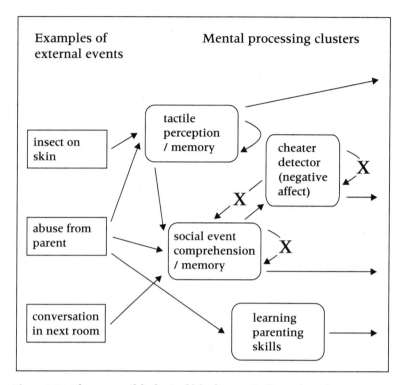

*Figure 5.7*   Three possible loci of blockages (indicated with an X) that are the result of disruption of normal integrative functions of processing and memory formation that depend on feedback loops and consolidation over time.

computations that take place over time, this sort of blockage could very likely produce amnesia for conscious episodic memories but intact sensory and affective memories (Browne 1990; Nelson 1993; Squire 1992). One could hypothesize that this lack of integration could also lead to the storage of essentially unprocessed information so that when memories are later "recovered" they are initially experienced as immediate events or "flashbacks" that lack episodic interpretation (Siegel 1992).

Our control of social interactions often involves consciousness. Thus, information about trauma often needs to be blocked from consciousness as well. In some cases this may be achieved by dissociating affective information from episodic knowledge. However, in other cases the event may be entirely blocked from consciousness and those related mechanisms that control social behavior.

Finally, at the other end of the continuum, initial event processing does not have to be disrupted for amnesia to take place. In this case, which perhaps most closely resembles the classic concept of "repression," the forgetting occurs after the event is fully encoded and a memory is successfully stored. This type of forgetting might be adaptive if an event becomes identifiable as a betrayal only some time after it occurs. Fugues, post-hypnotic amnesias, and traumatic amnesias that occur substantially after successful encoding may involve the same low-level cognitive mechanisms used in laboratory studies of directed forgetting and memory inhibition.

The processes by which memories are recovered depend on the nature of the dissociative conditions that produced the amnesia. In the case of very early dissociation of incoming information, where some information is selectively not attended and declarative memories are not formed in the first place, memory recovery can occur only in certain ways. Procedural memories may be identified and interpreted; or sensory and affective traces may be activated, leading to a flashback experience, which may allow the integrative, narrative-forming functions of episodic memory to take place much later. This sort of memory recovery also may invite distortions of interpretation. Though sensory and affective memories might be more enduring and accurate than normal episodic memory, the interpretation of those sensory and affective memories may be open to error, especially if the sensory information is limited or impoverished. For example, if a young child was sexually abused in a dark and quiet room (say by a father at night) and only affective and kinesthetic memories were created, the recovery process may require reconstruction and extrapolation. Some affective memories may never be interpretable in the sense of recovering a knowable event; nonetheless, a person may become conscious of the fact that he or she experienced something that can be remembered for the feelings it evoked and for associated aspects of the event, such as body size at the time, smells, or sounds.

At the other end of the continuum, in cases where previously well-encoded events have become blocked from consciousness, memory recovery may be fairly similar to normal "remembering"—that is, subject to the distortions of reconstruction. While such a recovered memory may be remarkable for its content, it may not be remarkable for the process by which the memory was recovered. If inhibition is released and an episodic memory is recovered, the remembering may be nothing like experiencing a flashback, but more like reminiscing. The sorts of amnesia that are associated with some cases of dissociative identity disorder and fugue states (in which a person suddenly cannot remember his or her identity) seem to fit features of this "well-encoded" end of the continuum, in which episodic memories are unavailable to consciousness but are later fully recoverable. Returning briefly to the distinctions between implicit/explicit memory on the one hand and procedural/declarative memory on the other, one could speculate that these inaccessible, but initially well-encoded, memories may be a good example of declarative memories that are only measurable implicitly.

*Amnesia for Nontraumatic Memories*

A psychogenic fugue is characterized by amnesia for extensive aspects of autobiographical history, not just amnesia for a particular set of trauma-related memories. People with multiple personalities often have states of consciousness in which they have no access to memories of mundane events that are accessible in other states of consciousness. Also, many incest survivors report "missing" segments of their childhood, where they are unable to remember not only incest or trauma but also childhood teachers, friends, and other nontraumatic aspects of their life. Recently researchers have documented generalized autobiographical memory impairment in traumatized people (Kuyken and Brewin 1995; McNally, Lasko, Macklin, and Pitman 1995; McNally, Litz, Prassas, Shin, and Weathers 1994). According to Richard Loewenstein, who reviewed the literature on psychogenic amnesia in a 1991 issue of the *American Psychiatric Press Review of Psychiatry,* these sorts of "complex psychogenic amnesia symptoms" were reported about a century ago by Breuer and Freud: "For example, patients such as Anna O and Emmy von N were described as having blackouts; episodes of disremembered behavior; extensive amnesic gaps for the life history; fluctuations in handwriting, handedness, and language and spontaneous age regression with amnesia" (pp. 197–198).

Why would incest survivors forget nontraumatic aspects of their childhood? The cognitive model presented in this chapter suggests some possibilities. If the amnesia is a result of very early information blockage, the blockage is possibly a kind of "overkill," where large aspects of reality are not attended. If the amnesia is a result of retroactive inhibition of well-encoded material, the inhibition may affect large sections of associated memories. This may occur in some cases of psychogenic fugue and in some cases of multiple personality. Loewenstein reported that Janet had a similar explanation: "[Janet] viewed amnesia as a basic part of the dissociative process in which complex subsystems of memories, feelings, thoughts, and ideas became autonomous through disconnection from the overall executive control of the total personality with failure to recognize these as part of the patient's own consciousness" (p. 197).

### Memories of Early Childhood

It is commonly said that most adults cannot remember their infancy or very early childhood. This lack of memory is sometimes called "childhood amnesia." Occasionally, however, adults claim to have memories from very early ages. When an adult reports memories of abuse that allegedly took place during infancy or toddlerhood, the authenticity of the memories is often challenged. However, the cognitive perspective on amnesia and memory recovery for abuse, as well as research in the area of childhood memory, suggests that the jury is still out, that we cannot conclude that all reports of even infantile memories are necessarily false or not authentic remembrances. In exploring this topic, it is important to keep in mind the distinctions between different kinds of memory. "Childhood amnesia" is generally used to refer to a lack of episodic memory of childhood. Perhaps procedural memory can exist for early childhood, even when declarative memory does not.

The recognized cutoff point for childhood amnesia for episodic memories has been slowly decreasing with time. One way of determining the cutoff point is to ask adults for their earliest memories (see, for example, Kihlstrom and Harackiewicz 1982; Waldfogel 1948). Such surveys suggest that the average age for the beginning of autobiographical memory is approximately three and a half years. More recently JoNell Adair Usher and Ulric Neisser (1993) examined childhood amnesia by asking college students about events that were known to have occurred in each participant's childhood, such as the birth of a sibling, a hospitalization, the death of a family member, or a family move. The participants were asked if they remembered one of these early childhood events and, if so, how old they were when it happened. Some participants reported remembering events from age two, especially hospitalizations and the birth of a younger sibling. The participants' mothers were then contacted for corroboration. Most of the mothers indicated that the reports were accurate. The most common inaccuracy was for participants to overestimate their age (for example, a hospitalization that actually took place when the participant was three years old was reported by the participant to have occurred at age five). Usher and Neisser also found that childhood amnesia seems to drop off at different ages depending on the nature of the event:

> These results indicate quite clearly that the offset of childhood amnesia, or the earliest age from which an event can be recalled, depends on the nature of the event itself. In particular, the birth of a younger sibling and a hospitalization are significant events in the life of a preschool-age child and are likely to be recalled into adulthood. The offsets of these events occur at age 2, after the second birthday and before the third. Thus some memories are from a substantially earlier point in childhood than previous research would have suggested. On the other hand, little or nothing was remembered from events at age 1, before the second birthday. (pp. 163–164)

If Usher and Neisser are correct that childhood amnesia depends on the type of event, it is possible that some sorts of trauma might have an even lower cutoff for childhood amnesia than the events the researchers studied. A crucial variable for episodic memory of events may be the extent to which the event was verbally encoded at the time, and this is likely to be at least partly a function of the behavior of family members. Perhaps a death in the family is not remembered as well as a hospitalization or a sibling birth not because it is intrinsically less significant but because it was not talked about as much. If this variable is important, and the research on the relationship between verbal encoding and autobiographical memory suggests it is (Nelson 1993), then traumas that were extensively discussed at the time might be remembered from an even earlier age than two for those children able to comprehend the discussion. (To test this possibility it would be necessary, of course, to distinguish memory for the events that were discussed at the time from memory for discussions that occurred later.)

One explanation that is often offered for childhood amnesia is that the brain is too immature to create long-term episodic memories. Some researchers have argued that in a child's first few years of life the hippocampus, which is needed for the consolidation processes necessary for long-term episodic memories, is not fully mature, and that this explains childhood amnesia. However, as Usher and Neisser point out, this argument does not sufficiently account for childhood amnesia, because young children often have access to early memories that they later seem to lose. One study found that two-and-a-half-year-old children could recall events that took place half a year earlier (Fivush and Hamond 1990). And Patricia Bauer and her colleagues (Bauer and Dow 1994; Bauer, Hertsgaard, and Dow 1994) demonstrated episodic memory in children when they are tested at under two years of age. Usher and Neisser suggest that memories are lost to children as they get older because of changes in cognitive structure that accompany development. They point out that an autobiographical narrative changes substantially from early childhood to adulthood. Aspects of events that are significant to children (such as what was eaten on a family vacation) may be irrelevant to adults, whereas aspects of events that are significant to adults (such as to what destination the family traveled on a vacation) may be irrelevant to children. Usher and Neisser suggest that "any event in which the child's focus of attention does happen to fit adult schemata should be relatively easier to recall later on. The birth of a sibling may constitute one such event" (1993, p. 156).

However, even if the age for possible accurate recall of memory is pushed further downward, it is not common for adults to recall early events at the conscious, explicit level. What about sensory, affective, and procedural memories? Human infants and toddlers have an enormous intellectual challenge: they must learn a complex system of cultural rules and language within a few short years. They must form enduring relationships with their caregivers and family members, and they must learn a myriad of skills. All these challenges require some degree of intact procedural and implicit memory abilities. Some studies suggest that procedural or implicit memories of early childhood remain intact even when declarative or explicit memories are absent or inaccessible, although this possibility awaits a great deal of additional investigation. Furthermore, the nature of the remembering may involve enactments of events, experiences, or behavior learned that is outside of conscious understanding. Nora Newcombe and Nathan Fox (1994) studied nine- and ten-year-old children's memories of former preschool classmates. They found evidence of some explicit memory of the former classmates. But, more strikingly, they found that implicit memory of former classmates, as revealed through increased skin conductance in response to photographs of the classmates, was unrelated to explicit memory. Nancy Myers, Rachel Clifton, and Marsha Clarkson (1987) reported that five children who had participated in an experiment at ages six to forty weeks showed evidence that they had implicit memories for the experience two years later as demonstrated by their actions (and as compared with control children who had not previously participated in the experiment during infancy).

Procedural memories may be revealed in patterns of motor action and mannerisms, and learned likes, dislikes, and fears. As mentioned earlier, one sort of procedural memory from infancy may be revealed in parenting skills and styles. It is possible that sensory flashbacks of procedural memories of traumatic events can be recoded and interpreted with some degree of accuracy in adult life; however, even if the procedural, sensory, or affective memories are accurate, the interpretations may not be. (See also Purdy 1989 for a case study of flashbacks of abuse during infancy communicated by a bright four-year-old child.

According to the adoptive mother—the author of the case study—many of the reported events were corroborated by records and witnesses. Without access to the corroboration it is difficult to evaluate the evidence of this one study, but it suggests that under some circumstances flashbacks from early infancy and their interpretations may contain elements of truth.)

In a set of laboratory experiments reported by Carolyn Rovee-Collier (1993), young infants two, three, and six months of age were taught to kick in order to move a mobile suspended over their crib. Infants at each age were able to learn to operate the mobile in this way. Rovee-Collier tested the infants' memory by re-exposing the infants to the mobile after some delay. When the mobile and the surrounding context were exactly as they were during testing, infants displayed the motor response they had learned after short delays. However, if the mobile or the surrounding context were changed, infants were less likely to display the kicking motion. The retention of memory for the mobile activity decreased as delay time increased. However, if after some delay (such as two weeks) the infants were re-exposed to the mobile in response to their kicking, they rapidly relearned the kicking response. The reactivation treatment was highly dependent on the context being held constant (such as the room the infant was in), suggesting that infants are aware of and have memory for their locale. Rovee-Collier summarizes her findings:

> Infants' memories of events in which they have actively participated are highly enduring and become even more so after repeated retrievals, including repeated encounters with reminders. In addition, infants' memories are highly detailed and include information about the incidental context in which the event occurred. The longevity and specificity of infants' early memories are inconsistent with the widely held view that early memories are short-lived, highly generalized and diffuse, and devoid of place information for most of the first year of life. Despite their specificity, however, infants' newly acquired memories can be readily updated within a limited period of time following original encoding. In large part, this malleability may account for subsequent failures to remember events, although the strong contextual specificity required for retrieval may also play a major role.

The discovery that forgotten memories can be reactivated both directly and indirectly by reminders and can be substantially prolonged by repeated reactivations offers a mechanism by which infants' memories of their early experiences can influence their later behavior. (p. 135)

The possibility of infantile experiences influencing later experience was also suggested by an intriguing study by six medical doctors at the State Institute of Forensic Medicine in Stockholm, Sweden. The authors (Jacobson et al. 1987) tested whether obstetrical procedures affecting the newborn during birth are important for eventual adult behavior. Birth records were gathered for 412 alcoholics, drug addicts, or victims of suicide who were born in Stockholm after 1940 and who died there between 1978 and 1984. The hospital birth records of these victims were compared with the hospital birth records of 2,901 controls. The investigators found that suicides involving asphyxiation were closely associated with asphyxia at birth, suicides by violent mechanical means were closely associated with mechanical birth trauma, and drug addiction was associated with opiate and/or barbiturate administration to mothers during labor. For example, the rate of asphyxia during birth among those people who committed suicide by asphyxiation was 10%, whereas the rate of asphyxia during birth among the control subjects was 2.3%. In addition, the authors reported that the rate of asphyxia during birth was significantly lower for those who committed suicide by poisoning themselves than it was for those who committed suicide by asphyxiation. The researchers considered a number of possible explanations for the transference of a birth trauma to an adult behavior, including the possibility of what they called "imprinting" of the traumatic experience in the brain of the newborn such that eventually the trauma is reenacted by the adult. This finding deserves attempted replication and exploration; for now it is only suggestive, not conclusive, of the possibility of adults retaining procedural memories from birth. Even newborns may demonstrate procedural memories of prenatal experiences by their tendency to orient toward their mother's voice (which they have been exposed to inside the womb) over other voices (Querleu et al. 1984) and to recognize other sounds to which they had been exposed prenatally (Damstra-Wijmenga 1991). Consequently, there is good reason to entertain the possibility that we can store some sort of procedural, sensory, or affective memory for events experienced at birth or very early infancy.

The empirical studies and cognitive mechanisms discussed in this chapter suggest that at the very least we should keep an open mind about the possibility that reports of recovered memories of abuse in infancy or early childhood sometimes reflect actual abuse. Currently, the attitude of the general public toward these memories is one of disbelief. I myself experience disbelief when I hear such reports. Perhaps the disbelief is valid: some reported memories of sexual abuse during infancy may be, in part or whole, confabulations. But spontaneous disbelief may be a poor measure of what is possible: I also experience disbelief at the thought that some adult men enjoy jabbing their penises at the bodies of young children. Yet we know that some do.

Lenore Terr (1988) studied twenty children who suffered documented traumas before the age of five. The children's verbal and behavioral memories were compared to the documentation of the events. Terr found that while the ability to verbally recount the trauma was related to the child's age, at any age "behavioral memories of trauma remain quite accurate and true to the events that stimulated them" (p. 96). In some cases of sexual abuse, Terr had pornographic photographs of the children as part of the documentation. Terr described the behavioral reenactment of "Gloria" and "Sarah" (not their real names):

> Gloria was 0 to 6 months old when she was enrolled in her grandparents' day care program. She did not see them again after age 6 months because of a family feud. At age 2 years, 11 months, she came into my office and shyly opened the toy cabinet, taking out a doll and looking under the doll's dress . . . "I want to undress this baby," she said—and she quickly, efficiently took all the clothes off Little Bo Peep . . . She poked Bo Peep suddenly and violently in the vagina. (The photos show an erect adult penis poking the infant Gloria's vagina.)

. . . Sarah was 15 to 18 months old in the day care home. She was 5 when she entered my office jauntily. First she drew a picture of a naked baby. She explained: "This is my doll. She is lying on the bed naked [she hesitated], but covered up. I'm playing and yelling at my doll. She was bad! I yell at my doll [she hesitated again, looking up at me for some response]—not really yell—you get to bed, you!"

I asked whether Sarah ever felt scared . . . The child fingered her upper abdomen. I asked, "Did anybody ever scare you?" "Somebody scare me once," she said, "with a finger part."

A few weeks later I saw the pornographic photos. Expecting to find a man's penis in or at the baby's genitals, I saw instead an erect penis (to this child with a 15 to 18 month old vocabulary at the time of the experience, a "finger part") on Sarah's upper abdomen—jabbing at the very spot she touched in my office. (pp. 98–101)

# 6

# TESTABLE PREDICTIONS

When she was a child, Lana Lawrence was sexually, emotionally, and physically abused by her father. Later her father was arrested and convicted for abusing Lana when she was a teenager. Lana Lawrence forgot and later recovered memories of the abuse that had occurred to her as a child. While her father was in prison, in response to her questioning him over the telephone, he confessed to her childhood sexual abuse. She described one flashback she had of herself as a small child: "My arms are wrapped around my father's neck while swimming in a lake. I see the . . . joy . . . on my face . . . until my father reaches his hand under my swimsuit to fondle me . . . Today I am left with an image of horror and betrayal" (Lawrence 1987, p. 10).

Although some of her memories were forgotten and later recovered, Lana Lawrence always remembered some facts of the abuse: "On an intellectual level, I knew that I had been a victim of incest, along with physical and emotional abuse." But as she describes it, her memory was incomplete: "On an emotional level, I felt numb. When talking about my experiences, it was as though I were speaking about someone totally separate from myself" (p. 10).

Some people do not forget childhood sexual abuse; others, like Ross Cheit and Marilyn Van Derbur Atler, are not at all able to recall the abuse for long periods of time. Lana Lawrence remembered some of the abuse she experienced, but not many of the feelings of which she later became aware; she forgot and recovered memories for other abusive events. What causes such variability in remembering, and what factors determine when forgetting is likely to happen?

Betrayal trauma theory provides a framework that allows us to make testable predictions of when abuse is most likely to be forgotten. It posits that forgetting certain kinds of betrayal—such as sexual abuse by a trusted caregiver—is adaptive, and that this forgetting is understandable in terms of what is known about cognitive mechanisms. Thus, one significant variable suggested by betrayal trauma theory is the relationship of the abuser to the person abused. Other variables that suggest the probability of forgetting, such as the lack of explicit discussion of abuse, are also suggested. The theory thus generates testable predictions.

Betrayal trauma theory grows out of the following propositions:

- Pain, including the pain of detecting betrayal, motivates changes in behavior to promote survival.
- Sometimes the pain-motivated changes in behavior would be too dangerous; thus, pain and the information that prompts it sometimes need to be suppressed.
- Humans are dependent on caregivers. A rich and crucial system of attachment-forming and attachment-eliciting begins in human infants at birth.
- Detecting betrayal is an adaptive activity that leads to pain, which in turn prompts a change in behavior, such as a shift in social alliances.
- Detecting betrayal can be too dangerous when the natural changes in behavior it provokes would threaten primary dependent relationships. In order to suppress the natural reaction to betrayal in such cases, information blockages in mental processing occur.
- The cognitive mechanisms that underlie these blockages are dissociations between normally connected, or integrated, aspects of processing and memory.

Blockages may sometimes depend on mechanisms of selective attention; here, information is blocked from consciousness despite some degree of unconscious processing. In no way, however, do these blockages suggest that the information will not be processed by other less conscious mechanisms. Another way dissociation and amnesia may occur is in blocking the repeated processing of that information through feedback loops of various kinds. Lack of integration may lead to the storage of essentially unprocessed information, so that when memories are later recovered they are initially experienced as immediate events or flashbacks that lack episodic interpretation. Amnesia may result even if initial event processing is not disrupted. This could depend on cognitive processes activated in the "directed forgetting" laboratory paradigm.

Memory recovery depends on the nature of the initial memory loss. In cases of early dissociation of information, memory recovery may require verbal recoding of the sensory information and implicit memories. In cases where well-encoded material has been forgotten, memory recovery may require release of inhibition; then normal remembering may proceed.

As detailed in Chapters 4 and 5, evidence exists for many of the elements of betrayal trauma theory. For instance, experiments have shown that the human cognitive system is capable of knowing and not knowing information simultaneously, depending on which mental modules have access to that information. This supports the claim that explicit amnesia for abuse can go hand in hand with implicit abuse-specific learning. But what about evidence for the central prediction of betrayal trauma theory—that betrayal produces amnesia? This chapter considers the kinds of evidence we might seek and the evidence that is already available.

## Empirical Evidence for Betrayal Trauma Theory

Many, if not all, of the components of betrayal trauma theory focusing on the cognitive mechanisms underlying information blockage can be (and in many cases, have already been) studied in the laboratory under highly controlled conditions. When done carefully, such studies can produce evidence that is accessible to others, replicable, and, at best, able to support strong inferences about causality.

*Cognitive Components*

My colleagues and I in my laboratory at the University of Oregon are exploring the cognitive mechanisms underlying dissociative experiences (Freyd et al., in preparation). Using a college student population, we are measuring performance on cognitive tasks relating to selective attention, explicit memory, and implicit memory, and are then relating those performance differences to differences in dissociative experiences. Our goal is to determine the relationship, if any, between basic attentional and representational processes and dissociative experiences and disorders. A logical extension of this research would be to look for neuroanatomical underpinnings of the cognitive mechanisms implicated in dissociation. My colleagues and I (Freyd, Martorello, and Alvarado, in preparation) are also conducting experiments with clinical populations to test various other aspects of betrayal trauma theory, including the relationship between betrayal and unawareness.

One research instrument that we have found useful for studies with both college student and clinical populations is the Dissociative Experiences Scale (DES) developed by Eve Bernstein Carlson and Frank Putnam (Bernstein and Putnam 1986; Carlson and Putnam 1993; Coons et al. 1989; Branscomb 1989; Boon and Draijer 1993; Saxe et al. 1993). This twenty-eight-item individual difference scale is easy to administer and is not considered intrusive or painful to the participants. It measures the tendency to have common dissociative experiences, such as highway hypnosis or absorption during a movie, as well as more extreme sorts of dissociative experiences, such as amnesia for blocks of time.

In our research we instruct subjects as follows:

You will be given a questionnaire consisting of twenty-eight questions about experiences that you may have in your daily life. We are interested in how often you may have these experiences. It is important, however, that your answers show how often these experiences happen to you when you are not under the influence of alcohol or drugs. To answer the questions, please determine to what degree the experience described in the question applies to you and mark the line with a vertical slash at the appropriate place, as shown in the example below.

To provide a taste of the kinds of statements in the DES, here are the first four items (Bernstein and Putnam 1986, p. 733):

1. Some people have the experience of driving a car and suddenly realizing that they don't remember what has happened during all or part of the trip. Mark the line to show what percentage of the time this happens to you.

2. Some people find that sometimes they are listening to someone talk and they suddenly realize that they did not hear part or all of what was said. Mark the line to show what percentage of the time this happens to you.

3. Some people have the experience of finding themselves in a place and having no idea how they got there. Mark the line to show what percentage of the time this happens to you.

4. Some people have the experience of finding themselves dressed in clothes that they don't remember putting on. Mark the line to show what percentage of the time this happens to you.

Each item is followed by a rule 100 mm long, with 0% marked at the left end and 100% at the right end. The DES is scored by measuring the position of the slash mark for each of the twenty-eight questions, and then computing an average score. Thus, a score of 0 would indicate no dissociative experiences reported at all, and a score of 100 would indicate constant, total forgetting. The DES scores of 154 college students are presented in Figure 6.1. The distribution of DES scores is not typically characterized as a "normal distribution" or "bell curve," but instead, as in Figure 6.1, is typically a skewed distribution. Most individuals have low scores. Those diagnosed with posttraumatic stress disorder or dissociative disorders typically have higher scores (Bernstein and Putnam 1986; Carlson and Putnam 1993).

We also collected data from 50 therapy clients. In our research with therapy clients, in addition to the DES and other instruments, we included a series of questions of our own that elicit information about experienced childhood abuse and sexual assault. We have found that DES scores are positively related to

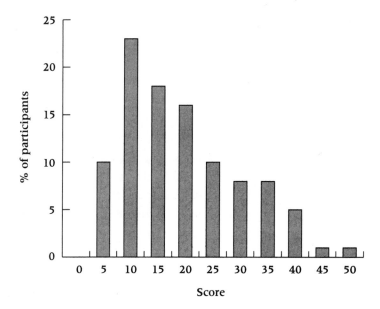

*Figure 6.1* DES scores for 154 college students (from Freyd et al., in preparation).

each of the types of abuse that we ask about (Freyd, Martorello, and Alvarado, in preparation). A positive relationship between DES and childhood abuse has been reported by other researchers as well (DiTomasso and Routh 1993; Chu and Dill 1990; Sanders and Giolas 1991).

Through our investigation of the relationship between betrayal trauma and dissociative episodes in a clinical population, we hope to arrive at a better understanding of the damage caused by the psychological components of abuse. As Spiegel (1989) comments: "Rape is a violation of both body and mind, transforming sensations associated with pleasure into pain, damaging a victim's sense of independence, personal safety, and capacity for future intimate relationships" (p. 295). We suspect that extensive damage can also occur even when no physical or sexual contact has taken place between a perpetrator and a victim, that psychological torment caused by emotionally sadistic and invasive treatment or gross emotional neglect may be as destructive as other forms of abuse. Analyzing DES scores and measures of different types of abuse (childhood physical abuse, childhood sexual abuse, childhood emotional abuse, witnessing of violence, and adult sexual assault) reported by participants, we found that the correlation between DES scores and abuse experiences was highest for childhood emotional abuse (such as having privacy invaded, being lied to, and being threatened with abandonment). The correlation was lowest for childhood physical abuse (Freyd, Martorello, and Alvarado, in preparation). These findings are preliminary, however, based on exploratory analysis, and thus must be interpreted with caution until they can be replicated with a study designed to test specific hypotheses about the effects of types of abuse; but they do suggest that attention should be paid to the consequences of psychological and emotional abuse.

In our study involving college students, we have investigated cognitive mechanisms implicated in dissociative experiences by comparing the performance on cognitive tasks of the 40 participants with the highest DES scores with performance by the 40 participants with the lowest DES scores. We have found, for ex-

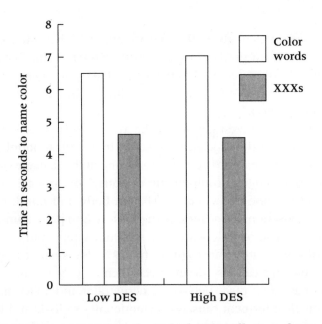

*Figure 6.2* Ink-naming times for 40 high DES college students and 40 low DES college students in a Stroop task (from Freyd et al., in preparation).

ample, that participants with high DES scores show more interference when attempting to name ink colors on a Stroop task
(see Chapter 5) than do participants with low DES scores. As
can be seen in Figure 6.2, the high DES participants took longer
to name the ink colors when the lists were conflicting color terms
(such as naming the color "yellow" when the word "red" was
printed in the ink color yellow) than did the low DES participants.

In future studies we will test more specific hypotheses about
the cognitive changes involved in dissociation. For instance, the
ability to dissociate current experience may depend partly on
representational structures that support spontaneous perceptual
transformations of incoming events. One such transformation
that could be studied is the creation of spatial representations in
which the observer's mind feels spatially distinct from his or her
body, as when people describe "leaving" their bodies during a
traumatic episode and viewing the scene as if from afar. One
could also investigate the role of mental recoding and restruc-
turing during memory recovery and psychotherapy. I would be
particularly interested in revealing transformations in knowledge structure as a result of shareability (Freyd 1983; 1993a),
such as an increase in categorical representations of what had
previously been analog sensory information.

### Social, Evolutionary, and Developmental Components

Forms of evidence other than the clinical need to be considered
when evaluating the social, evolutionary, and developmental
components of betrayal trauma theory. Here, case studies and the
reality we know through lived experience become important,
especially at this stage of our investigation of childhood sexual
abuse, because the phenomena of abuse and memory disturbance are so rich, because we lack other forms of evidence, and
because of the difficulty in collecting more systematic, scientific
data in an ethical way. We cannot randomly assign human participants to incest and nonincest experimental conditions, for instance, so as to study the effect of incest on memory. Each
person's life contains an endless number of unique, and interre-
lated, attributes that make it in some ways impossible simulta-

neously to observe the richness and complexity of the person's life as a whole and to measure the contribution of each variable.

Katy Butler (1995) gives a critique of inaccuracies in case studies used in recent books on the recovered memory controversy. I illustrate many of the ideas in this book by presenting various documented case studies. Except for examples from other authors' works, I include full, real names of the people involved. In this contentious area of research, case studies are most useful if the interested reader is able to corroborate the author's statements and selection of information.

Although case studies can provide essential information, converging scientific evidence is important. While it is not even remotely ethical to assign people at random to sex abuse and non–sex abuse conditions, one can nonetheless do systematic, scientific analyses of the naturally occurring responses of real-life victims of abuse. As mentioned earlier, the empirical limitations in this area of investigation are comparable to the limitations in many other sciences, such as paleontology or astronomy, where controlled experiments are not usually possible.

## The Role of Betrayal

Betrayal trauma theory differs from the prevailing conception of traumatic adaptation in its emphasis on the social utility of forgetting, in contrast to the more traditional explanations of forgetting to avoid being overwhelmed or to avoid unbearable pain. Some traumatic events may induce terror or pain and not involve betrayal (such as a natural disaster in which the victims cooperate to survive). Profound amnesia is not a likely response to traumatic events that do not involve betrayal, while other responses to traumatic events, such as increased arousal, generalized numbing, and intrusive cognitions (Horowitz 1986) would be expected. This suggests a testable prediction: that the degree of amnesia will be a function of the degree of betrayal (with betrayal defined as a conflict between reality and the need to trust the caregiver).

For example, we should see a higher rate of amnesia when the abuser is an essential caregiver, particularly a parent. However, we must take into account the fact that individuals traumatized by child abuse may employ defensive mechanisms they learned as a result of that early trauma to new traumas; thus, a learned dissociative response could lead to amnesia for even mildly traumatic events that occur later in life.

Eventually, experiences of betrayal will need to be evaluated with detailed analyses of the degree of dependency in the relationship. Among incest survivors, is forgetting related to degree of physical dependency or degree of emotional attachment? Do victims of child abuse by a nonparent who forget the abuse show evidence of more dependence on the relationship than those victims who remember the abuse? Similarly, is betrayal by a person or group with significant power over the victim (such that the victim feels dependent) a factor in amnesia for trauma experienced by adults (such as the battering of wives)? Some military trauma may include a component of perceived betrayal by those in authority (see Bartone and Wright 1990; Brende 1987; Glover 1988); is such trauma more likely to lead to amnesia than military trauma that lacks perceived betrayal?

A variety of factors related to betrayal by a close caregiver are predicted to increase the likelihood of forgetting childhood abuse. For instance, explicit threats and demands for silence from the abuser (statements such as "If you tell I'll kill you" or "I'll kill your mother") would hypothetically increase the advantages for the abused child in forgetting the betrayal in order to maintain critical attachment bonds and would thus increase the probability of amnesia (see Lister 1982).

Other factors could also make blocking information about the abuse more likely: the availability of alternative realities (abuse in the middle of the night, with "normal" family life during the day); isolation during abuse (lack of social validation for the experience, which would allow for cognitively consistent internal denial); young age at onset of abuse (reality defined by adults; lack of integrative functions; plasticity of nervous system); alternative reality-defining statements by caregivers ("This didn't happen"); the absence of any shared, explicit discussion of the abusive events (which could cause information to fail to enter the child's explicit autobiographical memory) (Nelson 1993). These factors, which contribute to the social utility and/or the cognitive feasibility of forgetting abuse, should be compared for their tendency to induce amnesia to the traditional components of trauma, such as stress, overwhelming terror, and intense psychological pain.

When I first articulated specific predictions based on betrayal trauma theory (Freyd 1994) I was not aware of any scientific evidence for these predictions. I had simply developed the theory to make sense of my own experiences, other people's reported experiences, and research findings. If a predicted correlation between one of the factors cited above and amnesia is confirmed, alternative explanations for the results will need to be considered. This will then require additional experimentation or systematic observation in which the competing explanations are specifically compared. For example, I argue in this chapter that I have found evidence that amnesia rates are a function of the closeness of the perpetrator to the victim. In future research, I will systematically compare explanations for this relationship that emerge from betrayal trauma theory with other sorts of explanations. This is the nature of the scientific enterprise. When a theory is new, indeed, when the field of inquiry is in its infancy, the theory is valuable for the ideas for analysis and research it provides. Without betrayal trauma theory, I would never have thought to look specifically for a relationship between incest and amnesia rates. Clearly, betrayal trauma theory is open to—indeed demands—extension, modification, and refinement in light of future research findings and analyses.

## Repeated Traumas

Lenore Terr (1991; 1994) has suggested that childhood traumas can be divided into two groups, based on whether the trauma is repeated or not. The first group, which Terr labels type I, consists of traumas "brought on by sudden shock"; type II traumas, by contrast, are "precipitated by a series of sudden blows" (1991, p. 19). According to Terr, "Type I trauma includes full, detailed memories . . . Type II trauma includes denial and numbing, self-hypnosis and dissociation, and rage" (p. 10). Terr also observes that "children who experience type II . . . may forget whole segments of childhood—from birth to age 9, for instance" (p. 16).

Terr's clinical observation seems paradoxical. Why would something that happens once be easier to remember than even a facet or single instance of something that has happened many times? According to Terr, type II traumas are more likely to be forgotten because repetition affords the opportunity to develop defenses:

> Type II disorders follow from long-standing or repeated exposure to extreme external events. The first such event, of course, creates surprise. But the subsequent unfolding of horrors creates a sense of anticipation. Massive attempts to protect the psyche and to preserve the self are put into gear. The defenses and coping operations used in the type II disorders of childhood—massive denial, repression, dissociation, self-anesthesia, self-hypnosis, identification with the aggressor, and aggression turned against the self—often lead to profound character changes in the youngster.
>
> . . . Children who have been victims of extended periods of terror come to learn that the stressful events will be repeated. Some of these children, the ones, perhaps, who have an innate ease of hypnotizablity, spontaneously fall upon the technique of self-hypnosis. This mechanism enables a child mentally to escape. (1991, pp. 15–16)

While anticipation and repetition are surely relevant to developing the ability to dissociate and forget traumas, I favor an alternative explanation of Terr's clinical observations. People forget repeated traumas because repeated traumas are more likely than single traumas to involve betrayals that contain many of the factors listed earlier as contributing to amnesia for abuse. Thus, it is the elements of betrayal, not anticipation of the event, that I contend induces forgetting. This could be investigated by disentangling the factors of repetition and betrayal by examining nonrepeated versus repeated betrayal traumas and nonrepeated versus repeated nonbetrayal traumas.

## Betrayal and Amnesia: The Centrality of Incest

In betrayal trauma theory, the nature of the relationship between victim and perpetrator is an important factor in determining whether forgetting is adaptive and therefore likely to occur.

Ideally this notion would be tested by gathering detailed information about the victim-perpetrator relationship, the degree of dependency, and so on, and whether the abuse was in fact forgotten. I am aware of no data sets that have this information in great detail. The closest approximation of degree of dependence in the relationship in published studies (Williams 1994a, 1995; Feldman-Summers and Pope 1994; Loftus, Polonsky, and Fullilove 1994) appears to be whether the abuse was perpetrated by a relative.

In the remainder of this chapter I review these data sets, focusing on the relationship between amnesia and incestuous abuse. In the cases of Linda Meyer Williams (1994a; 1995) and Elizabeth Loftus, Sara Polonsky, and Mindy Fullilove (1994) only sexual abuse was investigated. In the study by Shirley Feldman-Summers and Ken Pope (1994), both sexual abuse and physical abuse were studied. In all these cases I compare amnesia rates for incestuous abuse with amnesia rates for nonincestuous abuse. According to betrayal trauma theory, the seven factors predicting amnesia are more likely to occur in incestuous abuse than any other sort of abuse. These factors are:

1. abuse by caregiver;
2. explicit threats demanding silence;
3. alternative realities in environment (abuse context different from nonabuse context);
4. isolation during abuse;
5. young at age of abuse;
6. alternative reality-defining statements by caregiver;
7. lack of discussion of abuse.

In Chapter 3 I discussed the commonly held belief that forgetting childhood sexual abuse is rare, or at least less common than always remembering abuse. The extent to which people are more likely to forget incest than other sorts of abuse is an important factor in estimating the frequency with which abuse is generally forgotten. If incestuous abuse is likely to be forgotten, and if incestuous abuse is significantly underreported, then rates of forgetting abuse generally are underestimated. (It is interesting to note that memory of sexual abuse perpetrated specifically by a parent is at the core of the delayed memory controversy, as reflected by the demographics of the membership of the False Memory Syndrome Foundation. See Landman 1993.)

We do not know what percentage of childhood sexual abuse is perpetrated by parents because there is almost certainly an enormous reporting bias. Similarly, we do not know what percentage of those who have suffered parental abuse have forgotten it because these are the cases least likely to be documented.

The best way to know whether people who are sexually abused as children forget that they were abused would be to work prospectively from a representative sample of sexually abused individuals. However, obtaining a representative sample of sexually abused individuals for prospective study is virtually impossible: the nature of incestuous abuse means it is less likely to be documented; indeed, in many cases the abuse remains a secret even within the family. Still, the available retrospective data, presented in this chapter, suggest that amnesia rates for incest survivors are very high. In addition, available prospective data suggest that rates of amnesia for incest are higher than for other forms of sexual abuse.

The following list characterizes the studies that will be examined in this chapter by whether they show a relationship between incest and amnesia:

- Studies showing a positive relationship between incest and amnesia:
  Feldman-Summers and Pope (1994) (retrospective study)
  Cameron (1993) (retrospective study)
  Williams (1994a, 1994b, 1995) (prospective study)
- Studies showing a negative relationship between incest and amnesia:
  none
- Studies claiming lack of relationship between incest and amnesia:
  Loftus, Polonsky, and Fullilove (1994) (retrospective study)
- Amnesia studies not testing the relationship between incest and amnesia:
  Herman and Schatzow (1987) (all incest survivors)
  Briere and Conte (1993) (most incest survivors)

*Table 6.1*   Respondents reporting abuse, categorized by type of abuse and whether abuse was ever forgotten.

| Type of abuse | Did you ever forget the abuse? | | |
| --- | --- | --- | --- |
| | Yes | No | Total |
| Physical abuse by relative only | 3 | 10 | 13 |
| Sexual abuse by relative only | 9 | 14 | 23 |
| Sexual abuse by nonrelative only | 8 | 20 | 28 |
| Sexual abuse by both relative and nonrelative | 3 | 1 | 4 |
| Physical and sexual abuse by relative | 4 | 2 | 6 |
| Physical abuse by relative and sexual abuse by nonrelative | 2 | 0 | 2 |
| Physical and sexual abuse by relative, and sexual abuse by nonrelative | 3 | 0 | 3 |
| Total | 32 | 47 | 79 |

*Source:* From data collected by Feldman-Summers and Pope 1994.

Shirley Feldman-Summers and Ken Pope (1994) sent a simple ten-item survey to a national sample of 500 psychologists. Of these, 330 returned usable surveys. Of those responding, 79 (24%) indicated they had experienced some form of childhood sexual or physical abuse.

Participants who had been abused were asked to indicate whether they had been sexually abused by a relative, sexually abused by a nonrelative, physically abused by a relative, or physically abused by a nonrelative. Some respondents reported more than one category of abuse, but none reported being physically abused by a nonrelative. The sixth item on the survey asked, "Was there ever a period of time when you could not

*Table 6.2* Respondents reporting abuse (*n* = 79), categorized by whether they were sexually abused by a relative and whether abuse was forgotten.

| Sexually abused by relative? | Did you ever forget the abuse? | |
| --- | --- | --- |
| | Yes | No |
| Yes (incest victims) | 19 (53%) | 17 (47%) |
| No (all other abuse victims) | 13 (30%) | 30 (70%) |

*Source:* From data collected by Feldman-Summers and Pope 1994.

remember some or all of the abuse by someone?" From the raw data supplied to me by the authors I have prepared a table (Table 6.1) that categorizes participants based on the kind of abuse reported and the constancy of their memory for being abused. Table 6.1 reveals two significant points: the importance of abuse by a relative over a nonrelative in determining forgetting (which may relate to Factors 1 and 5 from the list of betrayal trauma abuse predictors); and the importance of the physical/sexual abuse distinction on amnesia (which may relate to Factors 2, 3, 4, 6, 7, as sexual abuse is more likely to occur in isolation and with demands of silence).

In an attempt to determine whether the data showed a difference between incestuous and nonincestuous abuse as it relates to memory, I categorized the 79 abuse survivors according to two questions: "Was the person sexually abused by a relative?" and "Was forgetting reported?" Table 6.2 shows the results. While 53% of the incest survivors had a period of forgetting the abuse, only 30% of the other abuse survivors did (see Figure 6.3). According to a chi square test of independence, the interaction between type of abuse (incestuous versus nonincestuous) and forgetting is statistically significant ($\chi^2 = 4.13$; $p < .05$).

Thirty-two participants in Feldman-Summers and Pope's (1994) survey reported having had a period in which they could not remember some or all of the abuse. In other words, these participants had recovered memories of abuse. Feldman-

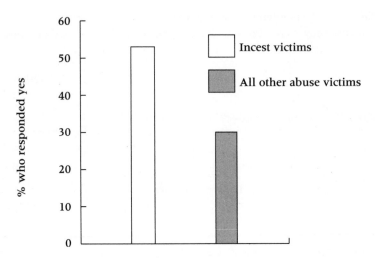

*Figure 6.3*   Percentage of respondents reporting they had forgotten abuse (from data collected by Feldman-Summers and Pope 1994).

Summers and Pope asked these participants to answer four questions about their recovered memories. The questions concerned the type of abuse forgotten, the period of forgetting, the trigger that caused them to recover the memories, and any sources of corroboration of recovered memories. Feldman-Summers and Pope found that of the 32 participants reporting recovered memories, 90% reported that at least one event or circumstance was believed to have triggered the recollection, and 46.9% reported they had found some corroboration of the abuse.

Of most interest to my analysis are the responses to the survey question about the type of abuse that had been forgotten. The question was: "If you checked more than one kind of abuse in question 5 above, please check the kind(s) of abuse that you were unable to remember during some period of your life," and the choices were: sexual abuse by relative, sexual abuse by nonrelative, nonsexual physical abuse by relative, nonsexual physical abuse by a nonrelative. Feldman-Summers and Pope reported that of the 32 participants who recovered memories of abuse, 56.2% reported that the forgetting involved sexual abuse by a relative, 37.5% reported that it involved sexual abuse by a nonrelative, and 21.9% reported that it involved nonsexual physical abuse by a relative. (The percentages total more than

*Table 6.3* Respondents reporting recovered memories of abuse, categorized by type of abuse and whether abuse was ever forgotten.

| Abuse experienced | Did you ever forget this type of abuse? | |
|---|---|---|
| | Yes | No |
| Incest (*n* = 19) | 18 (95%) | 1 (5%) |
| Sexual abuse by nonrelative (*n* = 16) | 12 (75%) | 4 (25%) |
| Physical abuse (*n* = 12) | 7 (58%) | 5 (42%) |

*Source:* From data collected by Feldman-Summers and Pope 1994.

100% because some participants reported having forgotten more than one type of abuse.)

That sexual abuse by a relative—incest—was the most frequently reported sort of recovered memory according to the Feldman-Summers and Pope data supports the notion that incest is more likely to be forgotten than sexual abuse by a nonrelative or physical abuse by a relative. However, one problem with interpreting the results this way is that the type of abuse recovered in memory must be considered in respect to the type of abuse actually experienced. The analysis presented earlier showed that, of the 79 participants who reported some form of abuse, memories of incest were more likely to be forgotten than memories of other sorts of abuse. Now let us focus on the 32 participants with recovered memories, comparing the kind(s) of abuse they experienced with the kind(s) of abuse they always remembered or at some time forgot. (Feldman-Summers and Pope did not report such an analysis in their paper.)

Of the 32 participants who recovered memories, there were 19 reports of experienced incest, 16 of experienced sexual abuse by a nonrelative, and 12 of experienced physical abuse. (These total more than 32 because some participants experienced more than one type of abuse.) Table 6.3 shows the types of abuse forgotten for each type of experienced abuse among those who recovered memories; Figure 6.4 displays graphically the percentages of those who forgot each type of abuse.

The results displayed in Table 6.3 and Figure 6.4 strongly suggest that among people who have recovered memories, incest

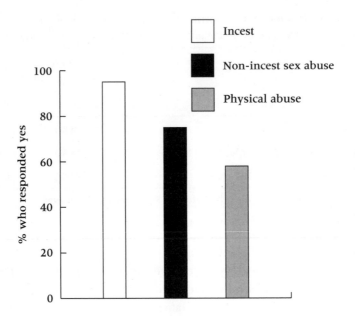

*Figure 6.4* Percentage of respondents reporting they had recovered memories of a particular type of abuse (from data collected by Feldman-Summers and Pope 1994).

is forgotten and recovered at a much higher rate than other forms of abuse. To simplify the analysis we can examine the 32 participants in terms of type of abuse. Of the 32, 9 experienced incest only; 10 experienced incest plus some other form of abuse; and 13 participants did not experience incest, but did experience at least one other form of abuse. All 9 participants who experienced only incest also forgot the incest (since the total population consists of participants with recovered memories). Similarly, the 13 participants who experienced only nonincestuous abuse also forgot their nonincestuous abuse.

But what of the 10 participants with recovered memories who experienced both incest and nonincestuous abuse? Each of these participants could have forgotten either or both the incest or the other form of abuse. The results are displayed in Figure 6.5. Strikingly, 9 of the 10 (90%) reported having forgotten the incest, but only 3 (30%) reported having forgotten one of the other forms of abuse. Although the number of participants is too low

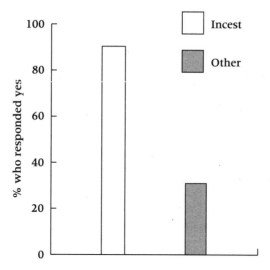

*Figure 6.5* Results for the 10 respondents reporting both incestuous and nonincestuous abuse with recovered memories. Percentages are shown for reporting a period of forgetting the incest and for reporting a period of forgetting the nonincestuous abuse (from data collected by Feldman-Summers and Pope 1994).

for statistical analysis, these results are in line with the other analyses performed: Memories of incest are more likely to be lost and recovered than are memories of other forms of abuse.

Critics might argue that all my analysis of the Feldman-Summers and Pope data shows is that when people have false memories they have false memories of incest. It is thus crucial to analyze data from a prospective study. In Chapter 3 I discussed such a study: Linda Meyer Williams's ground-breaking investigation (1994a; 1994c; 1995), in which 38% of her sample of women with documented childhood sexual abuse were unable or unwilling to report the abuse as young adults (Williams 1994a) and an additional 10% reported recovered memories for the abuse (1994b; 1995). In addition to offering striking support for forgetting and remembering childhood sexual abuse, Williams's

*Table 6.4*  Abuse respondents (*n* = 120), categorized by relationship of perpetrator to victim and whether the abuse was recalled during the interview.

| Perpetrator | Was abuse recalled during interview? | |
| --- | --- | --- |
|  | No recall | Recall |
| Stranger | 6 | 27 |
| Acquaintance | 19 | 28 |
| Extended family | 12 | 14 |
| Nuclear family | 7 | 7 |
| Total | 44 | 76 |

*Source:* From data collected by Williams 1994a.

study provides important evidence of the relationship between degree of betrayal and amnesia for sexual abuse. (Williams considered the possibility that women failed to report abuse that they actually remembered. As discussed in Chapter 3, she rejected this possibility as accounting for her major findings after additional analyses and considerations of her data.)

Williams found that women who were molested by someone they knew were more likely to have forgotten the abuse than women who were molested by strangers. She reported, "Women with a closer relationship to the perpetrator were more likely to not recall the abuse" (1994a, p. 1172). In one analysis she coded the closeness of the relationship to the perpetrator (0 = stranger–relative stranger; 1 = acquaintance, peer–friend of family, 2 = extended family member, 3 = nuclear family member) and compared the average closeness for women who remembered with the average closeness for women with no recall, using a *t* test. Williams found that closeness of perpetrator to victim was significantly greater for those women who forgot the abuse than for those women who remembered the abuse (*p* = .008).

Williams kindly supplied her raw data to me so that I could independently analyze the effect of perpetrator-victim relationship on memory, similar to my analysis of the Feldman-Summers and Pope (1994) data. Table 6.4 summarizes the raw

*Table 6.5*   Abuse respondents (*n* = 120), categorized by whether the perpetrator was a relative of the victim and whether the abuse was recalled during the interview.

| Sexually abused by relative? | Was abuse recalled during interview? | |
| --- | --- | --- |
| | No recall | Recall |
| Yes (*n* = 40) | 19 (48%) | 21 (53%) |
| No (*n* = 80) | 25 (31%) | 55 (69%) |
| Total | 44 | 76 |

*Source:* From data collected by Williams 1994a.
$\chi^2 = 3.03$   $p < .10$

data Williams gave me (Williams 1994b). She explained that 9 participants were missing from her original 129 because in some cases the relationship could not be determined. Although Williams reports (personal communication, 27 July 1995) that more detailed information has since resulted in some slight revisions to the data set, this is the data that was reported in Williams (1994a).

I collapsed Williams's data to separate incestuous from nonincestuous sexual abuse (see Table 6.5 and Figure 6.6). Using a different statistical test (an odds ratio), Williams (1994a, p. 1172) reported no significant effect of family membership (*p* = .136). However, using a measure of "closeness to perpetrator," her analysis did produce a significant effect (*p* = .008); and my analysis, using a $\chi^2$ test on incestuous versus nonincestuous abuse, shows results similar to those of the Feldman-Summers and Pope data analysis: that incestuous abuse is likelier to be forgotten than nonincestuous abuse.

Williams (1994c; 1995) also investigated recovered memories. She wrote, "Of the women who do recall the abuse that was documented in their 1970s records, approximately one in six report some previous period when they forgot. When current accounts of the abuse and the records from the 1970s were compared, I found that the women with recovered memories had no more discrepancies in their accounts than did those women who reported that they always remembered the abuse . . . Some

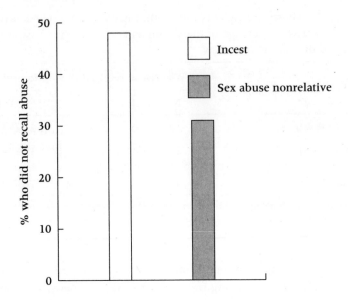

*Figure 6.6*   Female abuse victims categorized by whether the abuse was incestuous and whether the abuse was recalled during the interview (from data collected by Williams 1994a).

women, it appears, do reliably recover memories of child sexual abuse" (Williams 1994c, p. 1184).

Williams's results are highly congruent with betrayal trauma theory. As she noted in a later paper, "Those with a prior period of forgetting—the women with 'recovered memories'—were younger at the time of abuse and were less likely to have received support from their mothers than the women who reported that they had always remembered their victimization" (1995, p. 649). Also, "the closer the relationship to the perpetrator the more likely it was that the women had forgotten and then later recovered a memory of abuse" (p. 658). She has also presented data consistent with my predictions: "Women who were younger at the time of the abuse and those who were molested by someone they knew were more likely to have no recall of the abuse" (1994a, p. 1167).

Williams also reported that the veracity of recovered memories is not significantly different from the veracity of always-remembered memories (this is consistent with Feldman-Summers and Pope 1994), and that women with recovered memories (for documented events) are often very skeptical about their own memories, referring to them as possibly just "dreams."

At the meeting of the Western Psychological Association in April 1993, Catherine Cameron reported some of the results from a longitudinal study she conducted of women who entered therapy to deal with their childhood sexual abuse. Cameron conducted surveys in 1986, 1988, and 1992 on her group of participants. One of Cameron's conference presentations (1993) was on the topic of recovered memories for abuse.

She evaluated various factors that discriminated the women who had forgotten their abuse from the women who had not forgotten their abuse. Cameron's most striking result, based on data from her 1986 survey, was that women who forgot the abuse at some point were much more likely to report that one of their abusers had been their own fathers than were women who had never forgotten the abuse. Cameron reported that of the women who had amnesia for the abuse, 75% named their fathers as an abuser, whereas among women who reported no amnesia for their abuse only 24% named their fathers as an abuser. Cameron also reported that among the "total amnesia" group, 33% were abused by their mothers, and among the nonamnesic group, 14% were abused by their mothers. (Some women were abused by more than one person.)

I contacted Catherine Cameron to learn more about her survey results. She told me (1995) that in the mid-1980s she had asked therapists to refer patients to her for her research. She pointed out that her data thus are not from a probability sample, but from a purposive one, so one should not assume that the statistical properties of her sample generalize to any other sample. The participants were classified into one of three memory categories (amnesia, partial amnesia, and no amnesia) based on their answer to a 1986 question about the extent to which they had forgotten the molestation that they had experienced. The participants who indicated that they had previously (that is, some period previous to 1986) had no memory of the molestation were considered fully amnesic. Within this group some participants reported that they were not even aware of gaps in memory, while others had no memory of the molestation but were aware that

*Table 6.6*  Abuse victims categorized by whether the perpetrator was a relative of the victim and whether the victim was amnesic or nonamnesic for the abuse.

| Sexually abused by relative? | Amnesic | Nonamnesic | Total |
|---|---|---|---|
| Yes (incest victims) | 24 | 19 | 43 |
| No (all other abuse victims) | 0 | 2 | 2 |
| Total | 24 | 21 | 45 |

*Source:* From data collected by Cameron 1993.

there were gaps in their own memory. The participants who reported that they had never forgotten the molestation or who reported that they had always remembered it but had not labeled it as molestation were considered nonamnesic.

A small number of women fell between these two categories: they reported that they had always remembered some of the molestation, or had always remembered molestation by one perpetrator but not by another. Because Cameron was interested in the two polar groups of amnesic and non-amnesic participants, the analyses she presented in 1993 did not use the results from the small middle group of "partial" amnesics. I followed Cameron's lead and also dropped this group. However, I did look at the data for this group and confirmed that at the descriptive level, the partial amnesics fall between the amnesics and nonamnesics on the factors (incest, parent incest) that I discuss next.

Table 6.6 displays the results of the 45 participants for whom there was sufficient data to categorize on the basis of persistence of memory and whether each participant was or was not an incest survivor. Clearly, Cameron's sample was made up primarily of incest survivors: of 45 women, 43 (96%) were abused by at least one member of their family. With this high an incest rate it is impossible to test statistically the role of incest on amnesia, although it is interesting at the descriptive level that none of the nonincest sexual abuse survivors reported full amnesia for the abuse.

*Table 6.7*   Abuse victims categorized by whether the perpetrator was a parent of the victim and whether the victim was amnesic or nonamnesic for the abuse.

| Type of abuse | Amnesic | Nonamnesic | Total |
|---|---|---|---|
| Abused by parent | 21 | 8 | 29 |
| Not abused by parent | 3 | 13 | 16 |
| Total | 24 | 21 | 45 |

*Source:* From data collected by Cameron 1993.

   Approximately two-thirds of Catherine Cameron's survey participants were abused by one or both of their parents. Betrayal trauma theory would predict that amnesia rates for people abused by a parent would be higher than amnesia rates for people sexually abused by someone other than a parent. Based on data provided by Cameron, I created Table 6.7 and Figure 6.7, which categorize the 45 participants according to whether they were sexually abused by a parent or not and whether they were amnesic or nonamnesic for the abuse at any point in the past. From that table and figure it is clear that in Cameron's sample, there is a strong relationship between amnesia and parental abuse ($\chi^2 = 11.93$; $p < .001$). This finding supports betrayal trauma theory: sexual abuse by a trusted caregiver is the most likely sort of abuse to lead to amnesia.

   In a paper published in 1994, Elizabeth Loftus, Sara Polonsky, and Mindy Fullilove wrote that 54% of women in an outpatient substance abuse treatment group reported a history of childhood sexual abuse; of these, 19% reported that they forgot the abuse for a period of time and later recovered the memory. An additional 12% reported a period of partial forgetting. Thus, 31% of the participants in this study reported some disruption in their memory for the sexual abuse.

   Loftus, Polonsky, and Fullilove (1994) gathered data on the relationship between the victims and perpetrators. They wrote, "Another important finding from our research is that whether a woman remembers her abuse throughout her whole life or forgets then regains the memory is unrelated to a number of im-

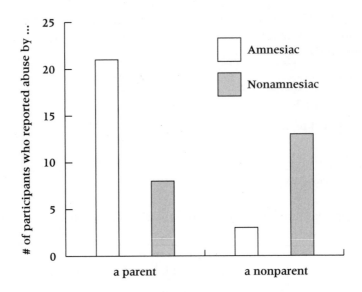

*Figure 6.7*  Female abuse victims categorized by parent and nonparent abuse and whether the victim was amnesic or nonamnesic for the abuse (from data collected by Cameron 1993).

portant factors, such as whether the abuse was violent or incestuous" (pp. 79–80).

To call this an "important finding" is an error. What these researchers have determined is that they have not found a relationship between incest and memory, measured in the particular way they considered each of these variables. This is not a finding, but the lack of a finding. In order to show the lack of a relationship between two variables researchers must demonstrate that their methodology would make it likely to find such an effect if one existed. The authors correctly report that they have not found a relationship between incest and memory in this study. Fullilove (1995) has noted that even if the data more clearly indicated lack of a relationship, she would urge caution in generalizing beyond this population given the extremely high overall rate of traumatization in this group (with a mean number of traumas per woman of 5) and the histories of substance abuse (many of the women had been free of drugs only briefly at the time of the interview).

Still, I am surprised that apparently no relationship between incest and memory is seen in this study, given the fact that such evidence exists in the results collected by Williams (1994a, 1994c), Feldman-Summers and Pope (1994), and Cameron (1993). Loftus, Polonsky, and Fullilove (1994) report, "Of those who always remembered their abuse, 56% claimed their experience involved incest. Of those with some degree of forgetting, 47% claimed it involved incest" (p. 79).

I contacted Elizabeth Loftus and Mindy Fullilove in order to analyze the data behind this summary. Fullilove provided me a list of the 57 women who reported one or more kinds of childhood sexual abuse, showing the relationship of the abuser and whether or not they always remembered the events. In the list Fullilove provided, the "memory" variable was reduced to either "always remembered" or some degree of forgetting. Participants had been asked to indicate whether the relationship of the abuser was a parent, stepparent, elder sibling, other relative or family member, family friend, or stranger. Data for both the relationship of the abuser to the victim and the memory question were available for 49 of the women (8 of the 57 women did not indicate the relationship of the abuser or did not answer the memory question). Of these 49 women, 29% had some degree of forgetting. In addition, 10% of the women reported being abused by a parent; 16% by a stepparent; 8% by a brother or sister; 37% by another relative or family member; 53% by a family friend; and 37% by a stranger. (These percentages add to more than 100% because many of the women reported more than one abuser relationship.) Loftus, Polonsky, and Fullilove defined incest as abuse by a parent, stepparent, brother or sister, and/or other relative or family member and found no evidence that women who had reported such abuse had a higher rate of forgetting. Unfortunately, it is not possible to determine the frequency of caregivers or parent-figures (e.g., live-in boyfriends of mothers) within the largest category of abusers, family friends, nor was it possible to determine the frequency of close versus distant relatives (e.g., cousin) within the largest "incest" category, "other relative or family member."

I inspected each of the categories of abuser relationship separately and found that of those women who reported abuse by a parent, 40% reported some degree of forgetting; of those who

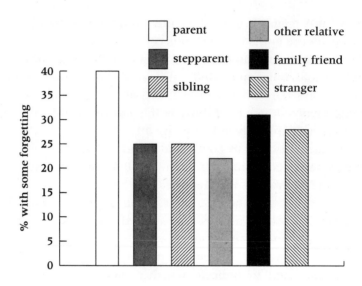

*Figure 6.8* Rates of forgetting based on relationship of victim to abuser (from data collected by Loftus, Polonsky, and Fullilove 1994).

reported abuse by a stepparent, 25% reported some degree of forgetting; of those who reported abuse by a sibling, 25% reported some degree of forgetting; of those who reported abuse by "other relative or family member," 22% reported some degree of forgetting; of those who reported abuse by a "family friend," 31% reported some degree of forgetting; and of those who reported abuse by a stranger, 28% reported some degree of forgetting. (Again, some women were in more than one of these categories due to their reporting abuse by multiple perpetrators.) Given the small numbers of women in many of these categories and the fact that many women reported abuse by multiple perpetrators, it is not possible to test for a statistical relationship between abuse by a parent and forgetting the abuse. The results, shown in Figure 6.8, indicate that the highest amnesia rates are among those women abused by a parent and that family relatedness per se does not predict amnesia; they are equivocal on the relationship between betrayal and amnesia.

I have not found any studies in which it is claimed that incest is negatively predictive of amnesia. That is, I have not found a study claiming that nonincestuous abuse has a higher rate of being forgotten than incestuous abuse. There are some studies of amnesia that do not report testing an effect of incest (for example, Herman and Schatzow 1987; Briere and Conte 1993). In each of these cases, the base rates of incestuous abuse in the sample may have been so high as to make it difficult to find a statistically significant relationship between incest and amnesia.

In Herman and Schatzow (1987), for instance, the women in the sample were participants in short-term therapy groups specifically for incest survivors. Of all the women in the sample, 75% were abused by their fathers or stepfathers, 26% by their brothers, 11% by their uncles, and 6% by their grandfathers. In addition, a small number of women were abused by female relatives. (The percentages total more than 100% because some women had multiple perpetrators.) Herman and Schatzow report one of the highest rates of amnesia overall: 62%. This high rate may well be a function of the fact that the women in the study were all incest survivors.

A similar pattern obtains in Briere and Conte's (1993) study of 450 adults who were referred by their therapists for reported childhood sexual abuse: 59.3% reported having forgotten some or all of their abuse. In Briere and Conte's sample, 89.8% of the participants reported at least one incident of incest. The relationship of incest to amnesia was presumably not testable, given this high a rate of incest. As with the Herman and Schatzow study, the high rate of amnesia overall may reflect the high rate of incest in the clinical sample.

The analyses presented in this chapter on the relationship between incest and amnesia tend to support predictions made by betrayal trauma theory. Ultimately, however, additional information is needed. Surveys are required that produce data relating each of the seven factors suggested by betrayal trauma theory to amnesia. Alternative explanations must be evaluated by separately testing the effects of correlated factors. To measure betrayal, enough detail must be elicited to distinguish relatives who are not in care-giving roles from relatives who are—and similarly, to distinguish nonrelatives who have a significant care-giving role from those who do not. A person sexually abused in childhood by a trusted teacher or nanny would be predicted to be more likely to have amnesia than a person sexually abused in childhood by a relative who is not in a trusted care-giving relationship, all other factors being equal.

In the meantime, in the absence of such data, it is instructive to return to a case study approach.

## "Why Didn't My Cheater Detector Work?" Betrayal Trauma Theory in Ross Cheit's Words

As related in Chapter 1, the adult Ross Cheit recovered memories of childhood sexual abuse he had suffered when he was a boy at the San Francisco Boys Chorus camp. The abuser was the camp administrator, William Farmer, a man he had trusted and admired. As the story was related in an article published in *U.S. News and World Report:*

> Compelled now to know more, Cheit began to dredge his past.
>
> From his parents, he recovered the letters he had written from camp, and reading them brought the most painful revelation yet. "He broke down and cried with his whole body, as if he would never stop," says his wife. "He came into the bedroom where I was half asleep, saying over and over, 'But he was such a great guy.' He was so hurt that someone he loved did this to him." It was only then, says Cheit, that he fully understood the damage that had been done. "These were not just perverse sexual acts," he says, "but the most profound betrayal possible for a kid." (Horn 1993, p. 55)

This realization of betrayal was as profound a feeling as Cheit had at any point in his process of recovering memories. In late October 1994, Cheit explained:

> I came to see my own ordeal primarily in terms of betrayal about three months after my first recollections of Bill Farmer. The day I read the letters I had written home from camp was about as close as I came to an epiphany in this entire ordeal. It certainly was a watershed, a turning point, a defining moment, back in

early December 1992. And the central concept was betrayal. But I came to this understanding almost viscerally; the feeling washed over me that night . . . After that night, I moved beyond the overriding sense of shame and embarrassment I had experienced for months.

Cheit has explained how his experience of childhood sexual abuse confirms aspects of betrayal trauma theory. On the primary factor of betrayal by a trusted caregiver, Cheit writes that the "central concept," the underlying injury, was specifically the betrayal. But why did Cheit not stop the abuse when it occurred? And why didn't he remember it later? He answered these questions in terms of three of the seven factors predicted to increase the probability of forgetting abuse: alternative reality-defining statements by the caregiver; a distinct abuse context; and an absence of discussion of the abuse. As Ross Cheit explained in October 1994 (unless otherwise noted, all subsequent quotes are from Cheit's October 1994 letter):

> The night of the almost-epiphany—Bill Farmer betrayed me!—was also the beginning of a dreaded feeling that the whole experience was somehow denied to me by Madi Bacon [the founder and leader of the San Francisco Boys Choir]. I have been wrestling with that issue almost ever since. It has seemed of monumental importance at several times over the last two years to know: did she or didn't she somehow deny this to me? Later I would wonder whether I just wanted to think that she somehow talked me out of this? There was plenty of reason to want that—if it was denied to me in some way by the very woman who embodied the organization, then I could explain my failure to do anything about it at the time. I could also apparently take solace in your prediction that this would help explain why I didn't remember the whole thing all along. But I'm actually more skeptical of this explanation—that I took the issue to Madi—than I was just a little while ago.

Cheit goes on to write about his anger at Madi Bacon for her symbolic role in tolerating the sexual abuse. Cheit's description of his feelings of rage for the kind of betrayal he describes on

Madi's part are reminiscent of what many father-daughter incest survivors report feeling toward their mothers. As Cheit says:

> I no longer think that Madi literally denied this to me in conversation at the time. Bill Farmer certainly never did. And I hadn't really thought about that in all my rage and anger against Madi. Bill Farmer never said it wasn't happening, or that it somehow hadn't happened. And I don't remember ever talking to him, or to anyone else at the time, about it. The rage at Madi is better understood, I think, in a less literal way: Madi stands for the institution. She founded it, she ran it. And the institution betrayed me, beyond Bill Farmer. It tolerated the whole thing. And I don't mean to say that I knew that then; but I sensed . . . that it was "in the air."

Ross Cheit also points out that the setting for his abuse was different from the nonabuse setting at the camp:

> My story is, quite literally, one of day and night. The abuse I remembered occurred on a nightly basis—but never during the day. Indeed, I don't remember even thinking about it in the day. That's when I did fun things with Bill Farmer. That's when he was my friend. That's when I wrote letters home . . . The disconnectedness of day and night has, in a way, been part of the nagging discomfort about my own story. I've never had any doubt about what I remember, but it has become haunting to be at such a loss to explain it. How could I act during the day as if nothing happened at night?

Marilyn Van Derbur Atler, who also forgot childhood sexual abuse for a period of time, reports a very similar situation. She came to refer to herself in terms of the "night child" and the "day child" (Van Derbur Atler 1991). The cognitive model developed in Chapter 5 suggests answers to why abuse restricted to the middle of the night, with a "normal" family or camp experience during the day, would be so forgettable. This situation allows for a small set of consistent constructions of reality. Each experience can be put into one of two separate contexts (day or night), with information blockage protecting the integrity of the abuse context. The normal triggers for remembering events, perhaps as in context-dependent memory, may then be restricted to the abuse context.

In addition, Cheit reports that, as far as he knows, "I never talked to anyone about this at the time (unless I talked to Madi!)." He told neither his parents nor, apparently, any of the other boys at the camp.

Cheit's adult investigation of his abuse led him to several additional victims of William Farmer. Katy Butler wrote about Cheit's case in the *San Francisco Chronicle:*

> [Cheit] hired a private investigator, spoke to dozens of former chorus members and found three others who said that Farmer had molested them. Cheit also found a nurse and a former camp counselor who said they had each discovered Farmer in bed with a [fourth] young boy and reported the incidents to the chorus' founder, Madi Bacon. (1994, p. A2)

In addition to corroborating Cheit's memories, the stories of the four additional victims show a correlation between explicit discussion and absence of forgetting. As Cheit explained, "The only one of the four (five, including me) who seems to have kept the memory intact and throughout is [P.W.]—who had no relationship with Bill Farmer and who discussed his ordeal most pointedly with several adults." Cheit also explained that the boy who had been discovered in bed with Farmer did not remember his abuse; he did not even remember William Farmer.

According to Katy Butler, after Cheit discovered that there were additional victims and that at least one of the incidents had been reported to Chorus founder Madi Bacon, Cheit approached her for an explanation:

> Cheit then interviewed Bacon, long retired, at her home in Berkeley. Much to his outrage, she told him that she had warned Farmer about "hobnobbing" with the boys but had not disciplined or fired him.
>
> Bacon, now 89, confirmed the substance of the conversation but said she had insufficient facts to support a firing. (Butler 1994, p. A2)

The fact that there were other victims, and even that some of the victims' abuse experiences seem to have been known about by the adults at the time, suggests yet another level of betrayal to Cheit:

> I have a strange kind of extension to offer to your prediction concerning the absence of any socially shared explicit discussion— inelegantly, the presence of implicitly socially shared perversity. In other words: a setting in which there is latent acceptance of what the broader society abhors. Imagine the cognitive consequences . . . The idea emanates from something [another victim of William Farmer] wrote to me in his incredibly poignant letter: "There were people all around us . . . even other counselors. It must have seemed safe/OK to me at the time." This sentence about knocked me over. It tapped into something I felt about the atmosphere then. Now, I felt some kind of pain that I would call institutional betrayal.

Ross Cheit offers a new twist on the lack of explicit discussion, the notion of institutional approbation. Cheit's insight is important, and seems to extend to a kind of family approbation or, more generally, social approbation that is perhaps inevitable when the truth is not discussed explicitly. It is perhaps why to speak no evil when evil is present is, in the end, so evil.

"Why does this matter now?" and "Why are you pursuing this old issue?" are questions commonly asked of survivors of childhood sexual abuse who are attempting to redress, or just discuss, their childhood victimization. Ross Cheit addressed these questions when he spoke about the return of his memories of sexual abuse, his realization of betrayal in childhood by a trusted adult, and the current betrayal he was experiencing as a result of the denial of his experiences:

> Why does this matter now? I've been asked that all too many times in the last year. Why are you pursuing this old matter? There are several reasons. The first is, pain endures. And this is not ancient history for me. I can barely look at my eleven-year-old [relative] right now without crying over his vulnerability. And I feel the stigma that's attached to this, to being a survivor of this crime . . . this is not ancient history. This is my life. Second, I just think healing requires that we confront and deal with the truth, that the truth helps restore social order and promotes healing, and that to me, denial is a continuing injury. And as long as they continue to deny it, they're still hurting me. Third . . . pedophiles rarely, if ever, stop. This man said to me on the telephone, "I know I shouldn't work with children." And he is working with children. (Cheit 1994a)

Cheit identifies some of the most central and vexing issues that our society faces about the epidemic of childhood sexual abuse: the injury is extensive; pain endures; victims are stigmatized; denial persists; victims are further injured through denial; and perpetrators continue to victimize children.

In this final chapter I consider betrayal trauma theory in relation to the pressing issues of injury and treatment, legal redress, and societal transformation. I also consider how betrayal trauma theory may extend to adult betrayal traumas and even to mundane facets of our daily lives.

## Injury and Recovery

Judith Herman (1992) proposes that "posttraumatic stress disorder" does not capture the complexity of the aftereffects of repeated traumas such as child abuse. Instead she introduces the concept of "complex posttraumatic stress disorder." She categorizes the symptomology of complex posttraumatic stress disorder into alterations in emotional control, alterations in consciousness, alterations in self-perception and the perception of others, and alterations in systems of meaning. Herman's account, like others in the literature (for example, Terr 1991), emphasizes changes in mental information processing ("alterations"), especially of memory and consciousness.

These symptoms of complex posttraumatic stress disorder can be understood in terms of betrayal trauma theory. While it would be inappropriate to apply the theory diagnostically, as if betrayal trauma is a disease or syndrome, it sheds light on common responses to interpersonal violence and child abuse.

In Chapter 4 I explained *why* people sometimes forget childhood sexual abuse. Humans are social beings, fundamentally dependent on relationships, alliances, and trust. Betrayal violates the basic ethic of human relationships, and though we are skilled at recognizing betrayal when it occurs, this ability may be stifled for the greater goal of survival. A child sexually abused by an adult who has power and authority over that child is in a bind. The child *needs* to trust his or her parents and caregivers. Child sexual abuse perpetrated by a trusted caregiver is therefore a prime example of the kind of event that can create information blockage in the mind of the victim. To know is to put oneself in danger. To not know is to align with the caregiver and ensure survival. Some degree of amnesia or unawareness of the abuse is thus a natural reaction to childhood sexual abuse. Forgetting occurs not for the reduction of suffering but to stay alive.

In Chapter 5 I explained *how* people sometimes forget (and later remember) childhood sexual abuse. To forget and to later remember are everyday aspects of human experience. Various degrees of amnesia, various times of onset, and various consequences can be understood in terms of what we currently know about memory and attention. Knowledge is multi-stranded. We can simultaneously not know and know about a betrayal. This knowing is often what cognitive psychologists call "implicit knowledge" or "implicit memory." While experiencing a complex traumatic event such as sexual abuse, multiple mental mechanisms are activated in the person's brain to process the information and determine responses. Many of those mechanisms operate outside of conscious awareness. Thus, some of the mental mechanisms normally operative during event perception could be disrupted, while other mechanisms are left intact. Conscious awareness or emotional responsiveness might be attenuated without necessarily disrupting physiological sexual responsiveness or memory for sensory and affective states. The survivor of childhood sexual abuse who "forgets" and "does not know" about the abuse may have implicit memory and knowledge of the events that surface in other ways: specific phobias, learned behaviors, a self-perception of being a "bad girl" or "bad boy." Memory disturbances—alterations in memory—are a likely result if sensory and emotional memories of a traumatic event are created in such a way that the information is blocked from other, more conscious and declarative, episodic memory stores. Betrayal trauma also is consistent with difficulties with trust, either in the form of too great a willingness to trust or an inability to trust, also a common result of child abuse (Browne and Finklehor 1986). This follows from the prolonged blockage of information into mechanisms that accurately assess cheating and betrayal.

With dissociations between different memory stores for the same event and the blockage of information about current reality to some processing units, a firm foundation for assessing reality using all available internal sources of knowledge cannot be laid (see Herman 1992; Kluft 1990; van der Kolk 1987). This lack of integration is likely to produce alterations in consciousness, dissociated states, and problems such as depersonalization—feeling detached from one's own body. Leslie Young (1992) has argued that the aftereffects of information blockage during abuse may create enduring and disturbing problems with awareness of one's own body:

> For the survivor of severe trauma, including the survivor of sexual abuse, a radical reformulation of the conditions of personal identity may be required . . . [E]vents which go on inside my body, which seem to be essentially physical and inescapably tied to embodiment such as sexual, sensuous, affective or proprioceptive experiences, no longer have anything to do with me, they are not me.
>
> . . . Whether by choice or blind necessity, the survivor can forget or wall off memories of traumatic events by consigning them to the body, and excluding all bodily sensations and intense affects from consciousness. But such a solution entails an enormous sacrifice, since it also makes problematic experiencing the everyday pleasures, sensations, and comforts of human embodiment. (p. 93)

With the "everyday pleasures, sensations, and comforts of human embodiment" denied to the survivor of childhood sexual abuse, and with other human mental capacities attenuated or dissociated from consciousness, it is no wonder that depression is such a common experience for abuse survivors (Browne and Finkelhor 1986). With sensory and affective memories missing episodic interpretation, and with reduced connectivity between different sorts of memory systems, we would also expect to see inexplicable mood states, hallucinations, flashbacks, nightmares, and bodily sensations that are easily interpreted as physical illness or somatization (van der Kolk 1987). Those experiencing betrayal trauma are also likely to exhibit specific learned behaviors. For instance, a child who has been beaten repeatedly may learn to flinch or to manipulate the timing of another person's aggressive tendencies. Similarly, a child who has been sexually abused may learn degrading sexual behaviors demanded by the perpetrator. Without conscious interpretation, the trauma survivor has no way of knowing the source of his or her behavior. Sadly, this may be especially true for behaviors learned during infancy and childhood and later expressed during parenting (Seay, Alexander, and Harlow 1964).

Ross Cheit recovered memories of sexual abuse when he was on vacation. He realized that he needed to address the effects of the abuse on his life, and he was motivated to heal, but he discovered what so many abuse survivors have discovered: that once the wall of amnesia begins to crumble, feelings of shame (an emotion common in response to both forbidden sexual experiences and betrayal by a parent or trusted authority figure) can become a new sort of wall.

I kept thinking about that man and the things he did to me. A few weeks later, I took the issue up with my therapist, who I hasten to add was entirely passive in this process. I had started seeing her in June, in fact, a month after the Father Porter stories started, and two months after I had learned my nephew was going to camp. But we had never discussed sexual abuse. I brought this to her. She never suggested anything to me. I've never been subject to any techniques for recovering memories. This happened on its own. There is no hocus-pocus here. It took a few months, then, before curiosity overcame shame. And it's really difficult, I think, to convey how isolated I felt in the interim. Because I knew what had happened, but I was alone in my experience. I had no one to talk to who shared my ordeal.

This prompted me to seek out a book of some sort, being the good academic that I am, something that would allow me to connect with other people, something that would allow me to do that while maintaining my privacy. So I went to a large bookstore in Cranston, Rhode Island. I can still feel this experience vividly. I had only talked to my wife and my therapist about sexual abuse for the previous few months. I had never even uttered those words to anyone else. And I went to the bookstore in search of a book, and there it was on the shelf, a book called *Abused Boys* [Hunter 1990]. And at first, I was just elated. There's actually a book about what happened to me, a book that's specifically about boys. And I was really delighted. Moments later, when I was walking through the bookstore to go to the counter and pay for this book, I was just overcome with a kind of panic and anxiety. "Oh, my God," I thought. "This book is about me." The connection that I had long since made intellectually had suddenly become emotional. And it just made me shudder. I didn't want anyone to see me even buying this book. And I wasn't sure I could go through buying it, let alone actually reading it. I did buy it, and I put it away for a little while before I read it. (1994a)

Ross Cheit was able to move beyond those feelings of shame and he has been successful at addressing his childhood experiences with sexual abuse.

Laura S. Brown (1995b), commenting on some of the political and social forces that have pervaded the public debate over recovered memories of abuse, has also drawn attention to the fact that healing is possible.

A collective societal effort at denial of all forms of private violence appears to be underway . . . It is not simply the truth about sexual abuse of children that risks being silenced in our present zeitgeist. So, too, is any of the hopeful information and consciousness-raising data emerging from the work of psychological scientists and science-practitioners, the data telling us that human beings can be harmed by abuses of power but that human beings can also change and heal. (p. 313)

Healing from childhood sexual abuse and other betrayals and trauma is possible, and good therapy—while not the only way to heal—can be a great help.

Psychotherapy has the potential to heal trauma wounds for a variety of reasons. In therapy the client has the opportunity to learn to build appropriate trust and set social boundaries in a healthy way. In other words, the abuse survivor learns to use social information processing mechanisms in a fully integrated manner. The potential for healing is dependent on the relationship between the therapist and client, suggesting that a focus on the nature of the therapeutic relationship is paramount. The potential for creating further harm to an abuse survivor in therapy is great because the survivor must use the very mental mechanisms that have been damaged in past relationships, such as those necessary for trust. Denial of a respectful, empathetic, empowering relationship, betrayal of trust, or violation of boundaries by the therapist can create more damage (see L. S. Brown 1994; Herman 1992; Pope 1994).

The potential for the abuse survivor to learn to use previously disconnected parts of him- or herself in a healing relationship may not only improve the survivor's sense of well-being and enhance the ability to function in relationships, but is also likely to generate a whole range of additional effects. Some of these effects may become new sources of pain. Increasing internal integration and removing barriers to knowing and feeling will almost surely increase awareness of societal injustices and other people's suffering (L. S. Brown 1994). Yet with the newfound pain that comes with empathy and social connectedness is the potential for spiritual healing.

The therapist can also help the abuse survivor interpret sensory memories, feelings, and behaviors. This can allow the client to make sense of negative feelings and maladaptive behaviors, and thus exert more control over those feelings and behaviors, which almost certainly will improve self-esteem. However, this aspect of psychotherapy and memory recovery also has the potential to lead to distortions in the interpretation of sensory, affective, and behavioral memories. It is especially important that the therapist attend to interpersonal boundaries and maintain a respectful stance, such that the client is aware that it is fundamentally the client's responsibility to recognize his or her own truth. This includes the responsibility to determine the extent to which external investigations will be pursued, and the responsibility to determine and live with doubt or ambivalence. At the same time, the therapist must be vigilant about the power of the therapist's conscious and unconscious suggestions in influencing beliefs. He or she must understand that explicit, declarative memories, including those developed in therapy, may not necessarily be accurate. The therapist should be informed about the nature of human memory and recall, including the power of suggestion in memory reconstruction and the fact that some things may never be known completely. (For additional treatment recommendations for recovered memories, see also Enns et al. 1995.)

Dana Jack has observed that "mind and self come into being through communication with others. One cannot heal the self in isolation" (1991, p. 205). The healing role of communication in psychotherapy may partially relate to the recoding of sensory and affective information in shareable ways, just as the original traumatic amnesia may relate to the blockage of such recoding. By talking or writing about the traumatic memories, the client spontaneously creates an episodic interpretation and integration of previously disjointed sensory and affective memories (see also Herman 1992; Nelson 1993; Pennebaker 1990; Squire 1992). Sensory information stored in a continuous way may be rendered more discrete and categorical because it is shared, and in turn the information may become more accessible to other cognitive modules that serve to integrate and control mental activity (Freyd 1983; 1993b). Some people seem to be able to do this sort of narrative recoding without actually speaking to a therapist or trusted other. For some it is enough to write the words down, or even to engage in mental dialogue about the memories, although for most people actual communication is important. The power of language is not only the external act, but it is also the internal act—the use of "voice" to reconstruct, to recode, to make new connections (see Enns et al. 1995; Jack 1991).

Psychotherapy may sometimes be effective in helping survivors heal from childhood sexual abuse, but in her provocative book *Rocking the Cradle of Sexual Politics,* Louise Armstrong identified a grave risk inherent in focusing heavily on damage to and treatment of the victim of sexual abuse. "It is the switch from the feminist to the therapeutic ideology," Armstrong writes, "with its muzzy-minded focus on incest survivors as the neurasthenics of the 1990s—that has framed a . . . destructive and potentially devastating experience as an individual disease, rather than as the result of an ingrained social disorder" (1994, p. 234).

In a review of *Rocking the Cradle of Sexual Politics,* Robin Abcarian asks, "Why . . . can't healing and political activism coexist?" (1994, p. E1). If only internal change, or only external change, is pursued, any progress made can be sabotaged by the problems that remain unaddressed. The potential for healing is greatest in the joining of the two movements, in pursuing internal recovery and external politics jointly and consciously. Determining the ideal balance between internal and external activities depends on many factors. Women in Allie Light's award-winning documentary *Dialogues with Madwomen* (1994) explain why it is sometimes essential to focus on healing internally before looking outward to the world. At other times it is necessary to change, or at least escape from, a toxic environment before healing can occur. And sometimes action on both fronts is required.

There is a long, sad history of psychiatry and other mental health fields silencing women and victims of oppression and abuse (Breggin 1991; Masson 1986, 1988). Many "healing" interventions can be understood as designed to cover up the very symptoms that point toward the oppression and victimization of women, children, and others. This history is directly counter to social activism. Worse, as voiced so eloquently by *Dialogues with Madwomen,* in too many cases the professionals endowed with the power of professional psychiatry or psychology not only implicitly cover up oppression and victimization but in some cases also exploit and sexually abuse their female patients (Pope 1994).

Louise Armstrong and Robin Abcarian do not direct their comments to the problem of actively abusive, or explicitly oppressive, mental health professionals. Their immediate concern is the internally focused aspects of the recovery movement, the self-help groups and books, and the therapists who may acknowledge oppression and victimization within the therapy room but take no role in promoting or encouraging political reform. I believe that this tendency of even gifted healers to avoid political activity and to infantalize women victims of interpersonal crimes may have its roots in the forces that have allowed psychiatry to silence victims of oppression and violence (see Masson 1988 for an insightful and provocative critique of psychotherapy). When the goal of therapy is reintegration into society, the assumption is that it is the individual who must adapt, and the society that is healthy.

While I agree with many of the concerns raised by critics of therapy, I believe that some therapy relationships can play an important role in some survivors' recovery. Perhaps the crucial factor for recovery is that the abuse survivor have a relationship (whether with a therapist or someone else) in which the truth can be told without recrimination, a relationship in which the survivor can trust that the truth will be heard and believed without the listener's subsequently abusing his or her power. According to Jonathan Shay, "Healing from trauma depends upon communalization of the trauma—being able safely to tell the story to someone who is listening and who can be trusted to retell it truthfully to others in the community" (1994, p. 4). With combat veterans in mind, Shay wrote,

> So before analyzing, before classifying, before thinking, before trying to *do* anything—we should *listen*. Categories and classifications play a large role in the institutions of mental health care for veterans, in the education of mental health professionals, and as tentative guides to perception. All too often, however, our mode of listening deteriorates into intellectual sorting, with the professional grabbing the veterans' words from the air and sticking them in mental bins. To some degree that is institutionally and educationally necessary, but listening this way *destroys* trust. (p. 4)

## Long-Lasting Damage

Although truth-telling and political activity are essential to ending crimes of sexual assault, interpersonal violence, and child abuse, and although the medicalization and pathologizing of victims of such crimes can become impediments to such external activities, the fact remains that those who have experienced such crimes may sustain long-lasting psychological injuries.

One sort of long-lasting injury that those abused may suffer is damage resulting from blockage of information to internal mental mechanisms designed to provide understanding of the world. Mechanisms that allow one to assess the trustworthiness of other people and the credibility of various claims are affected by the continual stifling of information into or out of them. Just as arm and leg muscles are damaged and even atrophied by underuse, so too may internal mental mechanisms suffer from underuse or inappropriate use.

Sexual abuse survivors also commonly suffer damage to their

ability to enjoy their sexuality. Their sexual behavior may be either excessively restricted or excessively promiscuous; either extreme can restrict both intimacy and pleasure (Buttenheim and Levendosky 1994; Maltz 1988). This damage to sexuality is similar to the damage to trust mechanisms, which is likely to lead to either an over- or an underwillingness to trust.

Damage to one's sexual being may cause a breakdown of the ability to freely consent to sexual activities with another person. Sexual behavior may look consensual on the outside but not really be consensual. How can sex *look* consensual, but not really *be* consensual? If a power differential exists (as it does in adult-child, teacher-student, and therapist-client sex), the free consent of the less powerful person is severely compromised (see Pope 1994). But even if there is no external power differential, sex that appears to be consensual may not be.

There are probably many mental mechanisms involved in determining whether sex is consensual or not, but for simplicity let us call the collection of these mechanisms the Consensual Sex Decision Mechanism, or CSDM. The CSDM is the set of mental functions that, in the absence of external force, allows a person to make a choice about whether to engage in sexual behavior (or continue to engage in sexual behavior, as this mechanism should be constantly active during sex). "External force" here includes not only implied or real physical force or obvious psychological force, but also the more subtle force of a power differential. Let us further assume that the CSDM has a natural maturation such that under healthy, ideal circumstances it becomes fully operational by early adulthood.

Consensual sex is possible only when two necessary conditions are met, neither of which alone is sufficient: the situation must be free from all external force, even subtle force; and each participant must have a functioning CSDM. A damaged CSDM may explain why some people are so vulnerable to subtle external forces. Women who were abused as children have a higher rate of adult sexual victimization than women who were not abused as children (Kluft 1990; Wyatt, Guthrie, and Notgrass 1992).

When fully working the CSDM has rich and thorough input: it is fully informed by all aspects of available reality. It also has rich and thorough output: the computation CSDM produces determines subsequent sexual behavior fully and completely. Furthermore, I propose, a fully operational CSDM produces conscious cognition about desire and choice that can be verbalized and shared.

Without fully operational CSDMs people dissociate in some way (that is, they fail to have normally connected mental processing, and they fail to integrate that processing with conscious awareness). I suspect that a great proportion of sexual encounters in our society take place between people without fully operational CSDMs, so that even without external force they are not *internally* free to say no or yes.

One may consent with mixed feelings; to consent does not guarantee no ambivalence. By analogy: James may consent to meet Montgomery in a smoky bar even though James is aware he does not like to breathe smoke. But consent does include the assumption that one has the power to make a choice: if Leonard agrees to meet Montgomery in a smoky bar without realizing that he could have proposed an alternative place or even had a choice in whether or not to meet, Leonard cannot be said to have consented to the meeting. A working CSDM implies only the ability to evaluate and make a choice in a complete and full way; it does not imply that all choices will be easy to make or will be made without ambivalence. In addition, a fully functional CSDM does not necessarily imply that every sexual act is preceded by conscious decision making.

What of the potential sexual partner of a person who may have an impaired CSDM? Do people have a legal, moral, or ethical obligation to assess their partner's CSDM (in other words, are they responsible for determining if the other person is able to make a choice)? If a person is drunk we recognize that he or she might not be able to make a free decision about having sex or not. We implicitly understand that intoxication can temporarily impair the functioning of the CSDM and that responsible behavior dictates that one not exploit an intoxicated person sexually. But intoxication is fairly easy to detect. When the CSDM is damaged because of previous victimization, issues of detection and responsibility are more subtle. And there are other questions: What if a young person's CSDM is not fully mature but his or her chronological age is beyond the cutoff point for statutory rape? What about degree—if the person is just a little bit intoxicated; just a little bit immature; just a little bit damaged from victimization? I don't know the answers (and I suspect that they would differ depending on whether legal or interpersonal responsibility is the issue), but the questions need to be considered. If we simply focus on whether external force or coercion was used at the time of the sexual event itself, we miss another, equally important determinant of nonconsensual sex, one that is internal.

Perhaps the existence of impaired CSDMs explains the extent of trancelike sexual behavior, which makes possible all sorts of hurtful acts, including the use of sex as violence. It appears that a person's sexual behavioral system is able to operate remarkably effectively even while the person suffers from dissociation, and that trancelike states of consciousness (and related ritualized repetitive behaviors) during sex are very common. From an evolutionary perspective, a very robust sexual behavior system, one that would work even under highly psychologically impoverished conditions, makes sense.

Why are so many people's CSDMs damaged so much of the time? I think the answer can be found in victimization and, more generally, a pervasive unhealthy socialization that has its roots in dysfunction within the family. I believe that the problem of damaged CSDMs is related to breakdowns in the mechanisms supporting decision making about trust—mechanisms that may also be damaged by victimization and betrayal. Victimization pits other survival needs against the natural maturation of the CSDM (or more generally the trust mechanisms) such that to survive, the developing child keeps out information that would allow the CSDM to develop. In other words, the child—or dependent adult, in some chronic marital rape situations—must disengage the CSDM to allow maintenance of crucial attachment bonds.

Thus, CSDMs fail because they must do so in order to protect the individual. It follows that a faulty CSDM is not a sign of pathology but a symptom of mistreatment that may turn into a source of continued problems. For instance, once the external situation is relatively free of force, it would be advantageous for a person to have a fully functioning CSDM. However, if the CSDM was sufficiently damaged by victimization or socialization, he or she might miss the opportunity to experience consensual sex. As in damaged or disengaged trust mechanisms, I think damaged or disengaged CSDMs can be healed effectively with appropriate support.

## Political and Forensic Connections

More than half a century ago the psychiatrist Milton Erickson published a short clinical note titled "Negation or Reversal of Legal Testimony" in the 1938 volume of the *Archives of Neurology and Psychiatry*. He began his paper with this observation: "The spontaneous, sincere and apparently completely unmotivated negation, reversal or alteration of condemnatory legal testimony previously given by credible witnesses constitutes a difficult and confusing problem" (p. 548). Erickson noted the serious legal difficulties that such recanting is likely to cause: "Such alteration of testimony is characterized by a complete change in the beliefs and understandings of the witness, effected by unrecognized factors within the personality. It occurs most frequently among the witnesses who are themselves the injured parties and, hence, have presumably every reason for telling only the truth, and it develops usually in relation to crimes of a personally horrifying, traumatic or repugnant character" (p. 548). Erickson suggested that because this type of recanting was significant for both psychiatry and the legal system, it should be studied and analyzed. In his article he presented two illustrative cases. Erickson explained that the two case histories cited were "selected from among others because of the fully established facts of the original crimes, the detailed, factual and fully corroborated testimony elicited initially and the absence of external motivation in the eventual development of significant and completely contradictory attitudes and beliefs" (p. 548).

Case 1 began with the arrest of two girls, aged nine and eleven, at a "bawdy-house" where they "worked." The girls' parents were the proprietors of the house of prostitution. (One hopes that in the 1990s minors would not be arrested for being the victims of such sexual abuse and slavery.) According to

Erickson, "Full confessions were obtained individually from all the prisoners, those of the adults corroborating fully the essentially identical accounts given by the two girls. In addition, medical examination of the girls disclosed numerous bruises and injuries, substantiating their accounts of beatings, and also revealed that they had been subjected to vaginal and rectal coitus and infected with syphilis and gonorrhea, both rectal and vaginal" (p. 548). The children were committed immediately to institutional settings where they were separated from each other, and kept for three months in quarantine isolation (for treatment of the venereal infections). During this time they were subjected to a series of interviews. During the first interview they readily acknowledged the story of their prostitution. As time progressed and with subsequent interviews, however, the girls became reluctant to discuss the sexual activities and ultimately began to deny them. According to Erickson, by the third interview, "rectal coitus was emphatically and resentfully denied by both. There were flat denials of ever having been nude or of having danced exhibitionistically, and they had forgotten the names of half the men. There were many vague statements of 'Ma didn't like those things' and 'Ma wouldn't let anybody do those things.' A few similar statements were made concerning the father" (p. 549).

By the final interview, six months after the first, the girls had made an almost complete retraction of their well-documented abuse: "Strong resentment was expressed over my interest in the story, and no information was given spontaneously except the emphatic inclusive declaration that it was 'all a lot of nasty lies.' A warm defense was given of both parents. The authorities were harshly criticized as unwelcome intruders into a private home, and the whole experience was minimized into the statement that 'some bad men came to the house, but nothing bad happened'" (p. 550). Erickson's interpretation of this retraction focused partly on what he thought was the girls' guilt for the pleasure they derived from the sexual activities. While this is a possibility, I identify a different source for the retraction, and that is the girls' need to regain their parents and to see them as protectors and nurturers, not abusers or people who would so blatantly betray them.

In Case 2, a young woman was in a man's automobile. According to Erickson their plans were clear, "their intention being to spend the night at a road-house of ill repute . . . During the course of the drive, as a result of recklessness, the car overturned, pinning the young woman beneath it, and burst into flames. The man freed himself but made no effort to rescue his companion, instead fleeing from the scene" (p. 550). The woman was rescued by passing motorists, but by then she was already severely burned. The man was arrested and at his trial for reckless driving admitted to his failure to rescue the woman. The woman later demanded a retrial because she believed that the man had been falsely accused, that he had tried to rescue her. The man did not agree with the woman's attempt to deny his wrongdoing, and a retrial never occurred. Erickson again suggests that the woman's guilt for sexual pleasure was a factor in her need to deny the events. However, it is not clear there was any sexual activity involved in this case. I think it is more significant that the woman was betrayed by a man she had apparently trusted, although in this case the meaning and significance of the attachment between the woman and man is unclear. A question suggested by this account is whether reversals of testimony are as likely for crimes perpetrated by strangers as for crimes perpetrated by trusted others.

While it would surely be illogical to use retraction as evidence of witness credibility, the question that arises is whether witness retraction should be used as prima facie evidence that the initial report was incorrect. Erickson commented that had the two cases he reported been brought back into court, the witnesses' retractions might have had serious implications for justice. "General experience . . . in similar cases suggests that the not unusual development of 'reasonable doubt' [results] from the recanting of testimony previously given by an otherwise credible witness and a consequent acquittal because of failure to prove again the guilt originally established" (p. 551). A similar sort of question may be asked about the reliability or credibility of alleged victims of childhood sexual abuse who claim to have had a period of not remembering the abuse.

Betrayal trauma theory suggests that forgetting abuse by a parent or trusted other is an understandable consequence of sexual abuse under some circumstances. The theory could be used to restore the credibility of a witness. It would, however, be a mistake to use the theory to contend that because someone alleged forgetting and remembering abuse, the abuse was more probable than if there had been no forgetting. A similar point has been made for the proper use of the Child Sexual Abuse Accommodation Syndrome (CSAAS, discussed in Chapter 3). It is inappropriate to use insights gained by the CSAAS, such as a child's delay or hesitancy in disclosing abuse or a child's retraction in the face of disbelief, as evidence for abuse. However, it might be appropriate to use such insights to restore the credibility of the child witness when his or her testimony has been impeached because of delayed, conflicted, or unconvincing disclosure, or retraction, by pointing out that such hesitancy and retraction is not inconsistent with actual abuse (see Myers 1996; Sorensen and Snow 1991). Similarly, for adult witnesses it might be appropriate to note the empirically high rates of forgetting sexual abuse, and, drawing on betrayal trauma theory, it might be appropriate to suggest that forgetting and remembering sexual abuse perpetrated by a trusted person is not inconsistent with the abuse having occurred. But it would be inappropriate to suggest that a pattern of reported forgetting and remembering is substantive evidence of abuse.

## The Delayed Memory Debate Revisited

"The dispute at the heart of the repressed memory debate," according to Loftus, Milo, and Paddock (1995), "is that people are claiming a mechanism that goes beyond normal forgetting, one that has not yet yielded empirical confirmation" (p. 303). Is this really the heart of the debate? I don't think so. What is at the heart of the repressed memory debate is whether the alleged sexual abuse occurred or not. This fundamental dispute then fans out to many other issues: Can traumatic memories be forgotten and later remembered? If so, is this rare or common? Can people come to believe that they were abused when in fact they were not? If so, is this rare or common?

Some have argued that psychogenic amnesia for childhood sexual abuse is impossible or unlikely and that, in contrast, false memories of abuse are both possible and likely (Loftus 1993;

Ofshe and Watters 1993). Some people now believe that a contested memory is more likely to be false than real—that errors of commission in memory later in life are plausible, while errors of omission earlier are not. Betrayal trauma theory does not directly address the issue of whether false memories for sexual abuse are possible. It also does not answer some more important questions: Assuming that some memories are largely false and some are essentially true, how frequently does the truth essentially prevail, and under what circumstances might inaccuracy dominate? What is the likelihood that an adult raised in a nonabusive family would come to believe, falsely, that he or she was sexually abused? These important questions deserve further investigation. However, individual cases of contested memories will always deserve open-minded scrutiny; individual truths can rarely be determined by group trends.

Betrayal trauma theory does address the issue of the plausibility of amnesia for actual childhood sexual abuse. In this book I have proposed that there is a logic to amnesia for childhood abuse. Under certain conditions, such as abuse by a close caregiver, amnesia for the abuse is an adaptive response, for amnesia may allow a dependent child to remain attached to— and thus elicit at least some degree of life-sustaining nurturing and protection from—his or her abusive caregiver. Furthermore, various degrees of amnesia with various times of onset and various consequences can be understood in terms of what cognitive science currently understands about memory and attention. Thus, we can reject at least one of the claims made by some critics of the legitimacy of delayed memories—namely, that memory repression for sexual abuse is impossible or implausible. In addition to the existing documentation of amnesia and memory recovery for verified traumas (for example, *Commonwealth of Massachusetts v. Porter,* 1993; Terr 1994; van der Kolk 1987; Williams 1992), betrayal trauma theory may serve to validate the experiences of survivors of childhood sexual abuse and other traumas who forget and later remember their abuse. Ultimately, however, a great deal of additional research is needed so that we can understand the nature of memories of childhood sexual abuse. Only with that understanding will we be able to make progress in evaluating contested memories. More important, only with additional knowledge and an understanding of how people naturally respond to actual childhood sexual abuse will we be able to end the epidemic of abuse that plagues our society.

## Breaking Silence and Pursuing Justice

Most sexual abuse survivors experience some period of feeling shame about their experiences. They fear being stigmatized and/or not believed should they tell their stories. Speaking to an audience of therapists at the Mississippi Conference on Child Abuse and Neglect in April 1994, Ross Cheit captured the feelings of many abuse survivors when he discussed his decision to act upon his memories of childhood sexual abuse:

> There was a time less than a year ago when I thought I could never speak publicly about what I'm going to say today. And my reluctance, I think, is testimony to the power of denial, the burden of shame, and the unsympathetic attitude that is displayed towards all too many adults who speak about being sexually abused as children. But it is clear to me that this topic demands public attention, that silence is part of the problem.

After describing his experience of remembering being sexually abused by William Farmer, the intensity of his shame in the bookstore when purchasing a copy of *Abused Boys,* and his reluctance to tell anyone, even his wife, about his experience, Cheit discussed how he managed to find the strength to pursue accountability and redress for the injuries he had endured:

> Memories of childhood sexual abuse are difficult to act on. Many people do not have the support, the resources, or the wherewithal to move beyond the kind of paralysis that I felt that day in the bookstore. I understand their predicament. And it's one of the challenges in our society to figure out how to reach out to these people. The alternating feelings for me were shame, and a strange kind of disbelief. Because I knew my memory was true, but I didn't want to believe it. It didn't really seem real, and I was wracked with fear that other people would not believe me.
> . . . I was terrified that my parents would not believe me. I worried that my wife didn't really believe me, that she was just

saying she did, but probably had her own doubts. And what I needed to do was prove it. I needed to somehow prove it to other people. So I began that process with the hardest phone call I've ever had to make, essentially telling my dear parents, out of the blue, to rewrite our family history, to include events that are so abhorrent, I could scarcely find the words to describe them to my own mother.

Fortunately—and I am fortunate; I got to go home from camp— my parents were exceptionally supportive. Unfortunately, I was soon to discover that the rest of the world, at least the part that mattered to me the most, the organization that I belonged to, could be much more callous.

After discussing matters with his parents and his wife, Cheit turned his efforts to investigation. "I wanted to know if the perpetrator was still alive, and I wanted to know anything else I could find out about why this happened," he explained. Cheit hired a private investigator, who found out that before the Boys Chorus hired William Farmer, he had abused children at a church in California. Cheit observed, "A simple phone call would have determined that from the people who hired him at my camp." When Farmer's activities were discovered at the church in 1968, he moved on to a second church in a different California town. In that town Farmer molested the son of a municipal court judge. "The judge told this man, leave town tomorrow or we'll go after you criminally," Cheit said. Farmer fled to Oregon, where he obtained teaching credentials. According to Cheit, the investigator reported that Farmer taught on and off in Oregon for "some twenty years," and "the investigator has turned up enough evidence to suggest that there are a number of cases in Oregon." Farmer then moved from Oregon to Texas, where he was employed as a teacher during 1994.

With the investigator's help Ross Cheit located fifty-five people who had attended Cheit's camp during the period Ross was attending. Cheit talked to most of his former campmates.

I started making phone calls to people I hadn't talked to in twenty, twenty-five years. And I quickly found another victim . . . What happened to him had been called to the attention of the people who ran the camp. The people who ran the camp didn't do anything about it. Their attitude apparently was that he had just been molested, that no action had been "consummated"—apparently the words of the perpetrator. And the person who ran the camp told this fourteen-year-old boy that she would talk to his parents about it. She never did. And when I found him twenty-five years later in Brooklyn, New York, he found out for the first time that his parents didn't know. And he had grown up thinking that his parents were unable to talk to him about this.

Within a month, I found another case that was completely verified. I found a nurse who had worked at the camp who had walked in on this man in bed with a child. She had called it to the attention of the people who ran the camp, whose attitude was apparently that he was a strong kid, and so they didn't need to do anything. They didn't talk to his parents. And that strong kid is on the edge of life in San Francisco. It took a long time to find him, and when we finally found him, he didn't remember this man. He has no memory of this man. But the nurse remembers vividly.

Some people have very vivid memories, and they describe to you, as if it happened yesterday, something that happened 24 years ago. A few other people, it's right below the surface. I called a guy in Southern California who said—I would call these people and I'd ask, "Do you remember this man?" I would give no pretext, although it's obviously an odd question to come out of the blue. And this guy said to me, he described him and gave a few descriptors, said, oh, he was a big guy, friendly, played the guitar, there was something kind of strange about him . . . And I said, "Something kind of strange about him? What?" And he said, "I don't know. I don't know." And I tried to push him, and he couldn't remember.

And I said, "Well, the reason I'm calling"—and I couldn't even finish that sentence. And he said, "Oh, I know," and proceeded to describe an incident where this man tried to get him into a sleeping bag on an overnight.

For some people, it was right below the surface. And for some people, memories are just convoluted. I reached someone else who told me a sleeping bag story, and told me that this man had tried to get him in a sleeping bag once. And he hadn't gotten in, because he had realized the man was naked. He wrote me a letter a few days later and said, "I feel really sheepish. What I told you the other night wasn't true. I did get into the sleeping bag. I just wish that the other story were the true one." Now, I think he carried the other story with him his whole life until I called him. But I have no doubt that he got into the sleeping bag, and that the story he now is telling is true.

In the course of his investigation, Ross Cheit found many victims of sexual abuse from the years he attended the summer camp. With a successful professional life and a healthy marriage, he considers himself one of the fortunate ones: "I've certainly encountered people in this process who are much less fortunate than myself, including a few who are now institutionalized and one who has committed suicide." What Cheit found most remarkable was that of "all the people I've identified—multiple perpetrators, multiple victims—none had ever come forward in a public way. The perpetrator had never in any way been confronted by law enforcement."

After amassing so much information about the abuses committed at the summer camp, Ross Cheit called William Farmer on the telephone and confronted him with his knowledge. Cheit tape-recorded Farmer's attempts to avoid accountability and his eventual confession during that telephone call. "Armed with this overwhelming evidence of verification, and consumed with some real desire for justice and accountability," Cheit "made the very difficult decision with my parents to take this evidence to the organization, seeking first and foremost a full and open accounting."

Cheit and his family took their complaint to the San Francisco Boys Chorus. But "in many ways," Cheit went on to say in his April 1994 speech, "what has been most disheartening is what has happened since then."

When I started talking about bringing legal action, I had another one of these moments of exhilaration followed by depression. Several people told me, "You'll be believed because you're a man."

And I was terrified of not being believed, so at first, again, I was exhilarated. "Oh, good. They'll believe me." It was a great comfort.

And then I quickly realized what the implications of that statement were. If the predominant victims of this crime, women, are automatically not believed—my God, what a situation we're in.

If there's a presumption that women cannot be believed—this is a presumption I find preposterous, given how difficult it is to speak about these things—then our society is just condoning sexual abuse right and left. The sad irony is that when it's all said and done, they don't really believe me either. So an organization that I loved and cared about, an organization that professes serious concern about sexual abuse—they even have a professional on their board who deals with sexually abused children—has completely turned its back on me, and on other survivors. They still are denying the obvious. Although they've spoken to three other victims, and they have in their possession a tape-recorded admission, they've said absolutely nothing to indicate their concern about the welfare of those who were abused in their care. And instead, they have attacked me. They have questioned my credibility. They have questioned my motives. And they even attached to a recent court filing in San Francisco that bizarre *New Yorker* article about satanic ritual abuse in the state of Washington, a case that leaves a lot of questions about what really happened.

But they know what happened in my case.

The first reaction we got from them when we sent them the letter was probably all levels possible of denial. First they said, "We don't think it happened." And they said, "Even if it did happen, we don't think we're liable." And then they said, "And even if we're liable"—and this is literally what they said—"we see little purpose that would be served by harming an organization that has done so much good for so many kids over so many years."

I was just stunned at that, because I felt like, well, so the kids who were lucky enough to not have this happen are the reason that you're not going to confront the kids that it did happen to?

Ross Cheit sued William Farmer and the San Francisco Boys Chorus. He was successful, winning a $457,000 damage judgment against Farmer (which he is exceedingly unlikely to collect). The San Francisco Boys Chorus settled the case with a $35,000 payment, an admission, and an apology. When he got his first payment from the San Francisco Boys Chorus, Cheit donated the money to a nonprofit organization advocating for survivors of childhood sexual abuse.

Ross Cheit's courageous actions are a ray of hope for those who are committed to holding child abusers accountable for their crimes, as a step toward preventing this devastating injury from happening to future generations of children. But, as Cheit noted to his audience of professionals in the child protection field, his case also illustrates that a great deal of work remains to be done to ensure such a societal transformation.

> Strangely, there seems now to be more concern about false accusations than there is about true ones. I certainly think we should worry about both problems—about believing false accusations, and about disregarding true ones. But I also think we're in desperate need of better evidence about the magnitude of both those problems. And I think there's plenty of reason to think that molesters who are never caught vastly outweigh the number of people who have ever been falsely accused.
>
> . . . One of the things I've discovered in this process of going forward—and a number of people asked me, "Couldn't you have exposed this without filing a lawsuit?"—there's a real bias in media, and it stems from libel law, the media will not write about an allegation of child abuse unless there's a lawsuit, to protect them against libel. But they'll sure write about someone claiming to be falsely accused. So I think the law has pushed the media towards doing that.
>
> My heart goes out to anyone falsely accused of child abuse. And I certainly applaud the efforts of professional societies that are now trying to address the proper protocols and parameters for dealing with issues about therapeutic relationships. But the challenge of our time is to reserve judgment and to evaluate evidence fairly on a case-by-case basis. It gives me hope to speak to people who are dedicated and concerned about addressing the formidable challenges posed by child sexual abuse.

Cheit is correct: the challenges are formidable. His story illustrates many of the obstacles childhood abuse survivors and political activists face when attempting to hold perpetrators accountable for their actions and when attempting to change institutions that have implicitly permitted the abuse to occur. Like other human rights struggles, the push for children's right to be protected from abuse meets resistance.

## The Issue of Children's Rights

In *The Little Prince,* Antoine de Saint-Exupéry observed, "All grown-ups were once children—although few of them remember it." Although at some intuitive level we all know the struggle and joy of childhood, for most of us, coming of age involves a disconnection from that childhood—a kind of culturally induced dissociation. The concept of the "inner child" that has emerged in popular culture is easy to ridicule (and there are indeed some versions of that concept that seem silly, and when it is used as an excuse for avoiding adult responsibility the concept has been twisted into something dangerous). Yet ridicule is often a response of those in power when they have little to say in defense of a challenge to the status quo; it is not children who ridicule the concept of the "inner child," but adults. The children I have spoken with about the continuity of childhood into adulthood consider this matter deeply important. As one child put it to me: "Yes, I understand that; I have a baby in me."

Western civilization has been moving slowly toward acceptance of children as human beings, worthy of human rights. This movement had been something like that of a wide, bending, slowly running river. Recently, however, that lazy river has suddenly become fast-moving and full of rapids. Carried along, we slam against the rocks, we get caught in swirling eddies. The river is taking us to a recognition of children's needs and rights, and we have entered particularly challenging waters. In addition, unlike other human rights struggles, the primary oppressed group in this case—children—cannot lead the movement. Instead, adults must take the lead.

The struggle for the freedom, dignity, and rights of children is also a struggle for the liberation of the human spirit in adults. If we free our children, they may mature into freer adults, living more fully, with more of an opportunity to fulfill their potential, thus making the world a better place for all. At the same time, by accepting the continuity between our adult selves and our childhood histories, we may help free the human spirit in our-selves and others. In this way, when we promote children's rights we are promoting our own freedom.

Although the concept of the inner child is easy to ridicule, it represents a profound change in society's understanding of human nature. Instead of perceiving adolescence as an abrupt trans-formation, producing adults who have left childhood in the past, we are increasingly perceiving the continuity of human experience from birth to old age. Although our needs change as we grow older, each of us represents the totality of our experiences, including those in our childhood. To be aware of this continuity decreases dissociation from childhood memories of self and thus promotes internal healing. To be aware of this continuity also leads us to realize that children deserve human rights too, and thus awareness of the continuity also promotes external action.

## Adult Betrayal Trauma and Betrayal Blindness

I have focused on childhood sexual abuse by a caregiver as the type of betrayal trauma most likely to lead to amnesia for the betrayal. Childhood sexual abuse by a caregiver is especially likely to contain the situational factors that make amnesia both adaptive (to maintain necessary attachment) and possible (it is kept secret, it is never discussed, alternative realities are presented). A possible additional factor that awaits future investigation is the relationship between sexual behavior and the likelihood of altered states of consciousness we may call "trance." We may be particularly vulnerable to entering dissociated states while engaged in sexual activity. This may help explain why otherwise inexplicable ritualized behaviors and fetishes are so often associated with sex. In addition, trance states may be somewhat contagious. Trance may beget trance. If an adult who is sexually abusing a child enters a dissociated state, that altered state of consciousness may be instrumental in inducing an altered state of consciousness in the child victim as well.

However, even if sexual abuse is the most likely sort of betrayal trauma to induce amnesia, it is not the only sort of trauma likely to have this effect.

*Combat Experience*

Combat veterans sometimes have amnesia for their combat experiences (see, for example, Archibald and Tuddenham 1965; Brende 1987; Henderson and Moore 1944; McFall et al. 1991; van der Kolk 1987). Jonathan Shay (1994) has suggested that betrayal is a key factor in the injuries that veterans suffer. He notes, "Armies, like families, are institutions that create a world. Both successfully engender the new member's respect, loyalty, love, affirmation, gratitude, and obedience. I speak of armies and families as creating social power, because the hold that each of these institutions has over its members comes to greatly exceed its moment-to-moment capacity to reward or punish and usually persists long after significant practical affiliation has ended" (pp. 150–151).

Soldiers may be fundamentally dependent on their army leaders. Shay identified a number of ways in which authority figures in armies have control over soldiers, much like authority figures in families have control over children (pp. 150–151). To begin with, there are barriers that keep the soldier from escaping. In addition, there are rules controlling the body and bodily functions; what and when to eat; when, where, and how much to sleep; what form the body can take (clothing, weight, haircut); and when and where to urinate and defecate. There is also a lack of privacy regarding bodily functions; prolonged daily contact with the power-holder in the group; and a combination of enticement, force, and intimidation. The power-holder is the source of small rewards, comfort, and approval. He or she may enforce the rules in an inconsistent, unpredictable, or capricious manner; may monopolize communication, resources, and control; and may be secretive about some activities and events. There is little alternative to seeing the world through the power-holder's eyes; and often there is required repetition of buzzwords, songs, slogans, and clichés, even if they are inwardly disbelieved and rejected. If a soldier is so completely controlled by a power-holder, and if that power-holder betrays him or her, betrayal blindness may be fundamentally adaptive. If the soldier is aware of the betrayal, he risks alienating the power-holder and endangering his or her life.

## Acquaintance Rape

In a landmark study, research psychologist Mary Koss (1988) reported that approximately one in four college women were the victims of rape or attempted rape. Not only did Koss discover striking levels of sexual assault, but she also found that 57% of the offenders were dates, and 84% of the victimizations involved an offender who was known to the victim. Acquaintance rape tends not to be reported, and is often not even considered rape by the victim, despite the fact that the events meet a legal definition of rape. In fact, the greater the intimacy, the less likely forced sexual intercourse is to be considered rape (Koss et al. 1988).

An unwillingness to tell others about the assault, or even to label the crime as rape when the offender is an acquaintance, suggests that victims of such events may be exhibiting a kind of betrayal blindness. In a recent study, Shannon Tromp and her colleagues (1995) studied memory for rape, using a community sample of rape victims who had not sought professional help. They reported, "The most powerful discriminator of rape from other unpleasant memories was the degree to which they [the rape memories] were less clear and vivid, contained a less meaningful order, were less well-remembered, and were less thought and talked about" (p. 607). This finding of diminished memory may depend partly on the high rate of acquaintance rape found within the base population of rape survivors (Koss 1988). Betrayal trauma theory suggests that the greater the intimacy (and especially the greater the perception of dependency on the relationship) between the rapist and adult victim, the more knowledge isolation and forgetting there would be. Being raped, even as an adult, by a trusted other is a betrayal trauma that can apparently lead to unawareness and forgetting. Being battered by an intimate partner may also lead to a kind of betrayal blindness (see also Burgess and Holmstrom 1974; Koss and Harvey 1991).

## Battered Woman Syndrome

Lenore Walker brought battered woman syndrome to the world's attention (1979, 1984, 1994). Battered women suffer from physical, sexual, or psychological abuse that is inflicted by their intimate partner. Walker, who interviewed many battered women, observed that the batterer's abuse is generally part of a pattern of obsessional behavior rather than an expression of sudden loss of control. Batterers are often prone to extreme sexual jealousy. Walker also reported that the abuse tends to become more violent and frequent, and tends to follow a three-step cycle of tension-building, violence, and contrition. The power of the emotional bond commonly found between a woman and her battering partner is a frustrating and perplexing phenomenon. According to Sarah Painter and Don Dutton (1985):

> It is not uncommon for a woman who has been beaten to the point of needing police intervention to save her life, who originally has pressed charges against the man who beat her, and who initiated an exit from the relationship, to change her mind, drop the charges, and resume the relationship. This pattern repeats itself often enough that police and legal professionals anticipate a change of heart and often attempt to discourage the initial laying of charges. Defense attorneys frequently point to the woman's unwillingness to leave the violent relationship as evidence of her culpability in contributing to her own victimization. Therapists and others counseling a battered woman may become frustrated when she suddenly discontinues therapy or leaves a shelter to rejoin her husband. (p. 363)

Why would an abused woman stay in such a relationship? Walker (1994) points out that women may be reluctant to leave because batterers often become more violent when women leave the relationship, that the woman may be financially dependent on the batterer, and that the woman may believe that she has no choice. Walker has conceptualized battered woman syndrome as a kind of posttraumatic stress disorder with cognitive and memory disturbances, avoidance, and heightened anxiety.

Mary Ann Dutton Douglas (Douglas 1987) proposed additional patterns of attitude and behavior: idealization of the abuser, denial of anger, and suppression of the victim's own anger. Dutton and Painter (1981, 1993) note that Anna Freud's (1946) description of the victim's identification with the aggressor may provide an explanation of how battered women survive a long-term relationship with a potentially lethal other. Dutton and Painter (1981, 1993) observe that the idealization of the abuser is related to the strength of the continued attachment after termination of the relationship. They also suggest that the battered woman's self-derogation and idealization of the abuser are related to two aspects of the relationship between the battered woman and her battering partner: the power differential and the "intermittency of abuse." By intermittency, Dutton and Painter mean the strength of the juxtaposition of positive and negative treatment. They find that battered women tend to have a greater attachment to the abuser when the abuse is rapidly followed by pleasant behavior.

This pattern of mistreatment followed by nurturing is critical to the abused woman's willingness to stay in the relationship. In one study of 75 abused women, Dutton and Painter found that "it is the extremity and juxtaposition of positive and negative behavior that contribute to battered woman syndrome, rather than predictability of abuse per se" (1993, p. 620). This finding suggests a testable application of betrayal trauma theory to adult relationships. Are the women in these relationships with high degrees of intermittency staying because they find a way to be blind to the betrayals they endure? Are their perceptions, memories, and projections of the future less accurate because of the intermittency than those of battered women who do not receive as much positive behavior after the negative behavior?

The sort of "traumatic bond" (Painter and Dutton 1985) that is observed between captive and kidnapper, battered woman and battering partner, and abused child and abusive parent may well be a consequence of betrayal blindness. In each of these cases the abused person is dependent on the abuser; to be blind to the betrayal may seem, or may actually be, necessary for survival.

### Betrayal Blindness

Betrayal trauma theory had its origins in observations about childhood sexual abuse. I saw the forgetting of sexual abuse to be an understandable response to an extraordinary situation that places a child in a horrible bind. To know about the abuse is sometimes itself a threat to survival. Thus, forgetting is adaptive, and given what is now known about cognitive architecture, the phenomenology of forgetting and remembering is better understood.

Everyday betrayal blindness is all around us. It is the systematic filtering of reality in order to maintain human relationships. It is the not knowing and not remembering the betrayals of everyday life and everyday relationships in order to protect those relationships. It includes the white lies—and the darker lies—we tell ourselves so as not to threaten our bonds. It is not seeing that your intimate partner is having an affair when others see it plainly. It is not being aware of your employer's exploitation of you, harassment directed toward you, or discrimination against you. It is believing your friend when he lies to you about why he cannot be with you on a significant occasion.

Carol Gilligan (1991) identified the irony that occurs when we must sever our relatedness in order to have relationships. She observed that in adolescence we learn to cut off components of our internal sources of knowledge in order not to speak unacceptable truths that would threaten relationships. According to Gilligan, this is something we learn to do; it is not the way we come into the world.

Must we be this way? And if this kind of behavior is so common is it perhaps acceptable, or even healthy? Perhaps. But I believe that a great deal of our habitual betrayal blindness is not necessary, and ultimately not healthy.

Recently I had a midair experience quite different from the near-miss I experienced over Denver. Immediately after taking off from San Francisco airport, and just moments after the flight attendant began her welcoming speech on the intercom, the plane was suddenly jerked about violently. The flight attendant stopped speaking. The airplane pitched dramatically, tipping toward the waters of San Francisco Bay not far below us. The event, though frightening, was over very soon; the turbulence stopped as abruptly as it had begun. Then, as in the incident over Denver, the stewardess resumed speaking, not referring to the frightening event. This time, however, I asked a flight attendant what had happened. She told me she did not know, but would ask the pilot. Half an hour later, the pilot spoke over the intercom to all of us. He explained that we had run into the wake of another plane that had taken off from a parallel runway. The wake, he explained, had blown into our trajectory. I felt relieved and reassured. In the end, he risked honesty and thereby engendered a much greater level of trust in his passengers.

## Removing Blinders, Becoming Connected

Love and joy are not the lack of pain, hurt, and fear. The world is simultaneously infinitely horrible and infinitely wonderful, and although it may be impossible for us to see beyond the horror or the wonder at any given time, one truth does not cancel out the other. Our mind is like our sense of taste: it sometimes deceives us by blending two sensations into one. Lemonade contains both sour acids and sweet sugars—it is only an illusion that it is neither very sweet nor very sour.

Sometimes we are so overwhelmed by the horror of our world that we are blind to its wonder; sometimes we are fortunate enough to be so overwhelmed by the wonder of the world that we are blind to its horror. When fragmented by betrayal blindness we sometimes see neither the horror nor the wonder. But whether we see them or not, both elements exist.

Psychological health and fulfilling, constructive relationships have in common wholeness, integration, and connection. Though a certain amount of divided consciousness may be adaptive, even necessary, for functioning, on the whole we are diminished by being separated from parts of ourselves and each other.

If you are blind to the evidence that your intimate partner is having an affair, you may manage to keep the relationship from ending. But what sort of relationship is it, and what purpose does it serve? Sometimes a perception of dependency is accurate; a woman—especially with young children—may be financially dependent on her husband. If that woman is blind to her husband's betrayal and abuse, she may be serving the immediate survival needs of her children and herself. But often the perception of dependency is the result of past or current psychological manipulation; escape and change may be possible, but the woman may not see those options at all. More often than not, I suspect, an adult's perception of dependence is erroneous. People are too easily manipulated into believing they have no options, and thus they collude in their own self-deception.

It is also tragic, and all too common, when a fear of trust limits intimate relationships between trustworthy individuals. This fear of trusting is a kind of betrayal blindness without the betrayal. The person is unwilling to look, for fear of finding betrayal. Thus, the blindness serves to protect the relationship, but at the price of intimacy.

Unawareness, not knowing, forgetting, dissociating—being less than fully connected internally—may be adaptive if the external situation is such that awareness, knowing, remembering, and integrating would be life-threatening. For a child dependent on abusive caregivers, lack of internal connection can help maintain some sort of external connection to necessary others. But I disagree with those such as Daniel Goleman (1985), who suggest that while truth is generally a good thing, sometimes even privileged members of our society are best served by living with "vital lies" in which the truth is best kept from oneself and one's intimate partners. And I disagree with Elizabeth Loftus's suggestion to therapists: "Instead of dwelling on the misery of childhood and digging for childhood sexual trauma as its cause, why not spend some time doing something completely different . . . A competent therapist will help others support and assist the client, and help the client direct feelings of gratitude toward those significant others" (1995, p. 28). Therapist-directed feelings of gratitude are not the stuff of connection and intimate relationships.

Blindness and lack of connectedness, whether truly needed or not, are ultimately tragic solutions to life. These adaptations keep us from knowing ourselves and others fully. We end up fragmented both internally and externally—impoverished spiritually and socially. We have learned this is the way to survive, a sort of minimum strategy. It may seem like a good solution when we are limited by the immediate context, but it seriously constrains human potential.

It takes courage to risk connection. Audre Lorde, a poet, a black woman who lived through oppression and betrayal, found a way to be deeply connected within herself, to others, and to the society around her. She did this without denying the horrors of reality and without giving up hope in the future. Her solution was both internal growth and external action: "When I dare to be powerful, to use my strength in the service of my vision, then it becomes less important whether or not I am unafraid" (1980, p. 15).

Survivors of childhood sexual abuse and betrayal trauma have learned to cope by being disconnected internally so as to manage a minimal kind of external connection. But with adult freedom and responsibility come the potential to break silence, to use voice and language to promote internal integration, deeper external connection, and social transformation. Through communication—integration within ourselves and connection between individuals—we can become whole: embodied, aware, vital, powerful.

I first began to develop betrayal trauma theory in early 1991 to understand the phenomena of forgetting and remembering sexual abuse. In 1991 there was no false memory movement or noisy debate about recovered memories. A lack of information prevailed. I sought to understand the motivation for and the nature of the intrusive recollections of abuse once memories were first recovered. I sensed that areas of psychology that I had previously studied and in which I had a passionate interest, especially cognitive science, would prove useful in understanding these important questions.

My personal motivation for pursuing these intellectual questions was complex. In 1991 my inner life and professional work came together in an unexpected way. Memories of my childhood were coming back to me at the same time that my research was leading me to rethink the science of memory. This private meeting of the personal and professional was to play a role in touching off a heated public and political reaction.

For the first two years of my work on betrayal trauma theory, I did not discuss my private life in public. When asked by colleagues why I was interested in trauma and repression, a topic outside the standard boundaries of cognitive science at that time, I deflected the question in order to protect my privacy. A few times after being trusted with a disclosure of abuse, I have asked a colleague if he or she had considered making this information more public. Most have not. For some a desire for personal privacy is the determining factor. For others, fear of stigma seems most salient. One prominent senior male psychologist explained to me that he was reluctant to disclose his history of abuse, even though in his own case he did not feel a great need for privacy per se, because he was concerned that his current professional work might be discounted were it known that he was an abuse survivor.

In my own case I lost the ability to choose privacy. Approximately eight months after I first presented betrayal trauma theory, my parents, in conjunction with Ralph Underwager and others, formed the False Memory Syndrome Foundation (FMSF). Before the organization was formed, my mother, Pamela Freyd, had published an article presenting her version of family history under the name "Jane Doe" (Doe 1991). The Jane Doe article, when circulated to my professional colleagues and to the media by my mother, made public allegations about my professional and personal life, at the same time that it helped spawn the false memory movement. With the incorporation of the FMSF, my personal situation continued to become more public, and I began to receive almost daily queries and comments from my colleagues about this situation.

During the next two years I grew increasingly uncomfortable with the way in which my own efforts to work on betrayal trauma theory were constantly being undermined by personalized reactions from my professional colleagues, who had come to believe various things about me through the popular and national media (see, for example, Weiss 1993). I was also uncomfortable with the way a distorted version of my story was being used by the FMSF and the media to create the impression that most adult women who recover memories of childhood abuse are deluded, unstable, or under the undue influence of others. In August 1993, two years after my mother's Jane Doe article and a year and a half after the formation of the FMSF, I broke my public silence and, at a mental health continuing education conference in Ann Arbor, Michigan, presented my perspective on my family of origin and the formation of the FMSF (Freyd 1993b).

Having spoken my personal truth, and having addressed the

issues necessary to meet my own standards of integrity and honesty, I have since returned my attention to the development of betrayal trauma theory. Yet hardly a day goes by that my work is not interrupted by challenges to my integrity or attempts to derail my work. Sometimes these challenges are quite intrusive. Other times they are obtrusive: in 1994 an FMSF member picketed the front of the building in which I work.

This pattern of diverting attention from the message to the messenger has shown up in the academic and scholarly world at large (see Chapter 3). It emerges, too, when children and adult victims of sexual abuse who dare to attempt to communicate their experiences suffer attacks on their credibility. We see it in the current societal debate about recovered memories. This pattern is so pervasive and central that it ultimately demands explanation by the very theories that attempt to account for the psychological response to sexual abuse. If people who dare to speak about sexual abuse are attacked by those whom they have relied on and trusted, is it any wonder that unawareness and silence are so common?

I believe that human lives and scientific knowledge alike will benefit from an open, rational, creative, and humane atmosphere in which we can pursue awareness, connection, and truth. Some of us, in order to counteract attempts to undermine our credibility or distract our audiences from our scholarly work, may need to step forward to speak the truth of our experiences. I have addressed aspects of my personal history here with the goal of providing an open and truthful context in which the ideas and information in this book may be freely considered and questioned. My own history does not argue for or against betrayal trauma theory. The theory must stand or fall on its own evidence and logic.

Abcarian, R. 1994. "Incest: Sexual Politics or a Matter of Therapy and Recovery?" *Los Angeles Times,* November 27.

Ainsworth, M. D. 1989. "Attachments beyond Infancy." *American Psychologist* 44 (4): 709–716.

American Psychiatric Association. 1994. *Diagnostic and Statistical Manual of Mental Disorders.* 4th ed. Washington, D.C.: American Psychiatric Association.

Anderson, M. C., and R. A. Bjork. 1994. "Mechanisms of Inhibition in Long-term Memory: A New Taxonomy." In D. Dagenbach and T. Carr, eds., *Inhibitory Processes in Attention, Memory, and Language* (pp. 265–325). San Diego: Academic Press.

Anderson, M. C., R. A. Bjork, and E. L. Bjork. 1994. "Remembering Can Cause Forgetting: Retrieval Dynamics in Long-Term Memory." *Journal of Experimental Psychology: Learning, Memory, And Cognition* 20 (5): 1063–1087.

Anderson, M. C., and B. A. Spellman. 1995. "On the Status of Inhibitory Mechanisms in Cognition: Memory Retrieval as a Model Case." *Psychological Review* 102: 68–100.

Archibald, H. C., and R. D. Tuddenham. 1965. "Persistent Stress Reaction after Combat: A Twenty-Year Follow-Up." *Archives of General Psychiatry* 12: 475–481.

Armstrong, L. 1978. *Kiss Daddy Goodnight: A Speak-Out on Incest.* New York: Pocket Books.

———. 1994. *Rocking the Cradle of Sexual Politics: What Happened When Women Said Incest.* Reading, Mass.: Addison-Wesley.

Baker, R. A. 1992. *Hidden Memories.* Buffalo, N.Y.: Prometheus Books.

Ballard, P. B. 1913. "Oblivescence and Reminiscence." *British Journal of Psychology Monograph Supplements* 1: 1–82.

Barach, M. M. 1991. "Multiple Personality Disorder as an Attachment Disorder." *Dissociation* 4 (3): 117–123.

Bartlett, F. C. 1932. *Remembering: A Study in Experimental and Social Psychology.* Cambridge, England: Cambridge University Press.

Bartone, P. T., and K. M. Wright. 1990. "Grief and Group Recovery Following a Military Air Disaster." *Journal of Traumatic Stress* 3 (4): 523–539.

Bate, W. J. 1955. *The Achievement of Samuel Johnson.* New York: Oxford University Press.

Bauer, P. J., and G. A. Dow. 1994. "Episodic Memory in Sixteen- and Twenty-Month-Old Children: Specifics Are Generalized but Not Forgotten." *Developmental Psychology* 30 (3): 403–417.

Bauer, P. J., L. A. Hertsgaard, and G. A. Dow. 1994. "After Eight Months Have Passed: Long-Term Recall of Events by One- to Two-Year-Old Children." *Memory* 2 (4): 353–382.

Bechara, A., D. Tranel, H. Damasio, R. Adophs, C. Rockland, and A. R. Damasio. 1995. "Double Dissociation of Conditioning and Declarative Knowledge Relative to the Amygdala and Hippocampus in Humans." *Science* 269: 1115–1118.

Bernstein, E., and F. Putnam. 1986. "Development, Reliability, and Validity of a Dissociation Scale." *Journal of Nervous and Mental Disease* 174: 727–735.

Bettelheim, B. 1960. *The Informed Heart: Autonomy in a Mass Age.* Glencoe, Ill.: The Free Press.

Bjork, E. L., and R. A. Bjork. 1988. "On the Adaptive Aspects of Retrieval Failure in Autobiographical Memory." In M. M. Gruneberg, P. E. Morris, and R. N. Sykes, eds., *Practical Aspects of Memory: Current Research and Issues.* Vol. 1, *Memory in Everyday Life* (pp. 283–288). London: Wiley.

Bjork, R. 1989. "Retrieval Inhibition as an Adaptive Mechanism in Human Memory." In H. L. Roediger and F. I. M. Craik, eds., *Varieties of Memory and Consciousness: Essays in Honor of Endel Tulving* (pp. 309–330). Hillsdale, N.J.: Erlbaum.

Bjork, R. A., and E. L. Bjork. 1992. "A New Theory of Disuse and an Old Theory of Stimulus Fluctuation." In A. Healy, S. Kosslyn, and R. Shiffrin, eds., *From Learning Processes to Cognitive Processes: Essays in Honor of William K. Estes* (pp. 35–67). Hillsdale, N.J.: Erlbaum.

Boodman, S. G. 1994. "Advocacy Group for 'Aggrieved' Parents Fights Back." *Washington Post,* April 12, Health Section, p. 15.

Boon, S., and N. Draijer. 1993. "Multiple Personality Disorder in the

Netherlands: A Clinical Investigation of Seventy-One Patients." *American Journal of Psychiatry* 150: 489–494.

Bower, G. 1981. "Mood and Memory." *American Psychologist* 36: 129–148.

———. 1987. "Commentary on Mood and Memory." *Behavior Research and Therapy* 25: 443–455.

Bowlby, J. 1969. *Attachment and Loss.* Vol 1, *Attachment.* New York: Basic Books.

———. 1988. *A Secure Base: Parent-Child Attachment and Healthy Human Development.* New York: Basic Books.

Branscomb, L. 1991. "Dissociation in Combat-Related Post-Traumatic Stress Disorder." *Dissociation* 4: 13–20.

Braun, B. G. 1990. "Dissociative Disorders as Sequelae to Incest." In R. P. Kluft, ed., *Incest-Related Syndromes of Adult Psychopathology* (pp. 227–245). Washington, D.C.: American Psychiatric Press.

Breggin, P. R. 1991. *Toxic Psychiatry.* New York: St. Martin's Press.

Brende, J. O. 1987. "Dissociative Disorders in Vietnam Combat Veterans." *Journal of Contemporary Psychotherapy* 17: 77–86.

Brewin, C., B. Andrews, and I. Gotlib. 1993. "Psychopathology and Early Experience: A Reappraisal of Retrospective Reports." *Psychological Bulletin* 113: 82–98.

Briere, J. 1984. "Long-Term Clinical Correlates of Childhood Sexual Victimization." *Annals of the New York Academy of Sciences* 528: 327–334.

Briere, J., and J. Conte. 1993. "Self-reported Amnesia for Abuse in Adults Molested as Children." *Journal of Traumatic Stress* 6 (1): 21–29.

Brown, A. S. 1976. "Spontaneous Recovery in Human Learning." *Psychological Bulletin* 83 (2): 321–338.

Brown, L. S. 1994. *Subversive Dialogues: Theory in Feminist Therapy.* New York: Basic Books.

———. 1995a. Personal communication. January 25.

———. 1995b. "Toward Not Forgetting: The Science and Politics of Memory." *Counseling Psychologist* 23 (2): 310–314.

Brown, R. 1965. *Social Psychology.* New York: Free Press.

Browne, A., and D. Finkelhor. 1986. "Impact of Child Sexual Abuse: A Review of the Research." *Psychological Bulletin* 99: 66–77.

Browne, I. 1990. "Psychological Trauma, or Unexperienced Experience." *ReVision* 12: 21–34.

Bryer, J., B. Nelson, J. Miller, and P. Krol. 1987. "Childhood Sexual and Physical Abuse as Factors in Adult Psychiatric Illness." *American Journal of Psychiatry* 144: 1426–1430.

Buechner, F. 1990. *The Wizard's Tide.* San Francisco: Harper and Row.

Bunge, N. 1993. "Child Abuse and Creativity: A New Look at Sherwood Anderson's Breakdown." *Journal of Psychohistory* 20: 413–426.

Burgess, A. W., and L. L. Holmstrom. 1974. "Rape Trauma Syndrome." *American Journal of Psychiatry* 131: 981–986.

Burton, L. 1995. "We Shouldn't Hate Susan Smith but Relate to Her." *Register-Guard,* Eugene, Ore., March 19, pp. 1c, 4c.

Butler, K. 1994. "S.F. Boys Chorus Settles Abuse Case: Man's 'Recovered Memories' Supported by Five Witnesses, Tape." *San Francisco Chronicle,* September 1, p. A2.

———. 1995. "Did Daddy Really Do It? A Debate Rages over Incest-Recovery Therapies That Can Create False Memories of Sexual Abuse." *Los Angeles Times,* February 5, Book Review section, p. 1.

Buttenheim, M., and A. Levendosky. 1994. "Couples Treatment for Incest Survivors." *Psychotherapy* 31 (3): 407–414.

Cameron, C. 1993. "Recovering Memories of Childhood Sexual Abuse: a Longitudinal Report." Paper read at the Western Psychological Association Convention, Phoenix, Arizona, April.

———. 1995. Personal communication. April 14.

Campbell, B. 1995. "Mind Games." *The Guardian Weekend,* February 11, pp. 23, 25–27.

Carlson, E. B., and F. W. Putnam. "An Update on the Dissociative Experiences Scale." *Dissociation* 6: 16–27.

Cassiday, K. L., R. J. McNally, and S. B. Zeitlin. 1992. "Cognitive processing of trauma cues in rape victims with post-traumatic stress disorder." *Cognitive Therapy and Research* 16 (3): 283–295.

Charlton, B. 1995. "Can You Forget Sexual Abuse?" *(London) Times,* March 14, Body and Mind section, p. 15.

Cheit, R. E. 1994a. Paper presented at the Mississippi Statewide Conference on Child Abuse and Neglect, Jackson, April 29.

——— 1994b. Personal communication. October 30.

——— 1994c. "Down Memory Lane" (Letters Section). *New York Review of Books,* December 22, pp. 76–77.

Christman, J. In press. "Quieting Doubts: The Gift of Corroboration." *Moving Forward.*

Chu, J., and D. Dill. 1990. "Dissociative Symptoms in Relation to Childhood Physical and Sexual Abuse." *American Journal of Psychiatry* 147: 887–892.

Cloitre, M., J. Cancienne, B. Brodsky, R. Dulit, and S. Perry. 1996. "Memory Performance among Women with Parental Abuse Histories: Enhanced Directed Forgetting or Directed Remembering?" *Journal of Abnormal Psychology* 105: 204–211.

Constantine, L. L., and F. M. Martinson, eds. 1980. *Children and Sex: New Findings, New Perspectives.* Boston: Little, Brown and Co.

Coons, P., E. Bowman, T. Pellow, and P. Schneider. 1989. "Post-

Traumatic Aspects of the Treatment of Victims of Sexual Abuse and Incest." *Psychiatric Clinics of North America* 12: 325–335.

Cosmides, L. 1989. "The Logic of Social Exchange: Has Natural Selection Shaped How Humans Reason? Studies with the Wason Selection Task." *Cognition* 31: 187–276.

Cosmides, L., and J. Tooby. 1992. "Cognitive Adaptations for Social Exchange." In J. H. Barkow, L. Cosmides, and J. Tooby, eds., *The Adapted Mind: Evolutionary Psychology and the Generation of Culture* (pp. 163–228). New York: Oxford University Press.

Crewdson, J. 1988. *By Silence Betrayed: Sexual Abuse of Children in America.* Boston: Little, Brown and Company.

Crews, F. 1994a. "Down Memory Lane" (Letters Section). *New York Review of Books,* December 22, p. 77.

———. 1994b. "The Revenge of the Repressed." *New York Review of Books,* November 17, pp. 54–60.

———. 1994c. "The Revenge of the Repressed: Part II." *New York Review of Books,* December 1, pp. 49–58.

Damstra-Wijmenga, S. M. 1991. "The Memory of the New-Born Baby." *Midwives Chronicle* 104 (1238): 66–69.

Davidson, L. 1994. "A Mother-Daughter Confrontation." *SOFIE (Survivors of Female Incest Emerge),* February, pp. 13–16.

Davies, J. M., and M. G. Frawley. 1994. *Treating the Adult Survivor of Childhood Sexual Abuse: A Psychoanalytic Perspective.* New York: Basic Books.

DiTomasso, M. J., and D. K. Routh. 1993. "Recall of Abuse in Childhood and Three Measures of Dissociation." *Child Abuse and Neglect* 17: 477–85.

Doe, J. 1991. "How Could This Happen? Coping with a False Accusation of Incest and Rape." *Issues in Child Abuse Accusations* 3 (3): 154–165.

Dominelli, L. 1989. "Betrayal of Trust: A Feminist Analysis of Power Relationships in Incest Abuse and Its Relevance for Social Work Practice." *British Journal of Social Work* 19: 291–307.

Douglas, M. A. 1987. "The Battered Women Syndrome." In D. J. Sonkin, ed., *Domestic Violence on Trial: Psychological and Legal Dimensions of Family Violence* (pp. 39–54). New York: Springer.

Dutton, D. G., and S. L. Painter. 1981. "Traumatic Bonding: The Development of Emotional Attachments in Battered Women and Other Relationships of Intermittent Abuse." *Victimology* 6: 139–155.

———. 1993. "The Battered Woman Syndrome: Effects of Severity and Intermittency of Abuse." *American Journal of Orthopsychiatry* 63 (4): 614–622.

Eagle, M. 1984. *Recent Developments in Psychoanalysis: A Critical Evaluation.* New York: McGraw-Hill.

Eich, E. 1989. "Mood Dependent Memory for Internal Versus External Events." *Journal of Experimental Psychology: Learning, Memory, and Cognition* 15 (3): 443–455.

———. 1995. "Mood as a Mediator of Place Dependent Memory." *Journal of Experimental Psychology: General* 124: 293–308.

Enns, C. Z., C. McNeilly, J. Corkery, and M. Gilbert. 1995. "The Debate about Delayed Memories of Child Sexual Abuse: A Feminist Perspective." *Counseling Psychologist* 23 (2): 181–279.

Erdelyi, M. H. 1985. *Psychoanalysis: Freud's Cognitive Psychology.* New York: W. H. Freeman and Company.

———. 1990. "Repression, Reconstruction, and Defense: History and Integration of the Psychoanalytic and Experimental Frameworks." In J. L. Singer, ed., *Repression and Dissociation: Implications for Personality Theory, Psychopathology, and Health* (pp. 1–32). Chicago: University of Chicago Press.

Erdelyi, M. H., and J. Becker. 1974. "Hyperamnesia for Pictures but Not for Words in Multiple Recall Trials." *Cognitive Psychology* 6: 159–171.

Erickson, M. H. 1938. "Negation or Reversal of Legal Testimony." *American Medical Association Archives of Neurology and Psychiatry* 40: 548–553.

Faller, K. C. 1988. *Child Sexual Abuse: An Interdisciplinary Manual for Diagnosis, Case Management, and Treatment.* New York: Columbia University Press.

False Memory Syndrome Foundation. 1992. "How Do We Know We Are Not Representing Pedophiles?" *FMS Newsletter,* February 29, p. 1.

Feinauer, L. L. 1989. "Comparison of Long-Term Effects of Child Abuse by Type of Abuse and by Relationship of the Offender to the Victim." *American Journal of Family Therapy* 17: 48–56.

Feldman-Summers, S., and K. S. Pope. 1994. "The Experience of 'Forgetting' Childhood Abuse: A National Survey of Psychologists." *Journal of Consulting and Clinical Psychology* 62 (3): 636–639.

Femina, D. D., C. A. Yeager, and D. O. Lewis. 1990. "Child Abuse: Adolescent Records vs. Adult Recall." *Child Abuse and Neglect* 14: 227–231.

Finkelhor, D. 1979. *Sexually Victimized Children.* New York: The Free Press.

Finkelhor, D., ed. 1986. *A Sourcebook on Child Sexual Abuse.* Beverly Hills, Calif.: Sage Publications.

Finkelhor, D., and A. Browne. 1985. "The Traumatic Impact of Child Sexual Abuse: A Conceptualization." *American Journal of Orthopsychiatry* 55: 530–541.

Fitzpatrick, F. L. 1994. "Isolation and Silence: A Male Survivor Speaks Out about Clergy Abuse." *Moving Forward* 3 (1): 4–8.

Fivush, R., and N. Hamond. 1990. "Autobiographical Memory across the Preschool Years: Toward Reconceptualizing Childhood Amnesia." In R. Fivush and J. A. Hudson, eds., *Knowing and Remembering in Young Children* (pp. 223–248). New York: Cambridge University Press.

Foa, E. B., U. Feske, T. B. Murdock, M. J. Kozak, and P. R. McCarthy. 1991. "Processing of Threat-Related Information in Rape Victims." *Journal of Abnormal Psychology* 100 (2): 156–162.

Fodor, J. A. 1983. *The Modularity of Mind.* Cambridge, Mass.: MIT Press.

Fraser, S. 1994. "Freud's Final Seduction." *Saturday Night* 109 (2, March): 18–21, 56–59.

Freud, A. 1946. *The Ego and the Mechanisms of Defence.* Trans. Cecil Baines. New York: International Universities Press.

Freud, S. 1913. *The Interpretation of Dreams.* 3rd ed. Trans. A. A. Brill. New York: Macmillan.

———. 1923. *Introductory Lectures on Psycho-Analysis.* Trans. J. Riviera. London: Allen and Unwin.

———. 1936. *The Problem of Anxiety.* Trans. H. A. Bunker. New York: Psychoanalytic Quarterly Press and W. W. Norton and Company.

———. 1949 (original work published 1940). *An Outline of Psychoanalysis.* Trans. J. Strachey. New York: W. W. Norton and Company.

———. 1954. *The Origins of Psycho-Analysis.* New York: Basic Books.

———. 1959 (original work published 1925 [1924]). "An Autobiographical Study." In J. Strachey, A. Freud, A. Strachey, and A. Tyson, eds., *The Standard Edition of the Complete Psychological Works of Sigmund Freud,* Vol. 20. London: The Hogarth Press and The Institute of Psycho-Analysis.

———. 1962 (original work published 1896). "Heredity and the Aetiology of the Neuroses." In J. Strachey, A. Freud, A. Strachey, and A. Tyson, eds., *The Standard Edition of the Complete Psychological Works of Sigmund Freud,* Vol. 3. London: The Hogarth Press and The Institute of Psycho-Analysis.

———. 1963 [1915]. "Repression." In P. Rieff, ed., *General Psychological Theory: Sigmund Freud's Papers on Metapyschology* (pp. 104–115). New York: Collier Books.

Freyd, J. J. 1983. "Shareability: the Social Psychology of Epistemology." *Cognitive Science* 7: 191–210.

———. 1987. "Dynamic mental representations." *Psychological Review* 94: 427–438.

———. 1990. "Natural selection or shareability?" *Behavioral and Brain Sciences* 13: 732–734.

――――. 1993a. "Five Hunches about Perceptual Processes and Dynamic Representations." In D. Meyer and S. Kornblum, eds., *Attention and Performance 14: Synergies in Experimental Psychology, Artificial Intelligence, and Cognitive Neuroscience—A Silver Jubilee* (pp. 99–119). Cambridge, Mass.: MIT Press.

――――. 1993b. "Theoretical and Personal Perspectives on the Delayed Memory Debate." *Proceedings of the Center for Mental Health at Foote Hospital's Continuing Education Conference: Controversies around Recovered Memories of Incest and Ritualistic Abuse,* August 7, Ann Arbor, Mich. (pp. 69–108). Jackson, Mich.: Foote Hospital.

――――. 1994. "Betrayal Trauma: Traumatic Amnesia as an Adaptive Response to Childhood Abuse." *Ethics and Behavior* 4: 307–329.

Freyd, J. J., and D. H. Gleaves. 1996. "Remembering Words Not Presented in Lists: Implications for the Recovered/False Memory Controversy?" *Journal of Experimental Psychology: Learning, Memory, and Cognition.*

Freyd, J. J., S. R. Martorello, and J. S. Alvarado. In preparation. "Betrayal Trauma and Dissociative Experiences."

Freyd, J. J., S. R. Martorello, A. E. Hayes, J. C. Christman, and J. S. Alvarado. In preparation. "Cognitive Mechanisms Associated with Dissociative Tendencies."

Fried, S. 1994. "War of Remembrance." *Philadelphia* (January): 66–71, 149–157.

Fromm-Reichmann, F. 1950. *Principles of Intensive Psychotherapy.* Chicago: University of Chicago Press.

Fullilove, M. 1995. Personal communication. April 18.

Fuster, J. M. 1995. *Memory in the Cerebral Cortex.* Cambridge, Mass.: MIT Press.

Ganaway, G. K. 1993. Untitled Paper. *Proceedings of the Center for Mental Health at Foote Hospital's Continuing Education Conference: Controversies around Recovered Memories of Incest and Ritualistic Abuse,* August 7, Ann Arbor, Mich. (pp. 42–61). Jackson, Mich.: Foote Hospital.

Gardner, R. A. 1991. *Sex Abuse Hysteria.* Creskill, N.J.: Creative Therapeutics.

Geiselman, R. E., R. A. Bjork, and D. L. Fishman. 1983. "Disrupted Retrieval in Directed Forgetting: A Link with Posthypnotic Amnesia." *Journal of Experimental Psychology: General* 112 (1): 58–72.

Geraci, J. 1993. "Interview: Hollida Wakefield and Ralph Underwager." *Paidika: The Journal of Paedophilia* 3 (1): 2–12.

Gilligan, C. 1991. "The Psyche Lives in a Medium of Culture: How Shall We Talk of Love?" Paper read at the American Psychological Association, 99th Annual Convention, August 16–20, San Francisco, Calif.

Glover, H. 1988. "Four Syndromes of Post-Traumatic Stress Disorder: Stressors and Conflicts of the Traumatized with Special Focus on the Vietnam Combat Veterans." *Journal of Traumatic Stress* 1 (1): 57–78.

Godden, D. R., and A. D. Baddeley. 1975. "Context-Dependent Memory in Two Natural Environments: On Land and Underwater." *British Journal of Psychology* 66: 325–31.

Goffman, E. 1967. *Interaction Ritual.* Garden City, N.Y.: Doubleday.

Goleman, D. 1985. *Vital Lies, Simple Truths: The Psychology of Self-Deception.* New York: Simon and Schuster.

———. 1992. "Childhood Trauma: Memory or Invention?" *The New York Times,* July 21, pp. B5–B8.

Goodwin, J., R. Attias, T. McCarty, S. Chandler, and R. Romanik. 1988. "Reporting by Adult Psychiatric Patients of Childhood Sexual Abuse." *American Journal of Psychiatry* 146: 1183.

Grant, L. 1994. "Tricks of the Memory: A New Group Concerned about Child Sex Abuse Is Taking Up the Fight against the Doctrine of False Memory Syndrome. Linda Grant Reports." *The Guardian,* April 25, pp. 8–9.

Green, L. 1992. *Ordinary Wonders: Living Recovery from Sexual Abuse.* Toronto, Ontario: Women's Press.

Greenson, R. R. 1967. *The Technique and Practice of Psychoanalysis.* Vol. 1. New York: International Universities Press.

Greer, C. 1994. "I Know There Is Help." *Parade Magazine,* September 11, p. 4–7.

Griggs, R. A., and J. R. Cox. 1982. "The Elusive Thematic-Materials Effect in Wason's Selection Task." *British Journal of Psychology* 73: 407–420.

Gross, L. 1994. "Facing Up to the Dreadful Dangers of Denial." *Cosmopolitan,* March: 190–194.

Harlow, H. F. 1959. "Love in Infant Monkeys." *Scientific American* 200 (6): 68–74.

Harvey, M. R., and J. L. Herman. 1994. "Amnesia, Partial Amnesia, and Delayed Recall among Adult Survivors of Childhood Trauma." *Consciousness and Cognition* 3: 295–306.

Hendersen, R. W. 1985. "Fearful Memories: The Motivational Significance of Forgetting." In F. R. Brush and J. B. Overmier, eds., *Affect, Conditioning, and Cognition: Essays on the Determinants of Behavior* (pp. 43–53). Hillsdale, N.J.: Lawrence Erlbaum Associates.

Henderson, D. J. 1975. "Incest." In A. M. Freedman, H. I. Kaplan, and B. J. Sadock, eds., *Comprehensive Textbook of Psychiatry,* 2nd ed. (pp. 1530–1539). Baltimore: Williams and Wilkins.

Henderson, J. 1983. "Is Incest Harmful?" *Canadian Journal of Psychiatry* 28: 34–39.

Henderson, J. L., and M. Moore. 1944. "The Psychoneuroses of War." *New England Journal of Medicine* 230: 273–279.

Henley, N. M. 1977. *Body Politics: Power, Sex, and Nonverbal Communication.* The Patterns of Social Behavior series, ed. Z. Rubin. Englewood Cliffs, N.J.: Prentice-Hall.

Herman, J. L. 1992. *Trauma and Recovery.* New York: Basic Books.

———. 1994. "Ethics on Trial: Tabloid Trash and Flash Threaten to Corrupt the American Media." *Nieman Reports: The Nieman Foundation at Harvard University* 48 (1): 43–45.

Herman, J. L., and E. Schatzow. 1987. "Recovery and Verification of Memories of Childhood Sexual Trauma." *Psychoanalytic Psychology* 4 (1): 1–14.

Hilgard, E. R. 1986. *Divided Consciousness: Multiple Controls in Human Thought and Action.* New York: John Wiley and Sons.

Hinton, G. E., and J. A. Anderson, eds. 1981. *Parallel Models of Associative Memory.* Hillsdale, N.J.: Erlbaum.

Holmes, D. S. 1990. "The Evidence for Repression: An Examination of Sixty Years of Research." In J. L. Singer, ed., *Repression and Dissociation: Implications for Personality Theory, Psychopathology, and Health* (pp. 85–102). Chicago: University of Chicago Press.

Homer. 1995. *The Odyssey.* Trans. A. T. Murray. Rev. by D. E. Dimock. Cambridge, Mass.: Harvard University Press.

Horn, M. 1993. "Memories Lost and Found." *U.S. News and World Report,* November 29, pp. 52–58.

Horowitz, M. J. 1978. *Image Formation and Cognition.* 2nd ed. New York: Appleton-Century-Crofts.

———. 1986. *Stress Response Syndromes.* 2nd ed. Northvale, N.J.: Jason Aronson.

Hunter, M. 1990. *Abused Boys: The Neglected Victims of Sexual Abuse.* Lexington, Mass.: Lexington Books.

Jack, D. J. 1991. *Silencing the Self: Women and Depression.* Cambridge, Mass.: Harvard University Press.

Jacobson, B., G. Eklund, L. Hamberger, D. Linnarsson, G. Sedvall, and M. Valverius. 1987. "Perinatal Origin of Adult Self-Destructive Behavior." *Acta Psychiatrica Scandinavica* 76: 364–371.

Jacoby, L. L., and C. M. Kelley. 1992. "A Process-Dissociation Framework for Investigating Unconscious Influences: Freudian Slips, Projective Tests, Subliminal Perception, and Signal Detection Theory." *Current Directions in Psychological Science* 1: 174–179.

James, W. 1890. *Principles of Psychology.* New York: Holt.

Janet, P. 1919/1925. *Les Medications Psychologiques.* Paris: Felix Alcan.

———. 1989. *L'automatisme Psychologique.* Paris: Felix Alcan.

Janoff-Bulman, R. 1992. *Shattered Assumptions: Towards a New Psychology of Trauma.* New York: Free Press.

Kaspi, S. P., R. J. McNally, and N. Amir. 1995. "Cognitive Processing of Emotional Information in Posttraumatic Stress Disorder." *Cognitive Therapy and Research* 19: 433–444.

Kelly, D. D. 1985. "Central Representations of Pain and Analgesia." In E. R. Kandel and J. H. Schwartz, eds., *Principles of Neural Science,* 2nd ed. (pp. 331–343). New York: Elsevier.

———. 1986. *Stress-Induced Analgesia.* New York: New York Academy of Sciences.

Kendall-Tacket, K. A., L. M. Williams, and D. Finkelhor. 1993. "Impact of Sexual Abuse on Children: A Review and Synthesis of Recent Empirical Studies." *Psychological Bulletin* 113: 164–180.

Kernberg, O. 1976. *Object Relations Theory and Clinical Psychoanalysis.* New York: Jason Aronson.

Kihlstrom, J. F. 1983. "Instructed Forgetting: Hypnotic and Nonhypnotic." *Journal of Experimental Psychology: General* 112: 73–79.

Kihlstrom, J. F., and J. M. Harackiewicz. 1982. "The Earliest Recollection: A New Survey." *Journal of Personality* 50: 134–148.

Kinsey, A. C., W. B. Pomeroy, C. E. Martin, and P. H. Gebhard. 1953. *Sexual Behavior in the Human Female.* Philadelphia: W. B. Saunders.

Klein, M. 1975. *The Writings of Melanie Klein.* Vol. 3. London: The Hogarth Press.

Kluft, R. P., ed. 1990. *Incest-Related Syndromes of Adult Psychopathology.* Washington, D.C.: American Psychiatric Press.

Kohut, H. 1983. "Selected Problems of Self-Psychological Theory." In J. D. Lichtenberg and S. Kaplan, eds., *Reflections on Self Psychology* (pp. 387–416). Hillsdale, N.J.: Erlbaum Associates.

Koss, M. P. 1988. "Hidden Rape: Sexual Aggression and Victimization in a National Sample of Students in Higher Education." In A. W. Burgess, ed., *Rape and Sexual Assault II.* New York: Garland Publishing.

Koss, M. P., T. E. Dinero, C. A. Seibel, and S. L. Cox. 1988. "Stranger and Acquaintance Rape: Are There Differences in the Victim's Experience?" *Psychology of Women Quarterly* 12: 1–24.

Koss, M. P., and M. R. Harvey. 1991. *The Rape Victim: Clinical and Community Interventions.* Newbury Park, Calif.: Sage.

Krystal, J. H. 1990. "Animal Models for Posttraumatic Stress Disorder." In E. L. Giller, ed., *Biological Assessment and Treatment of Posttraumatic Stress Disorder* (pp. 1–26). Washington, D.C.: American Psychiatric Press.

Kuyken, W., and Brewin, C. R. 1995. "Autobiographical Memory Functioning in Depression and Reports of Early Abuse." *Journal of Abnormal Psychology* 104 (4): 585–591.

Lakoff, R. T. 1976. *Language and Woman's Place.* New York: Octagon Books.

Landman, S. H. 1993. In *Proceedings of the The Center for Mental Health at Foote Hospital's Continuing Education Conference: Controversies around Recovered Memories of Incest and Ritualistic Abuse,* August 7, Ann Arbor, Michigan, pp. 1–26. Jackson, Mich.: Foote Hospital.

Lawrence, L. R. 1987. "Incest: One Woman's Story." *Washington Post,* September 1, pp. 10–11.

Levinthal, C. F. 1988. *Messengers of Paradise: Opiates and the Brain.* New York: Anchor Press.

Light, A. 1994. *Dialogues with Madwomen.* Film produced by I. Saraf and A. Light. Dist. by Women Make Movies, New York.

Lister, E. D. 1982. "Forced Silence: A Neglected Dimension of Trauma." *American Journal of Psychiatry,* 139 (7): 872–876.

Livingstone, D. 1857. *Missionary Travels and Researches in South Africa.* London: John Murray.

Loewenstein, R. J. 1991. "Psychogenic Amnesia and Psychogenic Fugue: A Comprehensive Review." In A. Tasmann and S. M. Goldfinger, eds., *American Psychiatric Press Review of Psychiatry* (pp. 189–221). Washington, D.C.: American Psychiatric Press.

Loftus, E. F. 1980. *Memory: Surprising New Insights into How We Remember and Why We Forget.* Reading, Mass.: Addison-Wesley Publishing Company.

———. 1993. "The Reality of Repressed Memories." *American Psychologist* 48: 518–537.

———. 1995. "Remembering Dangerously." Skeptical Inquirer 19 (2): 20–29.

Loftus, E. F., and K. Ketcham. 1991. *Witness for the Defense: The Accused, the Eyewitness, and the Expert Who Puts Memory on Trial.* New York: St. Martin's Press.

———. 1994. *The Myth of Repressed Memory: False Memories and Allegations of Sexual Abuse.* New York: St. Martin's Press.

Loftus, E. F., E. M. Milo, and J. R. Paddock. 1995. "The Accidental Executioner: Why Psychotherapy Must Be Informed by Science." *Counseling Psychologist* 23 (2): 300–309.

Loftus, E. F., S. Polonsky, and M. T. Fullilove. 1994. "Memories of Childhood Sexual Abuse: Remembering and Repressing." *Psychology of Women Quarterly* 18: 67–84.

Loftus, E. F., and G. Zanni. 1975. "Eyewitness Testimony: The Influence of the Wording of a Question." *Bulletin of the Psychonomic Society* 5: 86–88.

Lorde, A. 1980. *The Cancer Journals,* 2nd ed. Argyle, N.Y.: Spinsters, Ink.

Maier, S. F., L. R. Watkins, and M. Fleshner. 1994. "Psychoneuroimmu-nology: The Interface between Behavior, Brain, and Immunity." *American Psychologist* 49 (12): 1004–1017.

Maltz, W. 1988. "Identifying and Treating the Sexual Repercussions of Incest: Couples Therapy Approach." *Journal of Sex and Marriage Therapy* 14 (2): 142–170.

Martin, A., J. V. Haxby, F. M. Lalonde, C. L. Wiggs, and L. G. Unger-lieder. 1995. "Discrete Cortical Regions Associated with Knowl-edge of Color and Knowledge of Action." *Science* 270: 102–105.

Masson, J. M. 1984. *The Assault on Truth: Freud's Suppression of the Seduction Theory.* New York: Farrar, Straus and Giroux.

———. 1986. *A Dark Science: Women, Sexuality, and Psychiatry in the Nine-teenth Century.* New York: Farrar, Straus and Giroux.

———. 1988. *Against Therapy: Emotional Tyranny and the Myth of Psychological Healing.* New York: Atheneum.

McFall, M. E., M. M. Murburg, D. E. Smith, and C. F. Jensen. 1991. "An Analysis of Criteria Used by V.A. Clinicians to Diagnose Combat-Related PTSD." *Journal of Traumatic Stress* 4 (1): 123–136.

McHugh, P. R. 1992. "Psychiatric Misadventures." *American Scholar* 61: 487–510.

McLeer, S. V., E. Deblinger, M. S. Atkins, E. B. Foa, and D. L. Ralphe. 1988. "Post-Traumatic Stress Disorder in Sexually Abused Chil-dren." *Journal of the American Academy of Child and Adolescent Psychiatry* 27: 650–654.

McNally, R. J. 1992. "Psychopathology of Post-Traumatic Stress Disor-der (PTSD): Boundaries of the Syndrome." In M. Basolgu, ed., *Torture and Its Consequences: Current Treatment Approaches* (pp. 229–252). Cambridge, England: Cambridge University Press.

McNally, R. J., G. E. English, and H. J. Lipke. 1993. "Assessment of Intrusive Cognition in PTSD: Use of the Modified Stroop Para-digm." *Journal of Traumatic Stress* 6: 33–41.

McNally, R. J., S. P. Kaspi, B. C. Riemann, and S. B. Zeitlin. 1990. "Selective Processing of Threat Cues in Posttraumatic Stress Disor-der." *Journal of Abnormal Psychology* 99 (4): 398–402.

McNally, R. J., N. B. Lasko, M. L. Macklin, and R. K. Pitman. 1995. "Autobiographical Memory Disturbance in Combat-Related Post-traumatic Stress Disorder." *Behaviour Research and Therapy* 33: 619–630.

McNally, R. J., B. T. Litz, A. Prassas, L. M. Shin, and F. W. Weathers. 1994. "Emotional Priming of Autobiographical Memory in Post-Traumatic Stress Disorder." *Cognition and Emotion* 8: 351–367.

Miller, A. 1984. *Thou Shalt Not Be Aware: Society's Betrayal of the Child.* New York: Farrar, Straus, Giroux.

Miller, D. A. F., K. McCluskey-Fawcett, and L. M. Irving. 1993. "The Relationship between Childhood Sexual Abuse and Subsequent Onset of Bulimia Nervosa." *Child Abuse and Neglect: The International Journal* 17: 305–314.

Murthy, R. 1994. "Remembering Abuse: Professor Ross Cheit Discusses His Recovered Memories and Subsequent Legal Battles with Rekha Murthy." *Brown Daily Herald,* September 30, pp. 1, 13.

Myers, J. E. B. 1996. "Expert Testimony." In J. Briere, L. Buliner, J. Bulkley, C. Jenny, and T. Reid, eds., *American Professional Society on the Abuse of Children Handbook on Child Maltreatment* (pp. 319–340). Thousand Oaks, Calif.: Sage.

Myers, N. A., R. K. Clifton, and M. G. Clarkson. 1987. "When They Were Very Young: Almost-Threes Remember Two Years Ago." *Infant Behavior and Development* 10: 123–132.

National Victims Center. 1992. "Rape in America: A Report to the Nation." Washington, D.C.: National Victims Center.

Nelson, K. 1993. "The Psychological and Social Origins of Autobiographical Memory." *Psychological Science* 4 (1): 7–14.

Newcombe, N., and N. A. Fox. 1994. "Infantile Amnesia: Through a Glass Darkly." *Child Development* 65: 31–40.

Nissen, M. J., J. L. Ross, D. B. Willingham, T. B. MacKenzie, and D. L. Schacter. 1988. "Memory and Awareness in a Patient with Multiple Personality Disorder." *Brain and Cognition* 8: 117–134.

Novak, M. A., and H. F. Harlow. 1979. "Social Recovery of Monkeys Isolated for the First Year of Life: Rehabilitation and Therapy." *Developmental Psychology* 11: 50–61.

Ofshe, R., and E. Watters. 1993. "Making Monsters." *Society* 30 (3, March–April): 4–16.

Olio, K. A. 1994a. "Coping with Ritual Abuse Reports: Comments on the Case of Carla." Paper read at the American Psychological Association's 102nd Annual Convention, August 14, Los Angeles, Calif.
———. 1994b. "Truth in Memory." *American Psychologist* 49 (5): 442–443.

Painter, S. L., and D. Dutton. 1985. "Patterns of Emotional Bonding in Battered Women: Traumatic Bonding." *International Journal of Women's Studies* 8 (4): 363–375.

Pavio, A. 1990. *Mental Representations: A Dual Coding Approach.* New York: Oxford University Press.

Pavlov, I. P. 1927. *Conditioned Reflexes.* Trans. G. V. Anrep. London: Oxford University Press.

Payne, D. G. 1987. "Hyperamnesia and Reminiscence in Recall: A Historical and Empirical Review." *Psychological Review* 101: 5–27.

Pennebaker, J. W. 1990. *Opening Up: The Healing Power of Confiding in Others.* New York: William Morrow and Company.

Peters, S. D, G. E. Wyatt, and D. Finkelhor. 1986. "Prevalence." In D. Finkelhor, ed., *A Sourcebook on Child Sexual Abuse* (pp. 15–59). Beverly Hills, Calif.: Sage Publications.

Pezdek, K. 1995. "Planting False Childhood Memories: When Does It Occur and When Does It Not?" Paper presented at the 36th Annual Meeting of the Psychonomics Society, Los Angeles, November 10–12.

Pinker, S., and P. Bloom. 1990. "Natural Language and Natural Selection." *Behavioral and Brain Sciences* 13 (4): 707–784.

Pinker, S., and A. Prince. 1988. "On Language and Connectionism: Analysis of a Parallel Distributed Processing Model of Language Acquisition." *Cognition* (Special issue: *Connectionism and Symbol Systems*) 28 (1–2): 73–193.

Pope, H. G., and J. I. Hudson. 1995. "Can Memories of Childhood Sexual Abuse Be Repressed?" *Psychological Medicine* 25: 121–126.

Pope, K. S. 1990. "Therapist-Patient Sex as Sex Abuse: Six Scientific, Professional, and Practical Dilemmas in Addressing Victimization and Rehabilitation." *Professional Psychology: Research and Practice* 21 (4): 227–239.

———. 1994. *Sexual Involvement with Therapists: Patient Assessment, Subsequent Therapy, Forensics.* Washington, D.C.: American Psychological Association.

Purdy, A. J. 1989. *He Will Never Remember: Caring for Victims of Child Abuse.* Atlanta, Ga.: S. Hunter Publishing.

Putnam, F. W. 1989. *Diagnosis and Treatment of Multiple Personality Disorder.* New York: Guilford Press.

Putnam, F. W., J. J. Guroff, E. K. Silberman, L. Barban, and R. M. Post. 1986. "The Clinical Phenomenology of Multiple Personality Disorder: A Review of 100 Recent Cases." *Journal of Clinical Psychiatry* 47: 285–293.

Querleu, D., C. Lefebvre, M. Titran, X. Renard, M. Morillion, and G. J. Crepin. 1984. "Reaction of the Newborn Infant Less Than Two Hours after Birth to the Maternal Voice." *Gynecology, Obstetrics, and Biological Reproduction* (Paris) 13 (2): 125–134.

Quina, K., L. L. Harlow, P. J. Morokoff, and S. E. Saxon. In press. "Interpersonal Power and Women's HIV Risk." In J. Manlowe and N. Goldstein, eds., *Gender and the Politics of HIV.* New York: New York University Press.

Ramey, J. 1979. "Dealing with the Last Taboo." *Siecus Report* 7: 1–2, 6–7.

Reed, R. K. 1988. *Cognition: Theory and Applications.* 2nd ed. New York: Brooks/Cole Publishing Company.

Renshaw, D. C. 1982. *Incest: Understanding and Treatment.* Boston: Little, Brown and Company.

Roediger, H. L., III. 1990. "Implicit memory: Retentions without remembering." *American Psychologist* 45 (9): 1043–1056.

Romans, S. E., J. L. Martin, J. C. Anderson, G. P. Herbison, and P. E. Mullen. 1995. "Sexual Abuse in Childhood and Deliberate Self-Harm." *American Journal of Psychiatry* 152: 1336–1342.

Rovee-Collier, C. 1993. "The Capacity for Long-Term Memory in Infancy." *Current Directions in Psychological Science* 2 (4): 130–135.

Rowan, A. B., and D. W. Foy. 1993. "Post-Traumatic Stress Disorder in Child Sexual Abuse Survivors: A Literature Review." *Journal of Traumatic Stress* 6: 3–20.

Rumelhart, D. E., J. L. McClelland, and PDP Research Group. 1986. *Parallel Distributed Processing: Explorations in the Microstructure of Cognition.* Vols. 1 and 2. Cambridge, Mass.: MIT Press.

Russell, D. E. H. 1986. *The Secret Trauma: Incest in the Lives of Girls and Women.* New York: Basic Books.

Saint-Exupéry, A. de. 1943/1971. *The Little Prince.* Trans. Katherine Woods. San Diego: Harcourt Brace Jovanovich.

Salter, S. 1993. "Debating the Way Memory Works." *San Francisco Examiner,* April 10.

Sanders, B., and M. H. Giolas. 1991. "Dissociation and Childhood Trauma in Psychologically Disturbed Adolescents." *American Journal of Psychiatry* 148: 50–54.

Saxe, G., and J. Schwartz. 1993. "Dissociative Disorders in Psychiatric Inpatients." *American Journal of Psychiatry* 150: 1037–1042.

Saxe, G., B. A. van der Kolk, R. Berkowitz, G. Chinman, K. Hall, G. Lieberg, and J. Schwartz. 1993. "Dissociative Disorders in Psychiatric Inpatients." *American Journal of Psychiatry* 150: 1037–1042.

Schacter, D. L. 1992. "Understanding Implicit Memory: A Cognitive Neuroscience Approach." *American Psychologist* 47 (4): 559–569.

Schirmer, L. 1995. Personal communication. August 18.

Schooler, J. W. 1994. "Seeking the Core: The Issues and Evidence Surrounding Recovered Accounts of Sexual Trauma." *Consciousness and Cognition* 3: 452–469.

Seay, B., B. K. Alexander, and H. F. Harlow. 1964. "Maternal Behavior of Socially Deprived Rhesus Monkeys." *Journal of Abnormal and Social Psychology* 69: 345–354.

Shay, J. 1994. *Achilles in Vietnam: Combat Trauma and the Undoing of Character.* New York: Atheneum.

Siegel, D. J. 1992. "Memory and Trauma." Paper read at the Lecture Series in Cognitive Sciences and Mental Health, at the Institute of Cognitive and Decision Sciences, University of Oregon, April 13.

Sifford, D. 1991. "Accusations of Sex Abuse, Years Later." *Philadelphia Inquirer,* November 24.

————. 1992a. "Perilous Journey: The Labyrinth of Past Sexual Abuse." *Philadelphia Inquirer,* February 13.

————. 1992b. "When Tales of Sex Abuse Aren't True." *Philadelphia Inquirer,* January 5.

Smith, S. M. 1995. "Mood is a Component of Mental Context: Comment on Eich (1995)." *Journal of Experimental Psychology: General* 124: 309–310.

Sorensen, T., and B. Snow. 1991. "How Children Tell: The Process of Disclosure in Child Sexual Abuse." *Child Welfare* 70 (1): 3–15.

Spiegel, D. 1989. "Hypnosis in the Treatment of Victims of Sexual Abuse." *Psychiatric Clinics of North America* 12: 295–305.

Squire, L. R. 1992. "Memory and the Hippocampus: A Synthesis from Findings with Rats, Monkeys, and Humans." *Psychological Review* 99 (2): 195–231.

Stanton, M. 1995. "Bearing Witness: A Man's Recovery of His Sexual Abuse as a Child." *Providence Journal,* May 7, 8, and 9.

Steinem, G. 1994. *Moving beyond Words.* New York: Simon and Schuster.

Strick, F. L., and S. A. Wilcoxon. 1991. "A Comparison of Dissociative Experiences in Adult Female Outpatients with and without Histories of Early Incestuous Abuse." *Dissociation* 4 (4): 193–199.

Stroop, J. R. 1935. "Studies of Interference in Serial Verbal Reactions." *Journal of Experimental Psychology* 18: 643–662.

Summit, R. C. 1983. "The Child Sexual Abuse Accommodation Syndrome." *Child Abuse and Neglect* 7: 177–193.

————. 1988. "Hidden Victims, Hidden Pain: Societal Avoidance of Child Sexual Abuse." In G. E. Wyatt and G. J. Powell, eds., *Lasting Effects of Child Sexual Abuse* (pp. 39–60). Newbury Park, Calif.: Sage Publications.

————. 1992. "Abuse of the Child Sexual Abuse Accommodation Syndrome (Case Conference: Mental Health/Social Service Issues and Case Studies)." *Journal of Child Sexual Abuse* 1 (4): 153–163.

Summit, R. C., T. W. Miller, and L. J. Veltkamp. In press. "The Child Sexual Abuse Accommodation Syndrome: Clinical Issues and Forensic Implications." In T. W. Miller, ed., *Children of Trauma.* Madison, Conn.: International Universities Press.

Suomi, S. J., and H. F. Harlow. 1972. "Social Rehabilitation of Isolate-Reared Mokeys." *Developmental Psychology* 6: 487–496.

Terr, L. C. 1988. "What Happens to Early Memories of Trauma? A Study of Twenty Children Under Age Five at the Time of Documented Traumatic Events." *Journal of American Academy of Child and Adolescent Psychiatry* 27: 96–104.

————. 1990. *Too Scared to Cry: Psychic Trauma in Childhood.* New York: Harper and Row.

————. 1991. "Childhood Traumas: An Outline and Overview." *American Journal of Psychiatry* 148 (1): 10–20.

————. 1994. *Unchained Memories: True Stories of Traumatic Memories, Lost and Found.* New York: Basic Books.

Timnick, L. 1985a. "22 Percent in Survey Were Child Abuse Victims." *Los Angeles Times,* August 25, pp. 1, 34.

————. 1985b. "Children's Abuse Reports Reliable, Most Believe." *Los Angeles Times,* August 26, pp. 5, 12.

Treisman, A. M. 1960. "Verbal Cues, Language, and Meaning in Selective Attention." *Quarterly Journal of Experimental Psychology* 12: 242–248.

Tromp, S., M. P. Koss, A. J. Figueredo, and M. Tharan. 1995. "Are Rape Memories Different? A Comparison of Rape, Other Unpleasant, and Pleasant Memories among Employed Women." *Journal of Traumatic Stress* 8: 607–627.

Tulving, E. 1983. *Elements of Episodic Knowledge.* New York: Oxford University Press.

Usher, J. A., and U. Neisser. 1993. "Childhood Amnesia and the Beginnings of Memory for Four Early Life Events." *Journal of Experimental Psychology: General* 122 (2): 155–165.

Van Derbur Atler, M. 1991. "Say 'Incest' Out Loud." *McCall's,* September, pp. 78, 80–81, 148–149.

————. 1995. Personal communication. May 7.

van der Hart, O., and B. Friedman. 1989. "A Reader's Guide to Pierre Janet on Dissociation: A Neglected Intellectual Heritage." *Dissociation* 2: 3–16.

van der Hart, O., and E. Nijenhuis. 1995. "Amnesia for Traumatic Epxeriences." *Hypnos* 22: 73–86.

van der Kolk, B. A. 1987. *Psychological Trauma.* Washington, D.C.: American Psychiatric Press.

————. 1994. "The Body Keeps the Score: Memory and the Evolving Psychobiology of Posttraumatic Stress." *Harvard Review of Psychiatry* 1 (5): 253–265.

van der Kolk, B. A., J. C. Perry, and J. L. Herman. 1991. "Childhood Origins of Self-Destructive Behavior." *American Journal of Psychiatry* 148: 1665–1671.

van der Kolk, B. A., and O. van der Hart. 1989. "Pierre Janet and the Breakdown of Adaptation in Psychological Trauma." *American Journal of Psychiatry* 146: 1530–1539.

Victor, J. S. 1991. "Satanic Cult 'Survivor' Stories." *Skeptical Inquirer* 15: 274–280.

Wagenaar, W. A. 1986. "My Memory: A Study of Autobiographical Memory over Six Years." *Cognitive Psychology* 18 (2): 225–252.

Waldfogel, S. 1948. "The Frequency and Affective Character of Childhood Memories." *Psychological Monographs* 62 (4): 291.

Walker, L. E. 1979. *The Battered Woman*. New York: Harper and Row.

———. 1984. *The Battered Woman Syndrome*. New York: Springer.

———. 1994. *Abused Women and Survivor Therapy: A Practical Guide for the Psychotherapist*. Washington, D.C.: American Psychological Association.

Weinberg, S. K. 1955. *Incest Behavior*. New York: Citadel Press.

Weiss, E., executive producer. 1993. *All Things Considered*. July 8. Washingon, D.C.: National Public Radio.

Wheeler, M. A. 1995. "Improvement in Recall over Time without Repeated Testing: Spontaneous Recovery Revisited." *Journal of Experimental Psychology: Learning, Memory, and Cognition* 21 (1): 173–184.

Williams, L. M. 1992. "Adult Memories of Childhood Abuse: Preliminary Findings from a Longitudinal Study." *Advisor* (American Professional Society on the Abuse of Children) 5: 19–21.

———. 1993. "Recovered Memories of Abuse in Women with Documented Child Sexual Victimization Histories." Paper presented at the 45th Annual Meeting of the American Society of Criminology, Phoenix, Arizona, October.

———. 1994a. "Recall of Childhood Trauma: A Prospective Study of Women's Memories of Child Sexual Abuse." *Journal of Consulting and Clinical Psychology* 62 (6): 1167–1176.

———. 1994b. Personal communication. November 4.

———. 1994c. "What Does It Mean to Forget Child Sexual Abuse? A Reply to Loftus, Garry, and Feldman (1994)." *Journal of Consulting and Clinical Psychology* 62 (6): 1182–1186.

———. 1995. "Recovered Memories of Abuse in Women with Documented Child Sexual Victimization Histories." *Journal of Traumatic Stress* 8: 649–674.

Wright, L. 1993a. "A Reporter at Large: Remembering Satan (Part 1)." *New Yorker*, May 17: 60–81.

——— 1993b. "A Reporter at Large: Remembering Satan (Part 2)." *New Yorker*, May 24: 54–76.

———. 1994a. "Child-Care Demons: Why the Scapegoating of Those Who Look After Our Kids?" *New Yorker*, October 3: 5–6.

———. 1994b. *Remembering Satan*. New York: Knopf.

Wyatt, G. E., D. Guthrie, and C. M. Notgrass. 1992. "Differential Effects of Women's Child Sexual Abuse and Subsequent Sexual Revictimization." *Journal of Consulting and Clinical Psychology* 60 (2): 167–173.

Young, L. 1992. "Sexual Abuse and the Problem of Embodiment." *Child Abuse and Neglect* 16: 89–100.

Zeitlin, S. B., and R. J. McNally. 1991. "Implicit and Explicit Memory Bias for Threat in Post-Traumatic Stress Disorder." *Behavior Research and Therapy* 29 (5): 451–457.

## ACKNOWLEDGMENTS

Many people have shaped, inspired, and contributed to this book, and I am grateful to all. I thank by name just a few.

To my brave and triumphant friends Jill Christman, Frank Fitzpatrick, Lana Lawrence, Marilyn Van Derbur Atler, and especially Ross Cheit, thank you for permitting me to discuss aspects of your lives in this book.

To the four who gave so much to this project: Pam Birrell, Deb Casey, Jill Christman, and JQ Johnson—my gratitude goes beyond words, but perhaps you will recognize that your spirits have entered this book. To my uncle Bill Freyd, thank you for the tremendous gifts you give me: your belief and your love.

To researchers Catherine Cameron, Shirley Feldman-Summers, Mindy Fullilove, Ken Pope, and Linda Meyer Williams: thank you for making available the original empirical data you collected in your own studies so that I might reanalyze it for use in this book. Thanks also to Eileen McCornack for transcribing the audio tapes. I also wish to thank my students and colleagues for their constructive criticisms, suggestions, and encouragement, including (but not only) Jessica Alvarado, Mike Anderson, Laura Brown, Sara Brownmiller, Spark Campbell, Leda Cosmides, Susan Martorello, Ken Pope, Mike Posner, Kat Quina, Myron Rothbart, Roger Shepard, Roland Summit, and Mindy Tharan.

A special word of appreciation to my editor, Angela von der Lippe, Senior Editor for the Behavioral Sciences at Harvard University Press, for suggesting that I write this book and then helping turn that suggestion into a reality. I am also indebted to the Harvard University Press staff, and to the Press's two external reviewers, whose constructive comments helped shape this work. And for sharing her intelligence, attention, and grace in editing this book, I am especially thankful to Donna Bouvier.

I am grateful to the National Science Foundation, the Guggenheim Foundation, and the Center for Advanced Study in the Behavioral Sciences for earlier, crucial support. Thanks also to the University of Oregon and the National Institute of Mental Health for their longstanding and ongoing support.

The Lenore Terr quotes from her article "Childhood Traumas: An Outline and Overview," *American Journal of Psychiatry* 148 (1): 10–20, copyright 1991 the American Psychiatric Association, are reprinted by permission.

My greatest source of inspiration has been my partner and my sweet children. Thank you, family of my heart, for sharing your wisdom, gracing my life, and bringing me such joy.

# INDEX